SHARING KNOWLEDGE

Assertion is the central vehicle for the sharing of knowledge. Whether knowledge is shared successfully often depends on the quality of assertions: good assertions lead to successful knowledge sharing, while bad ones don't. In *Sharing Knowledge*, Christoph Kelp and Mona Simion investigate the relation between knowledge sharing and assertion, and develop an account of what it is to assert well. More specifically, they argue that the function of assertion is to share knowledge with others. It is this function that supports a central norm of assertion according to which a good assertion is one that has the disposition to generate knowledge in others. The book uses this functionalist approach to motivate further norms of assertion on both the speakers' and the hearers' side and investigates ramifications of this view on other questions about assertion.

Christoph Kelp is Senior Lecturer in Philosophy at the University of Glasgow. He is author of *Inquiry, Knowledge and Understanding* (2021), and co-editor of *Virtue Theoretic Epistemology* (with John Greco, Cambridge University Press, 2020).

Mona Simion is Professor of Philosophy at the University of Glasgow. She is author of *Shifty Speech and Independent Thought* (2021), and co-editor of *Reasons, Justification, and Defeat* (with Jessica Brown, 2021).

T0371540

CAMBRIDGE STUDIES IN PHILOSOPHY

General Editors

Nomy Arpaly
Brown University

Sanford Goldberg
Northwestern University

Cambridge Studies in Philosophy is the cornerstone of Cambridge University Press's list in mainstream, high-level analytic philosophy. It serves as a forum for a broad range of monographs on the cutting edge of epistemology, the philosophy of language and mind, ethics, and metaphysics.

Recent Titles

RICHARD FUMERTON *Knowledge, Thought and the Case for Dualism*

JAMIN ASAY *The Primitivist Theory of Truth*

CRAWFORD L. ELDER *Familiar Objects and Their Shadows*

SANFORD GOLDBERG *Anti-Individualism*

MICHAEL J. ZIMMERMANN *Living with Uncertainty*

LYNNE RUDDER BAKER *The Metaphysics of Everyday Life*

DAVID COPP *Morality in a Natural World*

JOSEPH MENDOLA *Goodness and Justice*

FOLKE TERSMAN *Moral Disagreement*

ALEXANDER R. PRUSS *The Principle of Sufficient Reason*

JOSHUA GERT *Brute Rationality*

NOAH LEMOS *Common Sense*

MICHAEL SMITH *Ethics and the A Priori*

KEITH FRANKISH *Mind and Supermind*

D. M. ARMSTRONG *Truth and Truthmakers*

WILLIAM S. ROBINSON *Understanding Phenomenal Consciousness*

ANDREW MELNYK *A Physicalist Manifesto*

JONATHAN KVANVIG *The Value of Knowledge and the Pursuit of Understanding*

SHARING KNOWLEDGE

A Functionalist Account of Assertion

CHRISTOPH KELP

University of Glasgow

MONA SIMION

University of Glasgow

Shaftesbury Road, Cambridge CB2 8EA, United Kingdom

One Liberty Plaza, 20th Floor, New York, NY 10006, USA

477 Williamstown Road, Port Melbourne, VIC 3207, Australia

314–321, 3rd Floor, Plot 3, Splendor Forum, Jasola District Centre, New Delhi – 110025, India

103 Penang Road, #05–06/07, Visioncrest Commercial, Singapore 238467

Cambridge University Press is part of Cambridge University Press & Assessment, a department of the University of Cambridge.

We share the University's mission to contribute to society through the pursuit of education, learning and research at the highest international levels of excellence.

www.cambridge.org
Information on this title: www.cambridge.org/9781009005791

DOI: 10.1017/9781009036818

First published 2022
First paperback edition 2023

A catalogue record for this publication is available from the British Library

ISBN   978-1-316-51713-0   Hardback
ISBN   978-1-009-00579-1   Paperback

For Max and Mia

Contents

vii

Acknowledgements

We have been thinking and writing about the nature and normativity of assertion for many years now, and we have benefitted from an extraordinary amount of support from our peers and mentors for this research. We would like to thank Kristoffer Ahlstrom-Vij, Bob Beddor, Sven Bernecker, Corine Besson, Alexander Bird, Michael Blome-Tillman, Emma Borg, Cameron Boult, Michael Brady, Elke Brendel, Fernando Broncano-Berrocal, Jessica Brown, Herman Cappelen, Adam Carter, Matthew Chrisman, Annalisa Coliva, Juan Comesaña, Robert Cowan, Marian David, Katherine Dormandy, Julien Dutant, Miguel Egler, Claire Field, Giada Fratantonio, Lizzie Fricker, Miranda Fricker, Manuel Garcia-Carpintero, Mikkel Gerken, Olav Gjelsvic, Sandy Goldberg, Emma Gordon, Peter J. Graham, John Greco, Patrick Greenough, Alex Gregory, Thomas Grundmann, Josh Habgood-Coote, Michael Hannon, Anandi Hattiangadi, Katherine Hawley, Frank Hofmann, Joachim Horvath, Christoph Jaeger, Jonathan Jenkins-Ichikawa, Matt Jope, Jesper Kallestrup, Klemens Kappel, Dirk Kindermann, Igal Kvart, Christos Kyriacou, Jennifer Lackey, Maria Lasonen-Aarnio, Janet Levin, Max Lewis, Clayton Littlejohn, Fed Luzzi, Jack Lyons, Susanne Mantel, Deborah Marber, Aidan McGlynn, Matt McGrath, Conor McHugh, Robin McKenna, Anne Meylan, Lisa Miracchi, Luca Moretti, Jennifer Nagel, Nikolaj Nottleman, Jonas Olson, Erik Olsson, Orestis Palermos, Carlotta Pavese, Andy Peet, Tommaso Piazza, Christian Piller, Duncan Pritchard, Andrew Reisner, Wayne Riggs, Sven Rosenkrantz, Lewis Ross, Sarah Sawyer, Susanne Schellenberg, Johanna Schnurr, Nick Shackel, Susanna Siegel, Martin Smith, Justin Snedegar, Ernie Sosa, Rachel Sterken, Ema Sullivan-Bisset, Kurt Sylvan, Alessandra Tanesini, Jonathan Way, John Webber, Alan Weir, Daniel Whiting, Asa Wikforss, Robbie Williams and Tim Williamson. We are convinced that we have missed people who deserve to be acknowledged by name and hope they will accept our apologies. Many thanks also to two anonymous referees from Cambridge University Press, who gave us excellent and very detailed comments on the book.

A few chapters of the book rely on previously published work: Chapter 2 draws heavily on our co-authored *Journal of Philosophy* article 'Criticism and Blame in Action and Assertion' (2017). Chapter 3 is based on Simion's *Synthese* article 'Assertion: Knowledge Is Enough' (2016), and Chapters 4 and 5 on Kelp's *Nous* article 'Assertion: A Function-First Account' (2018). Chapter 8 draws on Simion's 2019 *Mind & Language* article 'Assertion: The Context Shiftiness Dilemma'. Finally, Appendix A relies on our co-authored *Synthese* article 'Commodious Knowledge' (2017). We want to thank the editors of these journals as well as the anonymous referees who provided us with excellent comments on these articles.

Finally, many thanks to Sandy Goldberg and Hilary Gaskin at Cambridge University Press for all the excellent advice, support and efficiency.

Introduction

Imagine spending a day without asserting anything. For many people, this would be hard: we are asserting things all the time. When we do so, we are putting ourselves on the line in the sense that we make ourselves liable to criticism. 'You shouldn't have said this!' is one familiar way of criticising assertions. The fact that by asserting we make ourselves liable to criticism strongly suggests that assertion is governed by norms. This is in a way hardly surprising. After all, assertion is a speech act and action in general is governed by a variety of norms, including moral norms and practical norms. Suppose you say something mean to a friend. That's something you ought morally not to do. Or suppose you tell your supervisor at work that he is wearing ugly shoes. That's an imprudent thing to say, something that you ought practically not to do. 'You shouldn't have said this!' is one way of making just these points.

While all actions are governed by norms, including moral and practical ones, there are some types of act that are governed by specific norms. For instance, inner-city driving is governed by a norm that prohibits driving faster than 50 km/h, chess moves are governed by the rules of chess and so on. As a result, we are liable to further kinds of criticism when engaging in these types of acts. 'You shouldn't be driving so fast!' and 'You can't move the rook diagonally!' are ways of driving home such criticisms.

Is assertion governed by a norm that specifically governs assertion? We think that the answer to this question is 'yes'. More specifically, we take it that assertion is governed by an epistemic norm of the following form:

The C Rule of Assertion (CRA)
One must (epistemically): assert p only if p has C (Williamson 2000).

CRA proscribes assertions that do not satisfy a certain condition, C. In other words, CRA tells us that it is epistemically permissible to assert a proposition only if that proposition satisfies C. It states a necessary condition on epistemically permissible assertion. Another way of stating the content of the CRA is as follows:

The C Rule of Assertion (CRA)
It is epistemically permissible for one to assert p only if p has C.

One question that immediately arises at this stage concerns the identity of the crucial property C. And while there is broad consensus in the literature that assertion is governed by CRA, the identity of C is hotly debated. One prominent proposal, perhaps the most popular one at present, claims that C is the property of being known by the speaker. In other words,

The Knowledge Rule of Assertion (KRA)
One must (epistemically): assert p only if one knows p (e.g. Benton 2011, DeRose 2002, Hawthorne 2004, Kelp and Simion 2017b, Simion 2021, Slote 1979, Turri 2016, Unger 1975, Williamson 2000).[1]

To put our cards right on the table, one aim of this book will be to defend KRA.

Not far behind in terms of popularity is the following justification rule of assertion:

The Justification Rule of Assertion (JRA)
One must (epistemically): assert p only if one has justification for believing p (e.g. Douven 2006, Kvanvig 2009, Lackey 2008).

Not all champions of JRA use the term 'justification' in order to state the rule. Some use the term 'rationally credible' or 'reasonable to believe' instead. Crucially, however, when making the meaning of the relevant terms more precise, champions of these rules tend to come up with the same proposal: 'justification for believing', 'rationally credible' and 'reasonable to believe' are all unpacked as whatever turns ungettiered true belief into knowledge. Given that this is so, the differences between the various statements of the relevant rule are terminological. To keep things simple, we will henceforth use 'justification' for the property that turns

---

[1] Note that Williamson already notices a complication for KRA: '[I]f I know p and assert p, but the asserting is causally independent of the knowing, then something is wrong with the assertion. In some sense, in making my assertion I did not fully respect the knowledge rule, although I was lucky enough to get away without violating it' (Williamson 2000, 268, fn.99). Turri (2011) has since adduced some cases of assertion that fit the bill precisely. In order to deal with them he has proposed to endorse what he calls the express-knowledge rule of assertion, according to which one must assert p only if one's assertion expresses one's knowledge that p. Since the complication is of little consequence for our purposes, we will set it aside for the time being and allow the chips to fall however they may on this question.

ungettiered true belief into knowledge (unless otherwise noted) and work with JRA.[2]

While KRA and JRA are arguably the two leading views on the market, a number of further candidates have been defended, including the truth rule of assertion (e.g. Weiner 2005, Whiting 2013), the belief rule of assertion (e.g. Bach 2008, Hindriks 2007), the safety rule of assertion (e.g. Pelling 2013a, Pritchard 2014), as well as second-order accounts such as the believe-that-you-know rule of assertion (e.g. Thijsse 2000), the rationally-believe-that-you-know rule (e.g. Madison 2010), and contextualist accounts (e.g. McKinnon 2015, Goldberg 2015).[3] For the purposes of this book, we will largely bracket these alternatives and focus on JRA instead. The reason for this is (i) that our main arguments for KRA serve to favour KRA not only over JRA but also over the other rival views and (ii) JRA is the most serious competitor in that it not only has been worked out in most detail but also, in our opinion, has the strongest positive case in its support and the best alternative account of the considerations favouring KRA.

We evaluate assertions. Assertions can be good or bad. For instance, your assertion that London is the capital of the United Kingdom is a good one, whereas my assertion that my apartment is haunted by ghosts isn't. Under what conditions is an assertion a good one? There is a near-universal consensus that an assertion is good if and only if it complies with the rules governing assertion. Most importantly for present purposes, an assertion is epistemically good if and only if it complies with the epistemic rule of assertion. This gives us:

CRA-Good Assertion-Link
One's assertion that *p* is epistemically good if and only if it satisfies CRA.

[2] Crucially, several philosophers (e.g. Littlejohn Forthcoming, Sutton 2005, Williamson 2000) in the knowledge-first tradition take a view according to which a belief is justified if and only if it is knowledgeable (JB=K). As such, the notion of justification at work in JRA as discussed here comes in conflict with these views. On a JB=K account, JRA and KRA amount to one and the same norm. For now, for dialectical appropriateness, we are sticking to the 'traditional' notion of justification that the champions of JRA themselves endorse. See, however, Appendix B for discussion of JRA conceived along the lines of knowledge-first views of justification.

[3] Note, importantly, that some of these competing views do not, *stricto sensu*, come in conflict with KRA, in that they state necessary conditions for permissible assertion that are implied by knowledge. For instance, since the vast majority of views in the literature knowledge implies truth and justification, KRA champions agree with both JRA and a truth norm of assertion as stated (i.e. as necessary conditions on permissible assertion).

The disagreement amounts to what the strongest necessary condition for permissible assertion is. Champions of JRA, for instance, would deny that anything stronger than justification is needed, while champions of KRA will disagree with this claim.

CRA-Good Assertion-Link is highly popular,[4] in that it is widely assumed, although rarely if ever explicitly discussed in the literature.[5] Here, we aim

---

[4] Here is some textual evidence that CRA-Good Assertion-Link is presupposed both by friends and foes of KRA. Consider the following passage by Jonathan Sutton, a staunch defender of KRA:

> If the beliefs so transmitted meet the primary standards governing good belief for both speaker and hearer – that is, they are justified in an evaluative sense – and meet standards of permissible belief (as noted previously, it is hard to imagine the former standards being met without the latter), it would be mysterious if the assertions transmitting the beliefs failed to meet the standards governing good assertion. On the contrary, the assertions in question have to meet the standards governing good assertion impeccably since they transmit impeccable beliefs. It is not, however, the knowledge rule that is at fault; the arguments of Williamson and others for that rule are good ones. It is our initial supposition that was at fault. There are no justified true beliefs falling short of knowledge. (Sutton 2005, 376)

On the side of KRA's foes, here is McKinnon:

> There's an intuitive sense in which some assertions are good, whereas others are bad. Lies, for example, seem like good candidates for things we shouldn't say. But what's the difference between honest truth-telling and lying? Are all false assertions bad assertions? These questions concern whether there are any standards governing what it takes to assert well. We call these standards *norms*. (McKinnon 2015, 1)

It may also be worth noting that, in fact, anyone who grants that either of the standard cases of assertion from justified false belief and gettiered belief as well as selfless assertion serve to exert pressure on KRA because these assertions are intuitively epistemically good or, alternatively, permissible assertions (see Chapter 2, Sections 2.1.1 and 2.4.2) presupposes CRA-Good Assertion-Link. After all, if these philosophers were to deny CRA-Good Assertion-Link and to embrace a variety of normative pluralism instead, simply bringing forth cases of intuitively permissible assertions or, alternatively, intuitively good assertions, would not be enough to put pressure on KRA: after all, if knowledge is not necessary for permissible assertions, it might still be necessary for good assertions, and the other way around.

[5] That said, there are a couple of notable exceptions to the agreement on CRA-Good Assertion-Link. One is John Turri who defends a view that clearly distinguishes between good assertion and permissible assertions in (Turri 2014). According to Turri, roughly, good assertions must satisfy KRA and assertions that satisfy JRA but not KRA are permissible but suberogatory. Note that there are important differences between Turri's account and the one we will develop in Chapters 4 and 5. Most importantly, first, KRA is required for permissible assertion and, second, satisfying the norm for permissible assertion without satisfying the norm for good assertion does not amount to suberogation. Turri proposes this view to offer an alternative account of the standard counterexamples to KRA, i.e. one that deviates from the standard account in terms of blamelessness and that is more concessive to JRA. We think that this is a mistake. Suberogation is not the right way to deal with these cases. The reason for this is that suberogatory actions can be charged against the agent. The assertions in the classical counterexamples cannot. It might be said that suberogatory actions cannot be charged against the agent if the agent is blameless for performing them. We agree. However, if we need blamelessness anyway to deal with the standard counterexamples in a satisfactory way, it now looks as though the appeal to suberogation is simply redundant. We will not discuss Turri's view in any more detail here, however, due to the fact that, in more recent work he agrees that this view is too concessive to champions of JRA and has explicitly recanted it in his 2016 book.

Another possible exception to the wide endorsement of CRA-Good Assertion-Link is Ernie Sosa's (2011), who defends a normatively pluralistic view of the normativity of assertion, which, on the face of it, may allow him to be neutral on CRA-Good Assertion-link. Sosa distinguishes assessment norms of evaluation from minimal standards, and the latter from criticism norms (52–53). The

to tackle this issue head on: we aim to show that *CRA-Good Assertion-Link* is false.

Standard approaches to the normativity of assertion endorse (either implicitly or explicitly) both a version of CRA and *CRA-Good Assertion-Link*. The conditions for good assertion are then derived from CRA and *CRA-Good Assertion-Link*. In this way, standard approaches to the normativity of assertion qualify as *rule first accounts of assertion* (RFAA).

The central aim of this book is to defend an alternative to RFAA. Unlike RFAA, it derives the conditions for good assertion not from CRA but from the *epistemic function* of assertion. In this way, we are proposing a *function first account of assertion* (FFAA). More specifically, starting from a plausible etiological account of functions (henceforth e-functions for short), we argue that e-functions in general have normative import in the following sense: for tokens of e-functional types, there is such a thing as being *a good token of this type*. The sense of 'good' we have in mind is an attributive sense (e.g. Geach 1956), where 'good' functions as a predicate modifier, rather than as a predicate in its own right. For instance, 'Good knives are sharp' stands for the claim that knives *qua knives* are good only if they are sharp. It does not entail that good knives are good *simpliciter*, or good for some purpose or another.

We argue that a good token of an e-functional type is a token that has the disposition to fulfil its e-function. We then argue that assertion has the e-function of generating knowledge in hearers and in this way derive an account of good assertion. Roughly, the idea is that a good assertion is one that has the disposition to generate knowledge in hearers. We argue that FFAA's account of good assertion compares favourably with its RFAA rival.

Note that apart from the fact that the account of good assertion is derived from the e-function rather than the rule of assertion, the two views

assessment of a performance is the evaluative dimension, and from it one can establish minimal standards (in Sosa's view, in the case of assertion, the minimal standard in question is knowledge). In turn, criticisability can map on to either the evaluative or the minimal standards dimension, or both. Since the view is normatively pluralistic, Sosa's account can remain neutral on CRA-Good Assertion Link. Crucially, in spite of his pluralistic view, evidence that Sosa presupposes CRA-Good Assertion-Link derives from his treatment of selfless assertion cases. He grants that these cases cause trouble for any norm of assertion that features a belief requirement and offers an alternative explanation. Had he countenanced a distinction between good assertion and permissible assertion, this would have been too quick. He should (and we are very confident that he would) have stopped to consider the question of whether even though the assertion is impermissible by the belief entailing norm, it may still be a good assertion.

differ in orientation as well: whereas rule firsters propose a speaker-oriented account of good assertion in the sense that whether an assertion is a good one depends on whether the speaker satisfies certain conditions, our account is hearer-oriented in that whether an assertion is a good one depends on what it can do for hearers, as it were.

Given that FFAA arrives at a hearer-oriented account of good assertion, the question arises as to how speaker rules fit into the account. We offer a functionalist answer. We first argue that, when certain conditions are in place, it makes sense to govern production of tokens of e-functional types by rules. We show that the relevant conditions are met in the case of assertion and argue that, in fact, it makes sense to govern production of assertions by KRA. In this way, we offer a functionalist account not only of the status of KRA as derivative from its e-function, but also give a functionalist explanation of why assertion should be governed by KRA in the first place. In other words, we offer a functionalist rationale of KRA. In this way, we show that KRA actually fits rather nicely in the functionalist framework.

The questions of status and rationale of the epistemic rule of assertion are of independent interest. While this question has not been taken up as often as the question concerning the content of the rule, some accounts can be found in the literature. All of them are congenial to RFAA. We take a look at extant proposals in the literature and argue that they remain unsatisfactory. In this way, FFAA can score further points against RFAA.

FFAA is theoretically fruitful beyond its attractive accounts of good assertion and the status and rationale of KRA. One additional benefit of FFAA is that it serves to offer a rationale for a duty on the part of hearers to believe what is asserted. We argue that we must countenance this duty to make proper sense of testimonial injustice, one of the most important phenomena in recent epistemology, and we show why on FFAA it makes sense for there to be a duty to believe assertions.

Having made a case that FFAA can allow us to make progress on a number of key issues in the normativity of assertion, both old and new, we turn to broader issues about the relation between knowledge/KRA and language. Champions of KRA have argued that KRA can be used to argue for further substantive theses, especially in the philosophy of language. One important case in point is Williamson's claim that KRA is constitutive of assertion and that it allows us to give an account of the nature of assertion. Another, due to DeRose, is that KRA entails contextualism about knowledge attribution. While we are defenders of

KRA, we are more pessimistic about these attempts to use KRA to argue for substantive claims in the philosophy of language. In particular, we argue, pace Williamson, that the knowledge rule is not constitutive of assertion – at least not in the way in which he envisages the constitutivity relation, i.e. on the model of rules governing games and languages. And while we argue that an important premise of DeRose's argument is correct, i.e. that knowledge is not only necessary but also sufficient for epistemically permissible assertion, we show that it KRA does not provide support for contextualism about knowledge attributions. Even a biconditional version of KRA is entirely compatible with an invariantist semantics of knowledge attributions. In fact, we show that the argument can be turned on its head: KRA is in tension with contextualism.

0.1 Game Plan

Very briefly, here is a game plan for this book.

Part A defends KRA.

Chapter 1 outlines the positive argument for KRA. While quite a bit of the relevant evidence for KRA is familiar from the literature, we make a couple of additions that, we believe, serve to strengthen the case for KRA.

Chapter 2 discusses a number of classical problems for KRA and argues that these problems can be solved. Worth special notice here is a general normative framework with accounts of criticisability, blamelessness and blameworthiness that we develop. Applied to the case of assertion, this framework allows us to give a well-motivated and KRA-friendly response to some classical cases that are often thought to show that KRA is too strong.

Chapter 3 turns to the thesis that knowledge is sufficient for permissible assertion and defends it against recent objections by Jessica Brown and Jennifer Lackey.

Part B develops FFAA.

Chapter 4 introduces the first part of our function first account of the normativity of assertion. We introduce the account of e-functions and their normative import. We then argue for our thesis concerning the e-function of assertion and derive our preferred account of good assertion. We show that our account compares favourably with its standard rule first rival.

Chapter 5 fits KRA into the function first picture. We ask the question of why assertion should be governed by KRA, look at some proposals from the rule first camp, due, respectively, to Bach and Hindriks on the one hand, and Douven on the other, and show that they remain unsatisfactory. We then offer a functionalist account of the status of KRA as well as a function first rationale for it.

Chapter 6 turns to rules of assertion on the hearer side. One of the central aims of this chapter is to argue for one specific such rule which requires that hearers believe what is asserted. We argue that in order to make proper sense of testimonial injustice, we must countenance a duty to believe on the part of the hearer. Having looked at some proposals that emerge from recent literature on conversational pressure and found them wanting, we offer a functionalist account of this duty to belief.

Part C looks at a couple of further issues about the relation between knowledge and language.

Chapter 7 considers the question of whether KRA is a constitutive rule of assertion in the same way in which rules of games and languages are constitutive, and defends a negative answer.

Chapter 8 takes a closer look at the relation between KRA and the divide between contextualist and invariantist semantics for knowledge attributions. We argue that DeRose's influential argument that KRA demands contextualism fails and show how it can be turned on its head.

PART I

KRA
The Knowledge Rule of Assertion

CHAPTER I

The Case for the KRA

According to KRA, we need at least knowledge to be permitted to assert. In support of this thesis, champions of KRA have adduced three main pieces of evidence: lottery propositions, Moorean conjunctions and linguistic data. We will look at these in turn, starting with lottery propositions.

I.I   Lottery Propositions

You have bought a ticket in a fair lottery with one million tickets and exactly one winner. The winning ticket has already been drawn, but the result has not been announced. I know that you own a ticket and I know that the odds against winning are massive. Upon meeting you, I assert that your ticket did not win the lottery. My assertion in this case is not a good one.

The same goes for similar cases. Let a lottery proposition be any proposition of the form 'ticket x does not win lottery l'. When the only information one has about a given lottery concerns the odds against winning and when, for all one knows, those odds are non-zero, lottery propositions are not assertable. That is to say, if one does assert a lottery proposition, one's assertion is bound not to be a good one.[1]

Why not? Champions of KRA have an explanation ready to hand. When the only information about a lottery we have is the probabilistic information about the odds of winning, we are not in a position to know lottery propositions. If so, we don't know lottery propositions. If we assert a lottery proposition, we are bound to violate KRA. That's why our assertion is bound not to be good.

---

[1] This claim, while endorsed by the vast majority of epistemologists, is not universally accepted. See e.g. Gibbons (2013) and Sosa (2015) for notable exceptions.

At first glance, weaker rivals of KRA do not have an equally neat explanation available. Consider KRA's most prominent rival, JRA.[2] The reason why JRA will have a much harder time explaining why assertions of lottery propositions aren't good assertions is that lottery propositions appear to be exceptionally well justified.[3] If this isn't immediately obvious, notice that the probability of winning may be much lower than even one in a million. Already in an ordinary state lottery the odds are much worse than this. In fact, however, the odds can be as close to zero as you like. Given the prima facie plausible assumption that the degree of justification for a proposition is proportional to the probability of its truth, lottery propositions can enjoy as high a degree of justification as you like short of certainty. Even so, so long as there is a non-zero chance that a given ticket will win a lottery, the relevant lottery propositions won't be assertable. After all, the relevant ticket might just be the winner. As a result, lottery propositions appear to cause trouble for JRA.

On second thought, however, it is not so clear that lottery propositions serve to secure an advantage for KRA against the competition. In particular, there is reason to think that JRA will also be able to explain why

---

[2] Champions of the truth norm of assertion will have even more serious difficulties accommodating the intuitive impermissibility of asserting lottery propositions. After all, the truth norm predicts that, if one's lottery assertion is, as a matter of fact, true, it is permissible. One move available to champions of a truth norm would be to argue that it generates a subsidiary justification norm (Williamson 2000, 244–47). This could be done by arguing that the following principle holds in full generality: if one should φ only if some condition obtains, then one should φ only if one has evidence for thinking that that condition obtains.

Returning to the lottery case, however, since it is extremely probable on one's evidence that one's ticket lost, it would appear that lottery assertions would satisfy this derivative norm too. But see earlier discussion for further discussion of JRA and lottery assertions.

Matthew Weiner (2005), on behalf of the truth norm, attempts to explain the heard impropriety of lottery assertions by appealing to Gricean considerations; according to Weiner, when one makes a lottery assertion, one generates the implicature that one has inside information about the lottery (or, at any rate, more than just the probabilistic evidence), which, if false, renders the assertion impermissible. The problem with this attempt, however, is that the stipulated implicature fails to pass the cancellability test: an assertion of the form 'My ticket did not win but I don't know that my ticket didn't win' not only does not remove the heard impermissibility, but it adds Moorean paradoxicality to the mix. In a nutshell, the truth view has difficulties explaining why strong probabilistic support is insufficient for permissible assertion.

Daniel Whiting offers what we take to be the strongest defence of the truth norm to date; Whiting exploits the distinction between there being reason to *phi* and one's having reason to *phi* to argue that the truth of *p* generates warrant for asserting that *p*, even if the warrant in question is not *had* by the speaker. As such, according to Whiting, the heard impropriety of lottery assertions is generated by the speaker *not having* the warrant to assert, although, on the assumption that the assertion is true, there *is* warrant for it. See Whiting's (2015) exchange with Littlejohn (2014) for arguments for and against this defence of the truth norm.

[3] On the assumption that justification comes in degrees, and that a known high probability of *p* implies a high level of justification for *p*. However, see subsequent discussion.

lottery propositions are not assertable. To see this, consider, first, the lottery paradox according to which the following three very plausible propositions are jointly incompatible:

Sufficiency Thesis (ST)
If the probability of p on one's evidence is very high, then p is justified for one.

Conjunction Closure (CC)
If p is justified for one and q is justified for one, then so is their conjunction, p and q.

No Contradictions (NC)
No proposition that one knows to be a contradiction is justified for one.

To see that ST, CC and NC are jointly incompatible, consider a fair lottery with with n tickets and exactly one winner. For each ticket, the probability that it will win is $1/n$. Make n large enough that, for each ticket, the probability that it will lose qualifies as very high. By ST, for each ticket, the proposition that it will lose is justified for you. By CC, the proposition that all tickets will lose is justified for you also. Since, *ex hypothesi*, you know that there is exactly one winner, this proposition is also justified for you. By another application of CC, the proposition that all tickets will lose and that there will be a winner is justified for you. However, you know that this proposition is a contradiction. So, by NC, it is not justified for you. We now have derived a contradiction from ST, CC and NC.

Crucially, champions of JRA can (and have) argued that the culprit of the lottery paradox is ST.[4] Here is Douven:

> While some have proposed to abandon [CC] in response to this [i.e. the lottery paradox], a majority of philosophers nowadays think this is too high a price to pay and that the better option is to combine [CC] with some qualified version of [ST], or at least a principle akin to [ST]. (Douven 2006, 458)

Of course, if ST is the culprit of the lottery paradox, lottery propositions are not justified for us, even though they are highly probable on our evidence. As a result, assertions of lottery propositions are bound to violate JRA. JRA can also account for the unassertability of lottery propositions. Ultimately, there is no advantage for KRA here.[5]

---

[4] For a neat overview over the arguments, see Douven (2002). One of us has also argued that the lottery paradox shows ST to be false elsewhere (Kelp 2017, 2018).

[5] Note that Kvanvig (2009) and McKinnon (2015) also hold that we just don't have the kind of justification for lottery propositions they require for permissible assertion.

1.2   Moorean Conjunctions

Moorean conjunctions are a family of de se propositions that sound paradoxical when asserted (Moore 1942, 542–43; 1962, 277). The most famous examples are propositions of the form 'p but I don't believe that p' (belief version) and 'p but I don't know that p' (knowledge version). For instance, suppose I assert 'It is raining outside, but I don't believe that it is' or 'The morning star is the evening star, but I don't know this'. In both of these cases my assertions sound paradoxical. *A fortiori*, they are not good assertions.

It is widely acknowledged that KRA offers a very attractive explanation of why conjunctions such as 'It is Wednesday but I don't know that it is Wednesday' and 'It is Wednesday but I don't believe that it is Wednesday' are not assertable. If knowledge is the norm of assertion, on the plausible assumption that knowledge distributes across conjunctions, one is in a good enough epistemic position to assert 'p but I don't know that p' only if one knows both conjuncts. However, since knowledge is factive, one only knows the second conjunct if it is true that one does not know that p. But that contradicts the first conjunct. Thus, according to KRA, one cannot meet the conditions for making a proper assertion of a conjunction of the form 'p but I don't know that p'.

Furthermore, if KRA is true, it is plausible that when a speaker asserts that p, the hearer is led to believe that she knows that p; therefore, when one asserts the second conjunct of a Moorean conjunction, one denies what one has led one's hearer to believe by asserting the first conjunct. Thus, KRA explains not only why conjunctions of the form 'p but I don't know that p' are unassertable, but also why they sound paradoxical.

It is easy to see that, by similar reasoning, KRA scores equally well when it comes to Moorean conjunctions with belief. If, by KRA, one is supposed to know both conjuncts of the Moorean conjunction, given that knowledge implies belief, it follows that one has to (i) believe that p and (ii) know that one does not believe that p. Given, again, factivity of knowledge, one needs to (i) believe that p and (ii) not believe that p. Thus, Moorean conjunctions in the belief version are also not assertable. And, again, on similar grounds as discussed earlier, it makes sense that such assertions will sound paradoxical to the hearer.

At first glance, JRA does not seem to be able to give as good an explanation of the phenomenon, given that justification is not factive. In fact, even champions of JRA have acknowledged as much. In his 2006 paper, Douven concedes the superiority of KRA on this count. More specifically, he argues that, while JRA can also make sense of why Moorean conjunctions come with a paradoxical flavour, KRA scores better in terms of simplicity.

Douven's early explanation goes, roughly, along the following lines: first of all, he claims that champions of JRA need not hold that Moorean conjunctions are not assertable. All that is needed is a good explanation of the fact that they sound odd. Now, it is a fact that we do not encounter Moorean conjunctions every day. If that is the case, it also makes sense that they sound odd to us, due to lack of exposure. Why is it, though, that we do not hear Moorean conjunctions every day? Well, according to Douven, although KRA is strictly speaking false, it is the case that we typically know what we assert. That is, in normal, friendly environmental conditions, if p is justified for me, I also know that p. Given this, it will come as no surprise that Moorean conjunctions are extremely rarely asserted and therefore extremely rarely heard, which explains why they sound odd to us. As such, according to Douven, although JRA does not offer as straightforward an explanation of the oddity of Moorean conjunctions as KRA does, it is able to accommodate the data in a perfectly plausible way (2006, 474).

In later work, though, Douven (2009) comes back to the issue and concedes that his early explanation of the odd-soundingness of Moorean conjunctions is problematic. After all, there are many expressions that we do not often encounter and that do not seem to share the odd-soundingness of Moorean conjunctions. Consider, for instance, 'John seeks a unicorn'; surely we do not hear this every day. Still, it seems clear enough that whatever is happening when one hears a Moorean conjunction pertains to a completely different category of oddness than that of other sentences to which we have little exposure (2009, 363).

On the upside, Douven (2009) argues that a more careful examination reveals that JRA is able to do as good a job as KRA when it comes to accommodating the odd-soundingness of Moorean conjunctions. That is because, according to him, not only are the latter statements not knowable, but they are also not justified, and, therefore, unassertable even by the lights of JRA. In a nutshell, the argument proceeds along the following lines: first, Douven assumes that one plausible and fairly weak requirement on justification is that a person believes p justifiably only if it does not readily follow strictly on the basis of the assumption of her justifiably believing p plus some fairly uncontroversial doxastic principles[6] that her

---

[6] Here are the principles: (1) if you justifiably believe p and q, then you also justifiably believe p; (2) justifiably believing some p requires having a higher degree of belief in p than in its negation, and (3)

degrees of belief are not probabilities. Second, Douven proves that, if one assumes, for *reductio*, that one justifiably believes Moorean conjunctions, it does follow from these uncontroversial doxastic principles that one's degrees of belief are not probabilities. Thus, Douven argues, Moorean conjunctions cannot be justifiably believed, and therefore are not assertable.

Even if we accept Douven's unassertability diagnosis, however, there are still two major problems for his account. First, even if Moorean conjunctions are de facto not assertable on JRA, it is not clear that laymen would immediately 'feel' that Moorean conjunctions are unassertable if JRA is the norm of assertion. After all, by Douven's own lights, Moorean conjunctions may appear, at first glance, to be justifiably believable. For starters, Douven himself granted as much in 2006 when he conceded that they are assertable by JRA. Furthermore, proving that Moorean conjunctions are not justified, as we have seen, requires quite a bit of work as Douven also acknowledges: 'it is not immediately clear that it could never happen that, for some φ, φ is [justified for] to a person and at the same time it is [justified for] this person that she does not know φ' (2009, 363). But if it is not even immediately clear to specialists that Moorean conjunctions don't satisfy JRA, how can it be that they invariably and immediately trigger a strong feeling of paradox even in laymen?

Second, crucially, even if we set this problem aside, the mere unassertability of Moorean conjunctions will not do all the work that needs to be done here. Recall that the KRA explanation of why Moorean conjunctions sound paradoxical had two essential components: first, there was the unassertability; second, the heard contradiction triggered by it. Notice, also, that a fully adequate account of Moorean conjunctions will have to explain the heard contradiction as well. After all, there are other propositions that are guaranteed to be unassertable. Just recall the family of lottery propositions discussed earlier. However, just as in the case of 'John seeks a unicorn', the oddity involved in hearing someone assert 'Your ticket won't win the lottery', if any, is definitely of a completely different sort than the one at issue Moorean conjunctions. In particular, unlike Moorean conjunctions, lottery assertions clearly do not sound paradoxical. Given that this is so, just explaining the unassertability of Moorean conjunctions won't be enough. What is needed in addition is an explanation of why they sound paradoxical. KRA delivers on this front: knowledge is the norm

---

if you justifiably believe some p, then your degree of belief that you believe/know p is at least as high as your degree of belief that you don't believe/don't know p.

of assertion, therefore when one asserts that *p* one leads one's hearer to believe that one knows that *p*, which is contradicted by the second conjunct; hence, the heard contradiction. Can JRA do equally well?

McKinnon has recently offered an account of Moorean conjunctions that might do the trick for champions of JRA. Here goes:

> When one asserts that p, one both represents oneself as having the authority to assert that p *and* represents oneself as believing that p (and perhaps as knowing that p). That is, in representing oneself as having assertoric authority to assert a proposition, one *thereby* also represents oneself as believing the proposition. It is my view that the latter is derivative from the former. (McKinnon 2015, 134)

Now if McKinnon is right and by representing oneself as having the authority to assert that p one thereby represents oneself as knowing that p,[7] then KRA's explanation of why Moorean conjunctions sound paradoxical becomes available for champions of JRA.

The crucial question, however, is just why we should think that in representing oneself as having the authority to assert that p, one represents oneself as knowing that p. Of course, if KRA is true, then this makes perfect sense. After all, knowing that p is what it takes to have the authority to assert that p. No surprise, then, that in representing oneself as having the authority to assert that p one also represents oneself as knowing that p. However, McKinnon and champions of JRA alike reject KRA and so this answer to the crucial question is not available to them.

Here is another way in which they might try to respond. In general, if one represents oneself as having the authority to Xp, then one represents oneself as knowing that p. However, this avenue is also unpromising. When I command someone to do something, I do not thereby represent myself as knowing that this person will do the said thing. Suppose, for instance, that I am a fascist military general and command you, one of my officers, to shoot your spouse. Even if I now represent myself as having the authority to so command you, I surely do not thereby represent myself as knowing that you will comply with my demand. This becomes especially clear in cases in which it is common knowledge between us all along that you will not do what I command you to do. What comes to light, then, is that while McKinnon's account may well succeed in explaining why Moorean conjunctions sound paradoxical, it is unclear how it could do so unless KRA is assumed in the background.

---

[7] See also DeRose (1991) for an earlier defence of the view that when one asserts that p one represents oneself as knowing that p.

But perhaps there is a more direct alternative available for champions of JRA. Perhaps we can construct a JRA-based account of why Moorean conjunctions sound paradoxical that runs parallel to the KRA-based account. The key idea here is to exploit the fact that, on JRA, if I assert that p, I lead my hearer to believe that p is justified for me. However, the trouble with this account is that this does not contradict the second conjunct in any of the two Moorean schemas that we have been looking at. Take, for instance, the case of someone who is (irrationally) afraid of flying and consider her relationship to the proposition 'Flying is the least dangerous mode of transportation'. Even if the corresponding Moorean conjunctions are not justified for her, it certainly does not sound contradictory for that person to say that p is justified for her but she doesn't know or believe it. What comes to light, then, is that even if champions of JRA can secure the result that Moorean conjunctions are not assertable, they cannot successfully explain why they sound paradoxical. As a result, Moorean conjunctions do provide evidence favouring KRA over JRA.[8]

1.3   Parenthetical Position

Matt Benton (2011) has recently argued that the fact that 'I know' cannot be used in parenthetical position provides further support for KRA (see also Blaauw 2012). To see this compare:

B1.   I believe it is raining.

B2.   It is, I believe, raining.

B3.   It is raining, I believe.

K1.   I know it is raining.

K2.   ? It is, I know, raining.

K3.   ? It is raining, I know.

Following Slote (1979), Benton argues that constructions like B1 and K1 can be used to *ascribe* or *express* the relevant mental states, while parenthetical constructions like B2, B3, K2 and K3 unambiguously serve to *express* them. He claims that the oddity of K2 and K3 provides support for KRA because KRA has an explanation ready at hand. According to KRA

---

[8] For an overview of how the two candidate norms score on both empirical and theoretical considerations, see Simion (2016c).

flat-out assertion already serves to express knowledge. Parenthetical constructions like K2 and K3 sound odd because what is said in them is redundant.

The first thing to note about this is that it is far from clear that redundancy is what does the trick here. After all, since knowledge implies belief, on the assumption that KRA is correct, B2 and B3 are also redundant. More plausibly, what does the work here, if anything, is the intuitive permissibility of hedging assertions with 'I believe,' but not with 'I know.' However, even if Benton is right and K2 and K3 are odd, in a way in which B2 and B3 are not, this datum, in itself, does not solely support KRA: even if correct, all this datum shows is that the norm of assertion is stronger than belief – which is why 'I believe' is a proper way to hedge assertions – but weaker than knowledge – which is why 'I know' cannot serve this function. Needless to say, while this does serve to support KRA over Belief norms of assertion, several other norms of assertion will also be supported by this datum: for instance, a Justified Belief norm of assertion, as well as a True Belief norm of assertion will also stand to gain from Benton's argument.

Unfortunately, there is reason to think that, ultimately, these considerations do not provide special support for KRA against a Belief norm after all (McGlynn 2014, McKinnon and Turri 2013). There are similarly redundant uses of expressions in parenthetical position that are perfectly acceptable, including:

o1.   Why, I ask, should we do that?

o2.   It is raining outside, I claim. (McKinnon and Turri 2013)

Moreover, there are uses of 'I know' in parenthetical position that are perfectly acceptable. Consider, for instance:

K5.   It is, I know, a bad day to hold this meeting.

K6.   It is a bad day to hold this meeting, I know. (Ibid.)

It transpires that, even if some uses of 'I know' in parenthetical position are odd, others work perfectly fine. What's going on then? To answer this question, note that acceptability of sentences featuring 'I know' in parenthetical position seems to vary significantly with the length of the sentence. If this isn't sufficiently evident yet, compare:

K2.   ? It is, I know, raining.

K7.   It is, I know, raining outside but that's no reason not to go to the cinema.

к8.   It has been raining outside, I know, but that's no reason not to go to
       the cinema.

о3.   Why, I ask, is it raining here?
о4.   ? Is it, I ask, raining?

In conjunction, these considerations provide good reason to think that
redundancy is not the problem with K2, K3 and O4. In fact, once we
observe just how much sentence length seems to matter to acceptable,
an explanation in terms of prosody suggests itself: one possible reason
why these utterances might sound odd is that the rhythm just isn't
right.[9]

   That being said, we don't mean to settle the question of just why the
likes of K2, K3 and O3 sound odd. Rather, what we are interested in is the
question as to whether the oddity of K2 and K3 provides evidence for
KRA. We take it to be sufficiently clear at this stage that more work needs
to be done in support of this claim.

1.4   Challenges and Prompts

Another source of support for KRA stems from conversational patterns
(Unger 1975, Williamson 2000). As a first observation note that assertions
are susceptible to challenges. Consider the following exchange:

Exchange 1
A: The department will hire a new faculty member next year.
B: How do you know?

When B asks A how A knows that the department will hire next year,
B may just be requesting further information. However, B may also be
challenging A's assertion. B may suspect that A doesn't know this at
all. By putting his question to A, B invites A to put her cards on
the table.

   There are other ways of challenging assertions. Consider:

Exchange 2
A: The department will hire a new faculty member next year.
B: Do you know that?

When, in the first exchange, B asked A how she knows, B tentatively
granted that A does know what she asserted and challenged her assertion

---

[9] We owe this suggestion to the linguistics expertise of Gareth Roberts (pc).

by requesting information concerning how she knows this. B's challenge was implicit. In contrast, when B asks whether A does know, B does not grant A, even tentatively, that she knows. Rather B challenges A's assertion explicitly. Accordingly, this way of challenging an assertion is somewhat more aggressive than the first.

KRA can easily explain these challenge patterns. According to KRA, A is epistemically permitted – i.e. has the authority – to make her assertion only if she knows its content. Given that this is so, it is only to be expected that B can challenge A's assertion by asking how or whether A knows what she asserts. What B is effectively doing is asking whether A has the authority to assert (Unger 1975, Williamson 2000).

Assertions are challenged after the fact. They may be prompted beforehand. Again, prompting patterns provide further evidence for KRA (Turri 2010). To see this, consider a situation in which B asks A whether there is malaria in Laos. Here B prompts an assertion by asking a question about a piece of mind-independent reality. B presupposes that the addressee is in a position to answer this question, where this involves having the authority to answer. If this isn't immediately obvious, consider:

Exchange 3
B : Is there malaria in Laos?
A : I couldn't say.

Note that A's assertion will typically be an appropriate response to B's question. What A says here is that she does not have the authority to make the assertion prompted by B. That is to say, B is denying what A is presupposing in this exchange. Crucially, A might just as well have responded in the following way:

Exchange 4
B : Is there malaria in Laos?
A : I don't know.

What *Exchanges 3* and *4* highlight is that 'I don't know' and 'I can't say' can be used interchangeably by way of responding to an assertion prompt.

KRA can easily make sense of this. On KRA, only knowledge authorises assertion. While 'I couldn't say' explicitly states that A doesn't have the authority to assert on the matter, 'I don't know' explicitly states that A doesn't satisfy a necessary condition for having the authority to so assert, thus implying that she doesn't have authority. Unsurprisingly, each response will equally serve to point out that one does not have the authority to assert on the matter.[10]

Consider, next, the following exchanges:

Exchange 5

B: Is there malaria in Laos?

A: Yes, there is.

Exchange 6

B: Do you know whether there is malaria in Laos?

A: Yes, there is.

The main difference between these two exchanges is that, in *Exchange 5*, B presupposes that A has the authority to answer this question, whereas he doesn't do so in *Exchange 6*. As a result, B's question in *Exchange 6* will typically be perceived as somewhat more polite than in *Exchange 5*. Even so, the two ways of prompting assertions exemplified here can often be used interchangeably. Note also that A's response is an equally appropriate answer to either question.

Again, KRA can easily explain these data. Given that KRA holds, B's question in *Exchange 6* explicitly asks whether A has the authority to assert on the matter, whereas his assertion in *Exchange 5* already presupposes that he does. Note that given that this is so, it is unsurprising that the less presumptuous way should be perceived as more polite. Nor will be surprising that A's response is equally appropriate in both cases.

---

[10] By way of comparison, suppose an employee of a store, A, has reported a significant transgression to the manager, B. Suppose only the owner of the store has the authority to dismiss employees from their jobs. Now, consider the following exchange:

Exchange I
A: Fire that man.
B: I can't do that.

Exchange II
A: Fire that man.
B: I am not the owner.

Note that B can respond to A's request in either way. Given that only the owner has the authority to dismiss employees, this makes perfect sense. While in *Exchange I*, B states that he doesn't have the authority to dismiss the relevant employee, in Exchange II, he states that he doesn't satisfy a necessary condition for having the authority to dismissing the offender, thus implying that he doesn't have the authority to do so.

1.5 Legitimate Criticisms and Appropriate Responses

Consider any performance type that is governed by a rule to the effect that one must: φ only if one meets condition C. What we would like to suggest is roughly the following: When a performance type is governed by such a rule, we can *legitimately criticise*[11] agents for φing without satisfying C. Here is a slightly more careful statement of this idea:

> **Legitimate Criticism**
> For any performance type, φ, that is governed by a rule to the effect that one must: φ only if one meets C, if we criticise an agent who φs without satisfying C for φing without satisfying C, our criticism will be **prima facie**[12] **legitimate**. At the very least, it will be prima facie legitimate when we also satisfy the following two conditions: (i) we know that the agent φs but doesn't satisfy C and (ii) we can offer a reason to believe that the agent does not satisfy C when it isn't obvious that s/he doesn't.[13]

Consider, for instance, the performance type of playing one's penultimate card in a game of Uno. This performance type is governed by a rule to the effect that one must: call 'uno' when producing a token of the type. When we know that a player of Uno plays his penultimate card without calling 'uno', we can prima facie legitimately criticise him for not calling 'uno'.[14]

There is an important difference between legitimate criticisms that target violations of particular rules and criticisms targeting the all-things-considered status of the act under consideration. In particular, there may be cases in which an agent can be prima legitimately criticised for violating a certain rule, whilst the all-things-considered status of his act is not legitimately criticisable, not even prima facie. By way of example, suppose

---

[11] Importantly, we take it, in line with the relevant literature (for overview, see e.g. Kelp and Simion (2017b)) that there is a crucial difference between mere criticism and blame, in that the latter is the stronger act. What is at issue here is mere criticism, we discuss blame subsequently.

[12] Here and throughout the book we follow orthodox usage of 'prima facie' in epistemology, to mean 'that can be overriden or swamped' (compare, for instance, the wide spread usage of 'prima facie epistemic justification' as justification that can be defeated). We are aware that some philosophers in other subdisciplines employ this term differently, at times. In particular, in ethics 'prima facie' is sometimes used to designate a *perceived* obligation, in contrast to an obligation *simpliciter*.

[13] We don't mean to suggest that violations of rules only ever legitimise the kinds of criticisms mentioned above. On the contrary, other kinds of sanctions may be legitimate or even called for as well (perhaps given that further conditions are in place). Crucially, however, this fact does not affect the prima facie legitimacy of the aforementioned kinds of criticism. Rather, violations of rules always render these kinds of criticisms prima facie legitimate, whilst allowing for further kinds of sanction to exist alongside them.

[14] We take it that, in this kind of case, it will be obvious that our Uno player didn't call 'uno' when he didn't and so there is no need to produce a reason supporting the proposition that he didn't call 'uno'.

our Uno player doesn't call 'uno' because someone offered him a huge sum of money if he doesn't. In this case, he clearly did what, all-things-considered, he should have done, and so any criticism levelled against him that targets the all-things-considered propriety of his act will not be legitimate, not even prima facie. Even so, when we know he didn't call 'uno' and we criticise him specifically for that, our criticism will be prima facie legitimate. After all, the agent still did break the relevant rule of Uno.

As a result, certain ways of criticising agents for φing may at least not be legitimate in certain cases because they don't discriminate between violations of the particular rule and the all-things-considered permissibility of the act. 'You shouldn't have φed.' is a case in point. Accordingly, what is needed is a more discriminating way of stating our criticism. One option is to do so by saying 'You don't C!' (alternatively: 'You don't . . .!' where . . . is filled by an expression the semantic value of which is entailed by the addressee's satisfying C). Here it is clear that our criticism targets the particular rule proscribing φing without satisfying C. For instance, in the Uno case, we may in any case criticise the player by saying: 'You didn't call "uno"!' or 'You didn't say anything!'

Given that we can legitimately criticise violations of norms, it will come as no big surprise that there will also be a range of appropriate responses to such criticisms. In particular, we'd like to suggest that, when legitimately criticised, one may appropriately respond by saying, for instance, that one is sorry, that one couldn't help it, that one didn't know, and so on. Here is again a more detailed statement of this idea:

Appropriate Responses
For any performance type, φ, that is governed by a rule to the effect that one must: φ only if one meets C, if an agent has legitimately been criticised for φ-ing without satisfying C, a certain kind of response on the part of the defendant is prima facie appropriate, including (i) explanations invoking overriding norms, excuses appealing to (blameless) (ii) lack of control or (iii) ignorance, and (iv) apologies.

For instance, when you have legitimately been criticised for playing your penultimate card in a game of Uno without calling 'uno', it will be appropriate for you to respond by saying, for instance, that you are sorry (apology), that you didn't know you had to call 'uno' (excuse), that you didn't call 'uno' because someone threatened to shoot you if you did (explanation in terms of overriding norms) and so on.

Consider next performance types such that there is no rule to the effect that one must: φ only if one satisfies C. Here we would like to suggest, roughly, that criticisms of agents who φ without satisfying C will be prima facie *illegitimate*. Again, the following is a more careful expression of this idea:

Illegitimate Criticisms

For any performance type, φ, that is not governed by a rule to the effect that one must: φ only if one meets C, if we criticise an agent who φs without satisfying C for φing without satisfying C, our criticism will be **prima facie illegitimate**. Moreover, our criticism will be prima facie illegitimate, even when (i) we know that the agent φs without meeting C and (ii) we can offer a reason to believe that the agent doesn't satisfy C when it isn't obvious that s/he doesn't.

For instance, there is no rule of Uno to the effect that one must call 'duo' when playing one's antepenultimate card. Now suppose you played your antepenultimate card without calling 'duo' and we know this. It is hard to deny that any criticism levelled against you for playing your antepenultimate card without calling 'duo' will be prima facie illegitimate. By way of further evidence for this, notice that, unless there is special reason which renders our criticism legitimate after all, a direct rebuttal of the criticism as irrelevant or misplaced will be prima facie legitimate. When we criticise you for playing your antepenultimate card without calling 'duo', unless there is special reason rendering our criticism legitimate, you can prima facie legitimately rebut it as misplaced or irrelevant. 'So what?' is a prima facie legitimate response to 'You didn't call "duo"!', unless there is special reason rendering the criticism legitimate. Or, again, more carefully:

Legitimate Rebuttals

For any performance type, φ, that is not governed by a rule to the effect that one must: φ only if one meets C, if we criticise an agent who φs without satisfying C for φing without satisfying C, the agent **may prima facie legitimately rebut** our criticism as misplaced or irrelevant. At the very least the agent may do so if there is no special reason rendering our criticism legitimate. What's more, the agent may do so even when (i) we know that the agent φs without satisfying C and (ii) we can offer a reason to believe that the agent doesn't satisfy C when it isn't obvious that s/he doesn't.

To mount a case for KRA, we will argue first that the predictions KRA makes when combined with *Legitimate Criticisms* and *Appropriate Responses* are correct and, second, that the assumption that KRA is false leads to incorrect predictions when combined with *Illegitimate Criticisms* and *Legitimate Rebuttals*.

Suppose a speaker asserts that *p* but doesn't know that *p*. In this case, KRA combined with *Legitimate Criticisms* predicts that we can prima facie legitimately criticise the speaker for his assertion, for instance, by saying: 'You don't know that!'. At least, we may so criticise the speaker when (i) we know that he doesn't know that p and (ii) we can offer a reason to believe that the speaker doesn't know that p when it isn't obvious that he doesn't.

Since in this kind of case it will often not be obvious that the speaker doesn't know that p, we will do well to set up our test cases such that we can offer a reason of the relevant kind. Every case in which a speaker doesn't know that p falls in at least one of the following four categories: the speaker's environment is epistemically inhospitable for p; he doesn't have justification for p; p is false; or he doesn't believe that p. And, conversely, every case that falls in at least one of these four categories is a case in which the speaker doesn't know that p. Given that this is so, one way of offering a reason to believe that the speaker doesn't know that p is by pointing out that the speaker falls in one of these four categories of case. This can be achieved either by asserting 'You don't know that!' and then, by way of explanation, adding the reason why the agent doesn't know (e.g. 'There are too many indistinguishable fakes in the area.' to indicate that the agent is in an epistemically inhospitable environment); or else by offering a more specific form of criticism, which already wears the relevant reason on its sleeve (e.g. 'That's false!', 'You don't believe that yourself!' or 'You have no reason to believe that!').

When we know that some speaker doesn't know that p, then, KRA combined with *Legitimate Criticisms* predicts that we can prima facie legitimately criticise him for his assertion by saying 'You don't know that p!' with an addendum of a reason why he falls into one of the four categories of cases or else by producing one of the more specific criticisms just mentioned.

There is excellent reason to believe that KRA's predictions are correct. To see this, notice that, in all of these kinds of case, criticisms call for or at least make it appropriate for the speaker to apologise, offer an excuse or explanation, attempt to rectify the situation and so on. When it is pointed out that the speaker is in an inhospitable environment, he may offer an excuse: 'Oh, I didn't know that.'; when the speaker is criticised for not having knowledge-level justification, he may try to rectify the situation by weakening his assertion: 'Okay, okay, but there is good reason to believe that p.'; when the criticism concerns the truth-value of the assertion, the speaker may offer an explanation: 'You're right. But that guy threatened to shoot me unless I said this.'; when she is admonished for not believing what she asserted, she may offer an apology: 'I am sorry, I misspoke.'.[15]

Let's now assume that assertion is not governed by KRA. By *Illegitimate Criticisms*, we get the prediction that criticisms levelled against speakers for

---

[15] We do not mean to suggest that the various kinds of case invariably call for the kind of response described earlier. Different situations may make different responses appropriate. What matters is that some response in the range is always called for/made appropriate.

asserting what they don't know will be prima facie illegitimate, even when their critics know that they don't know what they assert and can offer a reason why they don't know. This prediction is manifestly incorrect. As the earlier discussion clearly indicates, when we know that a speaker doesn't know what he asserts and can offer such a reason, our criticisms of him for asserting what he doesn't know will be prima facie legitimate. If so, our criticisms will not be prima facie illegitimate.

In addition, assuming that assertion is not governed by KRA in conjunction with *Legitimate Rebuttals* leads to the prediction that, unless there is special reason rendering criticisms of speakers for asserting what they do not know legitimate after all, speakers can prima facie legitimately rebut these criticisms as irrelevant or misplaced, even when their critics know that they don't know what they assert and can offer a reason why they don't know. Again, this prediction is manifestly incorrect. Even when there is no special reason rendering such criticisms legitimate, speakers cannot prima facie legitimately rebut them as irrelevant or misplaced. 'So what?' is not a prima facie legitimate response to 'You don't know that!' and so on, at least not given that we know that the speaker doesn't know what he asserts and has offered a reason why he doesn't know.

Our argument for KRA is pretty abstract. To make things a bit more concrete let's take a look at how it plays out in the case of JRA. In conjunction with *Illegitimate Criticisms*, JRA predicts that when, in the cases just described, we criticise the agent accordingly, our criticism will be prima facie illegitimate. For instance, 'That's false!' turns out to be a prima facie illegitimate criticism, even when we know that what the speaker asserted is false. What's more, unless there is special reason rendering the criticism legitimate, in conjunction with *Legitimate Rebuttals*, JRA predicts that the criticism can be prima facie legitimately rebutted as irrelevant or misplaced. 'So what?' can be a prima facie legitimate rejoinder to 'That's false!'. It is easy to see that these predictions are manifestly incorrect.

Since KRA in conjunction with *Legitimate Criticisms* and *Appropriate Responses* makes correct predictions and the assumption that KRA is false (and e.g. JRA is true instead) in conjunction with *Illegitimate Criticisms* or *Legitimate Rebuttals* leads to incorrect predictions, there is reason to believe that assertion is governed by KRA.

1.6 Conclusion

This chapter has outlined the case for KRA. It has come to light that not all the evidence adduced by its champions support KRA. In particular, we have seen that lottery propositions do not really support KRA over its main rival JRA, as the lottery paradox provides reason to think that lottery propositions are not only unknown but also unjustified for us.

What's more, while Moorean conjunctions do support KRA, one needs to be careful about how they do so. It is not just that they seem inappropriate. As Douven convincingly argues, champions of JRA can explain this much. Rather the problem arises only once we take note of the specific way in which assertions of Moorean conjunctions seem improper: they sound paradoxical. Here KRA has a neat explanation ready at hand. However, even KRA's closest competitor, JRA, does not offer a satisfactory alternative.

The perhaps strongest support for KRA derives from conversational patterns. Challenging and prompting patterns support KRA. Most importantly, patterns of legitimate/illegitimate criticisms and appropriate responses/legitimate rebuttals not only confirm KRA but, in addition, disconfirm rival views such as JRA.[16]

One line of argument that we haven't looked at in any detail here concerns experimental data about people's judgements on assertability. Turri and his collaborators have argued extensively that the experimental data provide support for KRA (e.g. Turri 2013, 2015, 2016, and Turri, Freedman and Keefner 2017). While for the longest time, the experimental data may have seemed to offer further support for KRA, there has been some resistance in recent literature. In particular, Kneer (2018) and Reuter and Broessel (2018) not only raise worries about Turri's experiments but also argue that the experimental data really support JRA rather than KRA. One lesson we draw from this, at least for now, is that more time is needed before we can say with any degree of certainty what direction the experimental evidence points in.

Another reason why we did not spend much time on this issue is that we remain sceptical whether experimental data provide particularly good evidence in the first place. After all, it is just not clear just how much

---

[16] In our argument for KRA we have focused mainly on how KRA compares with its most prominent rival, JRA. It may be worth noting that, in virtue of what we take to be mere historical contingency, the vast majority of defenders of JRA also, at the same time, endorse traditional views on the nature of justification, according to which the latter is implied by knowledge. As such, all that we have said so far applies exclusively to such traditional accounts of the nature of justification and, *mutatis mutandis*, to JRA conceived along traditionalist lines. In recent years, however, several philosophers (e.g. Bird 2007, Jenkins Ichikawa 2014, Miracchi 2015, Reynolds 2013,) have proposed knowledge-first views of justification; on these accounts, knowledge is taken as a primitive and justification is analysed in terms of knowledge. We have, in fact, defended two varieties of this view ourselves in print extensively (e.g. Kelp 2016, 2017, 2018, Simion 2019b, 2020a). One might wonder what whether JRA might not be viable when combined with a knowledge first account of justification. We address this question in Appendix B.

evidential value people's judgements have when it comes to the normative facts on the ground. In particular, we take it to be highly plausible that normative arguments, especially of the kind developed in Section 1.4, and the relevant facts about our practice of assertion that bear out their predictions carry more evidential weight for ascertaining the normative facts than people's judgements.[17] But, of course, in that case our case for KRA stands, no matter where the chips fall on the experimental data.

---

[17] Note that it is not the *intuition* e.g. that assertions can prima facie legitimately be criticised by 'You don't know that!' that provides the relevant evidence here but the *fact* that we criticise assertions in this way in our everyday practice of making assertions. This fact, in turn, is justified for each of us by extensive (for readers of this book typically decades of) experience in participating in the practice of assertion on an everyday basis and the inductive evidence this experience provides. Of course, this is not to say that this fact cannot also be tested scientifically. Crucially, however, the way to properly do so is not by devising an experiment featuring a description of some case involving an assertion and asking people whether they'd agree that 'You don't know that' is a legitimate criticism of it. Rather, what we want to do is look at how people actually talk to one another and ascertain whether and perhaps how frequently they do respond to assertions in this way, what reactions such responses trigger and what happens to the standing of the assertion as a result.

CHAPTER 2

Problems for KRA

With the argument for KRA on the table, this chapter will look at some of the problems that KRA is said to encounter and will offer responses on behalf of KRA.

2.1   The Classical Counterexamples

The perhaps most prominent argument against KRA ventures to show that KRA's knowledge requirement on assertion is too strong. In order to achieve this, foes of KRA adduce cases in which a speaker is said to make a permissible assertion, whilst not knowing what they assert. Crucially, evidence that the assertion is permissible is supposed to reside in the fact that the relevant speakers are not deserving of criticism or alternatively that they are blameless. Here are some characteristic statements of the argumentative strategy:

> I shall show that there are cases in which a speaker asserts that *p* in the absence of knowing that *p* without being subject to criticism in any relevant sense, thereby showing that knowledge cannot be what is required for proper assertion (Lackey 2007, 595).

> [I]f breaching a rule makes one blameworthy, which typically it does, then, [in the relevant cases], on the knowledge account, the asserter comes out as being blameworthy, contrary to intuition (Douven 2006, 477).

2.1.1   The Cases

The classical cases that foes of KRA have adduced against KRA are cases in which speakers assert from (i) justified false beliefs and (ii) gettiered beliefs. By way of illustration, consider the following examples:

Fake Snow
[I]t is winter, and it looks exactly as it would if there were snow outside, but in fact that white stuff is not snow but foam put there by a film crew of

whose existence I have no idea … [I] assert that there is snow outside. (Williamson 2000, 257)

Fake Barns
[S]uppose that Wendy correctly sees the only real barn that, unbeknownst to her, is completely surrounded by barn facades and asserts to me 'There was a barn in the field we just passed' on this basis. (Lackey 2007, 544)

In both of these cases, the speakers are said not to be subject to criticism and not to be blameworthy. Since they violate KRA, it would seem that KRA makes incorrect predictions about these cases. Hence KRA is in trouble.

Champions of KRA often argue that speakers who assert justified false beliefs and gettiered beliefs violate KRA but do so *blamelessly*. In particular, they point out that when in doing something one breaks a norm because one reasonably believes that one does comply with the norm, then one is blameless. And since that's just what happens in cases like *Fake Snow* and *Fake Barns*, these speakers are blameless. The speakers here plausibly assert what they assert because they reasonably take themselves to know what they assert and, in consequence, to be permitted to assert as they do. If so, it is reasonable for them to believe that they comply with KRA. As a result, they are blameless when asserting as they do.

However, foes of KRA worry that the above response is ad hoc. Here is one very clear expression of this worry:

[A] general worry with excuse maneuvers is that they form very generic ways of immunizing proposed norms. Without a principled account of when an agent is excused, every counterexample to a norm may be rebutted by upholding that the agent is excused from violating the norm. As we have seen, the proponents of [KRA] have yet to provide a viable principled account of excusability. (Gerken 2011, 544)

We believe Gerken's (and others') worry of ad hocness is unmotivated, in that it gets the dialectic wrong. Here is why: First, note that all the defender of KRA needs for her defence to go through is the highly uncontroversial claim that blameless ignorance excuses. That ignorance excuses was already recognised by Aristotle in the Nichomachean Ethics (1110a–1111b4), and the vast majority of the theorists of blame agree that there is an epistemic condition on blame. Indeed, it is telling that there is an entire Stanford Encyclopedia entry dedicated to 'The epistemic condition on moral responsibility' (Rudy-Hiller 2018). If so, an account that employs the 'ignorance excuses' move in its defence is hardly ad hoc. On the contrary, it is independently plausible.

Second, insofar as it is possible to blamelessly violate norms due to ignorance, the cases adduced by critics will just not work as counterexamples to KRA to begin with. After all, the intuition of non-criticisability/blamelessness[1] that is meant to do the heavy lifting in these cases simply doesn't provide evidence that KRA has been violated.[2] And this is why Gerken's claim is dialectically problematic: it is not on the shoulders of the champion of KRA to produce a plausible full account of excusability in order to defend KRA from the cases in point. That's a task for colleagues working in the general theory of normativity. Instead, the onus is on foes of KRA to adduce cases in which speakers unequivocally conform with the norms of assertion but lack the relevant knowledge. Short of that, they simply won't have produced counterexamples to KRA to begin with. As a result of all this, the ad hoc-ness worry can be laid to rest.

By the same token, there is excellent reason to believe that champions of KRA do not need a fully fledged account of blameless norm violation. Nevertheless, to be on the safe side, we will take on Gerken's challenge in what follows. More specifically, we will develop an independently plausible general normative framework for action that offers champions of KRA exactly what Gerken claims champions of KRA are missing. It also predicts that the speakers in cases like *Fake Snow* and *Fake Barns* (as well as their unsophisticated counterparts) are indeed blameless.

One final thing to note before we move on: We have argued in the previous section that JRA fails to adequately account for intuitively legitimate criticisms of assertions. If the argument in the next section goes through, we will have also argued that widespread normative assumptions concerning the nature and normativity of blame and criticism are compatible with KRA. It is easy to see that these two arguments together will provide strong reason to believe KRA is normatively superior to JRA *tout court*.

---

[1] Note also that it won't help to replace the intuitions of non-criticisability/blamelessness by intuitions of appropriateness. After all, this intuition may be explained either in terms of conforming with KRA or in terms of blameless violations of KRA.

[2] On the contrary, if anything, these cases will serve to confirm KRA. To see why, note that if it is true in general that norms can be broken blamelessly, then if a norm N cannot be broken blamelessly, there is reason to think that N is not a genuine norm after all.

2.1.2 *Criticisms and Blame: A Basic Normative Framework*

a. Criticisability and Norm-Specific Blamelessness. It is widely acknowledged in the literature that, *ceteris absentibus*[3] a permissible action is a blameless action.[4] This applies at the level of specific norms such as the rule of Uno requiring players to call 'uno' when playing their penultimate card. If you do call 'uno' when playing your penultimate card, your action is permissible by this norm and so *blameless relative to this norm*.

Consider next a situation in which a particular norm is violated. Say, you played your penultimate card without calling 'uno'. You violated a rule of Uno. If so, you can, of course, be prima facie legitimately criticised for violating this norm. In the Uno case, we may do this for instance by saying: 'You didn't call "uno"!'

Even so, it may be that you violate a norm and yet you are blameless for so doing. If so, you are also, of course, *blameless relative to this norm*. More specifically, there are three ways in which this may happen.

One way of blamelessly violating a particular norm is through overriding (e.g. Chisholm 1964). This happens when the requirements of the norm you are violating are in conflict with the requirements of another norm that takes precedence in the situation. For instance, suppose you are playing a game of Uno and are required by the rules of Uno to call 'uno' when playing your next card. Suppose, at the same time, someone will kill your neighbour if you do so. What the rules of Uno require of you is in conflict with the requirements of moral norms, which take precedence here. In other words, moral norms override the rules of Uno. When, because of this, you go on to violate the rules of Uno, you do so blamelessly.

The second way of blamelessly violating a norm is by violating it because[5] your action is not under your control. Suppose, for instance, that you have been brainwashed by your guru not to call 'uno' when playing your penultimate card. Here you violate the rule, but you are clearly blameless for doing so.

---

[3] All else normatively relevant absent; that is, absent other breaches of other norms that may well be rendering the agent blameworthy. See e.g. Turri (2011).

[4] See e.g. Copp (1997, 2003, 2008), Fischer (2006), Smith (1991), Speak (2005) and Widerker (1991) in ethics and Bondy (2007) in epistemology. See (Turri 2011) for a view according to which one can be blameworthy while not being in breach of KRA. We agree with Turri's diagnosis of the cases. However, crucially, the claim defended here is weaker, in that it is restricted to a *ceteris absentibus* normative landscape.

[5] The 'because' here is crucial to blamelessness. See Frankfurt (1969).

Finally, the third way manifests itself in situations in which you violate a norm because you are unaware that this is what you are doing.[6] Suppose, for instance, that you are unaware that the rules of Uno require you to call 'uno' when playing your penultimate card. As a result, you do not do so. In this case you violate a rule of Uno. Again, you are blameless for doing so. Ignorance excuses also. Similarly, another way for you to be blameless due to ignorance is if you are not aware that you are not calling 'uno' (say, because, unbeknownst to you, the Evil Uno Demon makes it such that, whenever you believe that you are calling 'uno', what you actually utter is 'duo').

With regard to the second and the third way of blamelessly violating a norm, some qualifications are needed. To see why, suppose that you knew that you would undergo brainwashing were you to go back to your guru. You had also promised not to go back. However, you went anyway. The impermissible act you are made to perform may be out of your control. Even so, you are blameworthy (see subsequent discussion) for another act, going back to your guru, of which the impermissible act is a consequence. As a result, you are not blameless for violating the rule of Uno. Strictly speaking, then, lack of control excuses only when it is itself blameless.

Similarly, suppose that, in our toy case, you had promised to read up on the rules of Uno before playing but didn't do so. In this case, you are unaware of the relevant rule of Uno. Even so, you are blameworthy for another act (in this case an omission), your failure to read up on the rules of Uno, of which your failure to call 'uno' is a consequence. As a result, you are not blameless for not calling 'uno'. Strictly speaking, then, ignorance excuses only when it is itself blameless.[7]

In sum, then, we want to propose the following account of blamelessness with respect to specific norms:

Norm-Specific Criticisability
An agent is prima facie legitimately criticisable relative to a specific norm N for φ-ing iff φ-ing violates N

Norm-Specific Blamelessness
An agent is *ceteris absentibus* blameless relative to a specific norm N for φ-ing iff

---

[6] See e.g. Haji (1998) and Zimmerman (1997). However, that ignorance excuses was already recognised by Aristotle in the Nichomachean Ethics (1110a–1111b4).

[7] See Zimmerman (1997) on the distinction between direct and indirect blameworthiness.

(1) φ-ing is permissible by N or
(2) φ-ing violates N but the agent φs
    (2.a) in order to comply with the requirements of a (non-overridden) overriding norm or
    (2.b) because this is blamelessly out of her control or
    (2.c) because the agent is blamelessly ignorant that she is φ-ing/that φ-ing violates N.[8]

On this account, an action can be criticisable relative to a specific norm and, at the same time, blameless relative to that very same norm. While this may look odd at first sight, on reflection, it is entirely as it should be. Actions are often performed in the public sphere and, as such, are observable by others, who may pick up the forms of behaviour exhibited. When you fail to call 'uno' when playing your penultimate card and so violate a rule of the game, this may be observed by someone else who will pick up your behaviour and, as a result, may violate the rule in the future, too. By allowing for criticisms of actions that violate specific norms we can work against the spread of norm-violating forms of behaviour. Since this is a good thing, it makes sense for us to allow for such criticisms. At the same time, we may also want to grant that a norm has been broken blamelessly by the agent. We don't want to hold the norm violation against her: she was blamelessly ignorant, things were blamelessly out of control and so on. If so, there is excellent reason for us to allow criticisability relative to a specific norm and blamelessness relative to the very same norm to coexist.[9]

---

[8] Our view falls squarely into what Ishtiyaque Haji (1998) has dubbed the 'Objective View' of blameworthiness: necessarily, if S is blameworthy for A-ing, then it was objectively morally wrong for S to A. The Objective View is assumed in much recent work on moral responsibility. Notable exceptions include Capes (2012), Haji (1998) and Zimmerman (1997). The classical type of case thought to constitute a problem for the Objective View is one that features badly intended agents who end up doing morally good things by mistake. The thought is that these agents are blameworthy even though they do not do anything wrong. Note though that it is entirely compatible with Norm-Specific Blamelessness that an agent who intends to break N and fails is not blameless. Of course, the failed attempt will be blameless. Compatibly with that, however, the agent's may (and very often will) not be blameless for *intending to break N*. Another way of making the same point is that, when assessing the principle, we need to be careful that we substitute consistently for N and φ. The *ceteris absentibus* clause is meant to secure consistent substitution via restricting to one and the same action and norm.
  Another related worry one anonymous referee had concerns cases of risk: Suppose that I'm supposed to invest your money wisely. If I buy and lose money, that's bad. If I buy and make money, that's good. The agent might be non-culpably ignorant about whether an investment makes or loses money, but this blameless ignorance doesn't ensure that we're blameless for the investments we make. We agree with the referee's intuition here. Again, it is important to keep both the norm at stake and the relevant φ constant. If the norm at stake is N: 'Invest iff wise,' and the agent is blamelessly ignorant that their investment violates N, then they are blameless. We take it, though, that the case described earlier is one where the agent does not satisfy this requirement.
[9] This is also why we would not want to merge *Norm-Specific Criticisability* and *Norm-Specific Blamelessness* into one principle, where the latter specifies a defeat condition for the former. After all, that would mean that whenever someone is blameless for violating a specific norm, we will no

b. All-Things Considered Blamelessness and Blameworthiness. Thus far we have looked at the blamelessness of an action with respect to specific norms. However, it is common to distinguish between assessments of actions with respect to specific norms and all-things-considered assessments of actions. All-things-considered assessments take into account the entire normative profile of an action and assess whether the action was permissible, required or forbidden in view of its entire normative profile. Unsurprisingly, then, just as an action can be blameless relative to a specific norm, it can also be all-things-considered blameless. For that reason we now want to extend the above account to all-things-considered blamelessness.

An action is all-things-considered blameless if it is all-things-considered permissible. There are, in turn, two ways in which this can happen.

First, an action is all-things-considered permissible if it is permissible by all the specific norms that apply to it (henceforth also 'fully permissible' for short). Suppose you call 'uno' when playing your penultimate card and thus comply with the rules of Uno. Suppose, in addition, you do not thereby violate any practical and moral norms and that no other norms apply to your act. Then your calling 'uno' is all-things-considered permissible.

Second, an action is all-things considered permissible if it is permissible by all (non-overridden) overriding norms that apply to it. Suppose you don't call 'uno' when playing your penultimate card and thus violate a rule of Uno. Suppose, in addition, you violate a practical norm in so doing: you will be punished and are less likely to win. At the same time, your neighbour will die if you call 'uno' and so calling 'uno' is prohibited by moral norms. Suppose there are no further norms applying to your action. In order to save your neighbour's life, you don't call 'uno'. In this case, your action is all-things-considered permissible. The moral norms override the rules of Uno and the practical norms (without being themselves overridden by further norms) and your not calling 'uno' is permissible by the moral norms.

To repeat, what we have seen now are two ways in which an action can be all-things-considered blameless in virtue of being all-things-considered permissible. That said, even an action that is all-things-considered impermissible can be all-things-considered blameless. What we want to suggest is that an all-things-considered impermissible action is

longer be able to legitimately criticise her for violating that norm. Since, as we have just seen, it is useful for us to retain the right to criticise violations of a norm even when it is broken blamelessly, we will do well not to merge the two principles in the way envisaged.

all-things-considered blameless if the action is blameless relative to all specific norms that apply to it. Suppose that you play your penultimate card without calling 'uno'. However, this is because you are blamelessly unaware that there is a rule requiring to you call 'uno' when playing your penultimate card. Suppose that your action is permissible by moral and practical norms and that there are no further norms applying to your action. In this case, you are all-things-considered blameless for not calling 'uno'. Since your act is permissible by moral and practical norms, it is blameless relative to these norms. Since you do not call 'uno' because you are blamelessly unaware that there is a rule requiring you to do so, you are blameless relative to this rule. Since these are all the norms that apply to your action in this case, your action is blameless relative to all specific norms that apply to it. So, it is all-thing-considered blameless.

Finally, an agent is blameworthy if and only if she is not all-things-considered blameless.

In sum, we want to propose the following:

All-Things-Considered Blamelessness
An agent is all-things-considered blameless for φ-ing iff

(1) φ-ing is all-things-considered permissible (i.e. either fully permissible or permissible by all (non-overridden) overriding norms that apply to it) or

(2) φ-ing is all-things-considered impermissible but the agent's φ-ing is blameless relative to all specific norms that apply to it.

All-Things-Considered Blameworthiness
An agent is blameworthy for φ-ing iff she is not all-things considered blameless for φ-ing.

It may be worth noting that, according to this account, criticisability occurs at the level of assessments by specific norms. In this way, it is fine-grained, as it were. In contrast, blameworthiness occurs at the level of all-things-considered assessments and so is coarse-grained. Blamelessness can occur at both levels.

c. Blamelessness and Assertion. With our normative framework for criticisability, blamelessness and blameworthiness in play, let's return to assertion. First, *Norm-Specific Blamelessness* entails that an agent is blameless relative to a specific norm *N* for φ-ing if φ-ing violates *N* but the agent φs because the agent is blamelessly ignorant that φ-ing violates *N*. There are a number of ways in which one can be blameless for violating a specific norm in virtue of being blamelessly ignorant that one is doing so. One such way is if one does what one does because of a reasonable belief that what one is doing is permissible. If one believes that what one is doing is permissible, then one doesn't believe that one is violating a norm. If so, one is ignorant of the fact that one is violating a norm. If one's belief is reasonable, then one's ignorance is blameless. (2.c) is satisfied. And of course, this is exactly what champions of KRA have claimed is going on in cases like *Fake Snow* and *Fake Barns*. The speakers assert out of a reasonable belief that they know and so that asserting is permissible. This means that they are blamelessly ignorant for their assertions.[10]

In this way, the envisaged response by champions of KRA is borne out by our normative framework.

2.2 Conversational Patterns: Turning the Tables on KRA

2.2.1 Taking Back Assertions

Recall that champions of KRA take conversational patterns to provide evidence in support of KRA. More specifically, we found that both challenge and prompting patterns provided evidence for KRA as well as patterns of legitimate criticisms and appropriate responses.

a. Two Ways to Take Back Assertions? It may come as some surprise, then, that it has been argued that, on closer inspection, conversational patterns confirm JRA rather than KRA. In particular, Jonathan Kvanvig (2009, 2011) has ventured to turn the tables on this front. In order to achieve this, Kvanvig distinguishes two types of attitude a speaker has in

---

[10] Note that our account can also deal with a more concrete worry that Gerken raises for the standard version of the blamelessness response. Gerken points out that unsophisticated speakers who do not even have the concept of knowledge may also be in cases in which they assert justified false beliefs or gettiered beliefs. Since they don't have the concept of knowledge, they are not in a position to host reasonable beliefs about knowledge in the first place. As a result, the standard account of why they are blameless in terms of a reasonably held belief that they know won't work here (Gerken 2011, Sections 4–5).

To see how our account can avoid this worry, note first that while acting out of a reasonable belief that what one does is permissible is one route to blameless ignorance, it is not the only route. Others are available as well. To see this, recall our Uno case in which you are just blamelessly unaware of the fact that there is a rule requiring you to call 'uno' when playing your penultimate card. In this case you may have no belief either way on whether you are complying with the rules of Uno. (If this isn't immediately obvious, note that you may know that you haven't been filled in on all the rules of the game yet and are taught various rules as you go along.) So it's not as if you play in the way you do because of a reasonable belief that this is permissible. Rather, you blamelessly have no belief on the relevant rule of Uno whatsoever. Thus, according to the above framework, another way to blameless ignorance is via a blameless *lack of belief* concerning the relevant rules.

And this is of course exactly what we find with cognitively unsophisticated agents, such as agents who don't even have the concept of knowledge to begin with. Any such agent is incapable of even representing KRA. If they are blameless for not having this concept, as they typically will be, they, too, will satisfy (2.c) and so come out blameless for violating KRA.

response to his assertions being corrected. Kvanvig argues that 'in some cases of correction, we take back the content of our speech act, and in other cases we apologize for, and regret, the very act itself' (2009, 145–46). For example, if, in *Fake Snow*, we assert that it is snowing outside and then it is pointed out that our assertion is false and that what we are seeing is fake snow produced by a film crew, we take back the content of our speech act, but we needn't apologize for or regret the very act itself. 'In fact, were [we] to apologize, the natural response would be dismissive: Give it a rest, nobody's always right . . .' (2009, 147). According to Kvanvig, the same distinction plays out with gettiered assertions too. Thus, presumably, in *Fake Barns*, after Wendy asserts 'There was a barn in the field we just passed', and I point out to her that she can't possibly know that as we are in Fake Barn County, she would just take back *what* she said; she would not apologize for having said it.

Kvanvig argues that things are different when you don't have justification for what you say, even if, by some bizarre twist, you turn out to be right. In support of this, he offers the case of Billy Bob, a Texas Democrat, who, based on a headline on a tabloid, asserts to his friend Sue that George Bush is a communist. When Sue points out to him that he should not trust tabloids, Billy Bob apologizes: 'You're right, I shouldn't have believed that paper and I shouldn't have said what I did. I take it back'.

According to Kvanvig, in this situation, apologizing and taking back the speech act itself is the right thing to do. He argues that norms of assertion are norms governing a certain type of human activity, and thus relate to the speech act itself rather than the content of such an act. As such, we have reason to think that some norm of assertion is broken only when the speech act itself is at fault; when only the content of the assertion needs to be taken back, the assertion itself is not problematic.

While, at first glance, conversational patterns may appear to support KRA, a closer look suggests that they really support JRA. In particular, once we are clear on the distinction between taking back the content of a speech act and taking back the act itself, there is reason to believe that conversational patterns confirm JRA. There are thus two types of argument that provide evidence for JRA.

b. Only One Way to Take Back Assertions! On reflection, however, there is reason to doubt that Kvanvig's distinction works; speech act literature[11] distinguishes between the content of a speech act and the illocutionary

---

[11] See e.g. Green (2020).

force by which the content is being put forward. One can perform various speech acts on a proposition p: one can ask whether p, promise that p, threaten that p and so on. In the case of assertion, by uttering p the speaker presents p as true. Given that this is so, a *proposition* is itself communicatively inert; that is to say that to actually perform a speech act, one has to put forth a proposition with an *illocutionary force,* such as assertion, promise, command, etc.

But if the propositional content of a speech is inert, it is far from clear how Kvanvig envisages one being able to take it back in isolation. To see this, notice that assertion, as opposed to other types of actions – say, having vacationed in Hawaii – can be 'taken back'. Not in the sense that one can change the past so as to not have asserted in the first place, of course. Rather, to take back an assertion that *p* is to no longer stand behind the commitments implied by having asserted that *p*. Now, *p* itself, in isolation, does not imply any commitments whatsoever. That is, depending on illocutionary force, different commitments will follow. If I promise that *p*, for instance, I commit myself to a future course of action; if I assert that *p*, I commit myself to, at least, it being the case that *p*, and so on.

If that is the case, it becomes clear that in order to take an assertion back, that is, to be released from the commitments implied by it,[12] it has to be the case that I take back everything, force and content. I cannot only take back the content *p*, because *p* in isolation does not commit me to anything, inasmuch as I do not present p as true, or command *p*, or promise *p*, and the like. Also, I cannot only take the action back either, because presenting nothing as true, or promising nothing also fails to imply any commitments on my part.

What comes to light, then, is that there is only one way in which one can take an assertion back, to wit, by revoking the commitment toward the whole compound: having asserted that *p* is true. But given that this is so, Kvanvig's attempt to turn the tables on KRA with respect to conversational patterns fails. The distinction that is required to do the trick simply does not exist.

Since one of us first made this point in print (Simion 2016b), Jon Kvanvig has written and published a response piece where he argues that the distinction we contest holds, and gives further detail about how to understand it. According to Kvanvig,

---

[12] See Simion (2016c for discussion).

[O]ne side of the distinction applies to a speech act, for when one apologizes for, or regrets, an assertion, the object of one's attitude is the assertion itself, which is a speech act. But when one takes back only the content of an assertion, one does not have a speech act as the object of one's attitude nor of the act of taking back. Instead, the object of the taking back is whatever intellectual commitment to the claim led to the assertion in the first place, and what one is doing is countermanding that commitment. Thus, to take back the content of an assertion, as opposed to taking back the speech act itself, has as its object a commitment which is a mental state or act. In the usual case, such a commitment would be either a belief (a mental state) or the adoption of it (a mental act). (2017, 115)

On this way to look at things, then, what one takes back in cases in which one has asserted justifiably but not knowingly that p, is one's belief that p, but not one's assertion that p. The first question that arises, though, at this juncture, is why would this be so? Why would one, upon discovering that p is not known, merely take back their belief that p, but not their assertion that p? After all, by Kvanvig's own lights, justified belief is the norm of assertion. If so, it follows that justified belief and assertoric permissibility covary: one is present if and only if the other one is present as well. If so, however, it shouldn't be the case that we find scenarios in which one is required to take back one's belief but not one's assertion, since this would suggest that their permissibility conditions do not covary – in which case Kvanvig's own preferred norm of assertion would fail. In a nutshell, then, on this new reading of the distinction, Kvanvig is faced by a dilemma: either there are no scenarios in which one should take back one's belief but not one's assertion – in which case Kvanvig's explanation of retraction data fails – or, alternatively, there are such scenarios, but then his preferred norm of assertion is incorrect.

c. Diagnosis. Before moving on, we would like to spend a few moments on diagnosing what went wrong in Kvanvig's argument. First, Kvanvig seems to think that the only appropriate response to a legitimate criticism for violating a certain norm takes the form of apology and regret. Otherwise it is just not clear why the fact that apology and regret is appropriate in the Billy Bob case but not, for instance, in *Fake Barns*, serves to indicate that a norm has been violated in the former case but not in the latter. Now, in Chapter 1, we argued that the range of appropriate responses is much wider than Kvanvig would have us think. Appropriate responses to legitimate criticisms can take the form of apologies, but they can also take the form of explanations, excuses and so on. This raises the question as to who is right here. Fortunately, the normative framework from the previous section serves to adjudicate this issue. What the framework highlights is that there are various ways of breaking particular norms. A particular norm may be broken in a blameworthy fashion, in a way such that the action remains all-things-considered permissible or else in a way such that the action remains impermissible but blameless. Crucially, it is plausible that different ways of breaking particular norms render different forms of response appropriate. When one is blameworthy for breaking a norm, an apology may indeed be called for. That said, it is not hard to see that no apology is required when the action remains all-thing-considered permissible or when it is blameless.[13] In cases of all-things-considered permissible action, an explanation will typically be appropriate and in cases of blameless action an excuse. What's more, the fact that these responses are appropriate in those cases serves to *confirm* that a norm has been broken, rather than disconfirm it. In this way, there is reason to believe that Kvanvig's focus on apologies is too limited and that, as a result, his argument fails. While his observation that an apology is called for in the Billy Bob case provides reason to believe that the norm of assertion is broken here, the fact that in *Fake Snow* and *Fake Barns* no apology is called for does not serve to show that no norm has been broken here.

None of this is to say that Kvanvig is not latching on to any genuine distinction here. It's just not the distinction between conforming with the norm of assertion and violating it. Rather, we would like to suggest that the distinction Kvanvig is latching on to is the distinction between blameworthy and blameless violations of the norm of assertion. Billy Bob is blameworthy for violating the norm of assertion. While the speakers in *Fake Snow* and *Fake Barns* also violate the norm of assertion, they do so blamelessly. What's more, we believe that we are now in a position to explain why Kvanvig was misled into thinking that there are two different ways of taking back an assertion: that he confuses the distinction between blameworthy and blameless violations of a norm with the distinction between violating a norm and conforming with it.

2.2.2   The Target of 'How Do You Know?' Challenges

Here's another attempt at turning the tables on the evidence provided by conversational patterns. This time the focus is on 'How do you know?' challenges. The argument starts with the observation that when our

---

[13] This is not to say, however, that an apology may not also be appropriate, as Williamson (2009, 345) also points out.

assertions are challenged by asking 'How do you know?', we frequently respond by citing our evidence for what we asserted. And the thought is that this supports something like JRA rather than KRA.

By way of response to this worry, note first that the fact that we frequently respond to 'How do you know?' challenges by citing our evidence is just what we may expect if KRA is true. After all, given that 'How do you know?' constitutes a challenge to a speaker's assertion, the speaker would want to provide some evidence that she knows what she asserted. But of course, one excellent way of achieving this is by offering her evidence for what she asserted. Suppose, for instance, that you assert that Obama cried during his speech on gun violence in January 2016, and we challenge your assertion by asking how you know. If KRA is true, your response to our challenge had better produce some evidence that you know that Obama cried during the speech in question. One excellent way of providing such evidence is by citing your evidence for it, say that you saw him crying on a TV broadcast of the speech. But given that citing your evidence is an excellent way of producing the kind of evidence 'How do you know?' challenges call for, it will come as no surprise that we should frequently do so in response to such challenges.[14]

But perhaps the point is a slightly different one, to wit, that the fact that we frequently respond to 'How do you know?' challenges by citing our evidence provides reason to believe that, at the end of the day, 'How do you know?' challenges are really nothing more than 'What's your justification?' challenges. That might be a bit more troublesome for champions of KRA.

Fortunately, there is reason to believe that even this way of interpreting the objection will not refute KRA. To see why, note first that since knowledge entails justification, on KRA, we may expect that we can challenge assertions by challenging the speaker's justification. In order to turn this into a genuine problem for KRA, it would additionally have to be shown that assertions cannot be challenged in any of the other ways KRA

[14] Incidentally, we are not so sure just how frequently we actually do respond to 'How do you know?' challenges by citing our evidence. To see this, note that one perfectly legitimate response you may give in the Obama case is that you saw the speech on TV. It is hard to deny, however, that the fact that you saw Obama give a certain speech on TV is not evidence for the proposition that Obama cried during that speech. Rather, your evidence for this is that you saw him crying during the speech. But that is not what you offer in response to the challenge. What is going on here is that you cite the source of your belief that Obama cried – i.e. seeing a TV broadcast of the speech – implying that it is a source of knowledge for the proposition in question. These considerations suggest that we don't need to cite our evidence in order to successfully rise to a 'How do you know?' challenge. How frequently we actually do cite our evidence seems to us to be an open empirical question.

would predict. And this is just *not* what we find. On the contrary, as we have already seen, we can also challenge assertions by asking: 'Is that really true?' or 'Do you really believe that?' Moreover, we can also challenge them by querying whether the speaker's epistemic environment isn't inhospitable. For instance, Wendy's assertion that there is a barn in the field can be challenged by saying: 'But isn't this the part of the country that contains nearly only fake barns?' (In fact, given that assertions can be criticised by saying 'That's false!' and so on, it is unsurprising that it should also be possible to challenge them in these ways.) So, even if 'How do you know?' challenges did ultimately boil down to 'What's your justification?' challenges, this fact again does not serve to disconfirm KRA.

Here is another potentially troublesome datum for KRA. Suppose, before there was widespread consensus among expert scientists on the reality of global warming, you assert that global warming is happening and we criticise your assertion by saying: 'You don't know that! There still is a considerable number of scientists who would disagree.' Now suppose you reply along the following lines: 'Well, okay ... But still there is good reason to believe that it is' (cf. Douven 2006, 468, n.26). Isn't this exactly the kind of response that constitutes a legitimate rebuttal of our criticism? If so, KRA is in trouble. After all, as you also concede, you don't know that what you assert. If, nonetheless, you can legitimately rebut our criticism here, there is evidence that permissible assertion does not require knowledge, i.e. that KRA does not hold.

Fortunately for champions of KRA, there is reason to think that your response does not constitute a legitimate rebuttal of our criticism. To see why, note first that, *ceteris paribus*,[15] assertions that go unchallenged become part of the common ground of the conversation afterwards, as do assertions such that any challenge/criticism has been successfully met. If so, and if, in the above exchange, your response to our criticism is indeed a legitimate rebuttal, we may expect that the proposition that global warming is happening to become part of the conversation's common ground thereafter, at least assuming, as we may, that neither the original assertion nor the subsequent rebuttal are subject to any further challenges or criticisms. Crucially, however, this is not what is happening here. To see this, note that (i) subsequent assertions in the conversation cannot be defended by referring back to the proposition that global warming is happening, not even if they are obviously entailed by it. Moreover,

---

[15] Absent adverse conditions, for instance: epistemic injustice cases are paradigmatic cases in which this does not happen although it should.

(ii) attempted such defences can themselves be legitimately rebutted. For instance, suppose at a later stage you were to assert: 'Temperatures on Earth are on the rise.' Suppose that we also criticised this assertion and that you attempted to defend your assertion by referring back to the earlier assertion that global warming is happening, e.g. by saying: 'But didn't we already say that global warming is happening?' We could rightly point out here that the answer is negative: 'No, all that we said was that there is good reason to believe that global warming is happening.' There is thus reason to believe that the proposition that global warming is happening does not become part of the common ground after our exchange. But if your response to us had been a legitimate rebuttal, it would have done so. As a result, there is reason to believe that your response did not constitute a legitimate rebuttal.

Finally, there is another, more attractive interpretation of what is going on in our exchange. Rather than constituting a legitimate rebuttal of our criticism, your reply involves both a concession 'Well okay …' and subsequent weakening 'There is good reason to believe that global warming is happening' of the assertion. This interpretation avoids the problem of its competitor. After all, it at most predicts that the proposition that there is good reason to believe that global warming is happening becomes part of the conversation's common ground, which seems unproblematic. At the same time, this interpretation does not generate a problem for KRA. This is because if we drop the claim that your response constitutes a legitimate rebuttal of our criticism, we no longer have any reason against KRA's key claim that permissible assertion requires knowledge. On the more plausible interpretation of the case, then, KRA walks free once again.

2.3 A Priori Simplicity

In his 2006 paper, Douven offers an elaborate argument that aims to show that JRA is preferable to KRA because JRA is a priori simpler. Now, it might be thought that this argument will constitute a genuine problem for KRA only if JRA does an equally good job in explaining the evidence for KRA adduced in the previous chapter. And, it might be added, we have already seen that this is not the case. Even so, at the very least Douven identifies a count on which KRA might lose points against the competition. For that reason, it will still be good news for KRA if Douven's argument can be resisted.

Douven's argument starts from what he dubs 'the zeroth law of rationality' according to which one must: XY only if it is rational for one to XY. That one must: assert that p only if it rational for one to assert that p is a straightforward instance of this. Furthermore, Douven goes along with Jonathan Adler (2002) in endorsing the belief-assertion parallel – that is, the claim that belief is nothing but assertion to oneself. In the light of this, and by the plausible assumption that if it is rational for one to assert that p, then it is rational for one to assert p to oneself, he derives that one must: assert p only if it is rational for one to believe p. And this, of course, appears to just be Douven's formulation of JRA. As such, Douven argues, we are faced with the following situation: JRA seems to be a mere extension of a fundamental principle of rationality – to wit, the zeroth law of rationality – to which, he argues, we are committed anyway (2006, 456). Furthermore, the extension is obtained by an application of a principle Williamson (2000) also endorses – that is, the belief-assertion parallel. In this way, JRA is preferable to KRA, which does not just drop out of the zeroth law.

Unfortunately, Douven's argument remains ultimately unsuccessful. The reason for this is that, in the absence of a substantive account of rational believability, it simply fails to support any rule of assertion over any other. Of course, one could have an account according to which rational credibility just is whatever turns ungettiered true belief into knowledge. Otherwise put,

The J Account of Rational Credibility
p is rationally believable for one if and only if: if one has an ungettiered true belief that p, then one knows that p.[16]

The J account is, of course, what Douven has in mind: rational believability is just the sort of knowledge-level justification at issue in JRA. As such, it will indeed give him the kind of rule of assertion that he is aiming to derive. However, the J account is not the only account of rational credibility one can have, nor the only account of rational believability on the market. Importantly for our purposes here, consider the following alternatives:

The Strong K-Account of Rational Believability
p is rationally believable for one if and only if one knows that p.

The Weak K-Account of Rational Believability
p is rationally believability for one if and only if: if one believes that p, then one knows that p.[17]

---

[16] For purposes of simplicity, we will bracket the issue of basing here.
[17] Again, we are bracketing the issue of basing in the interest of keeping things simple.

It is easy to see that, when combined with *The Strong K-Account of Rational Believability*, Douven's derivation will lead straight to KRA. Even *The Weak K-Account* will deliver a rule of assertion that is quite different from the one Douven has in mind. What's more, it may seem as though its champions will be little more than an argument for a belief rule of assertion away from an argument for KRA. What's most important for present purposes is that a number of champions of KRA also accept at least *The Weak K-account of Rational Believability*.

What comes to light, then, is that KRA is perfectly compatible with the conclusion of Douven's derivation: one must, indeed, assert *p* only if *p* is rationally believable to one, where *p* is rationally believable for one only if one knows that *p*. Therefore, one must assert *p* if one knows *p*. Thus, in the absence of an argument for *The Standard Account of Rational Believability*, Douven's derivation fails to cause trouble for KRA.

2.4   Outstanding Problems

We have made good progress on a number of the central difficulties that KRA faces. It may be worth noting, however, that some problems remain. What's more, in order to properly address them, we will need the resources of the view that we will develop only in the next part. This is why we will now just state these problems and return to them later on in the book.

2.4.1   *Goals and Norms*

The first problem is again a theoretical one. It is due to McKinnon who states it in her 2015 book. The key thought is that, on many versions of KRA,

> the goal and the norm of the practice are satisfied by the same thing: knowledge. One aims to assert something that expresses knowledge, and thus the norm is that one ought to assert that *p* only if one knows that *p*. The goal of the act also counts as the norm. However, [...] this is a serious mistake: the norms and goals of a practice must be kept distinct, because norms are what it means to 'properly aim' at a goal. (McKinnon 2015, 170)

In a nutshell, the argument is this: if KRA is true, the goal and norm of the practice of assertion are one and the same. However, for any practice, its goal(s) and norm(s) must be distinct. Hence, KRA is false.

We have much more to say about the relation between the goal and the norm of assertion in the next two chapters. Once our view is sufficiently developed, it will be clear that it does not succumb to this objection. However, for the time being, we will simply take note of McKinnon's worry about KRA.

2.4.2 Selfless Assertions

While we have seen how champions of KRA can deal with the classical counterexamples, there is another kind of counterexample, which is said to make a more convincing case against KRA. Here is the most famous case:

> **Creationist Teacher**
> Stella is a devoutly Christian fourth-grade teacher [...] Part of this faith includes a belief in the truth of creationism and, accordingly, a belief in the falsity of evolutionary theory. Despite this, Stella fully recognizes that there is an overwhelming amount of scientific evidence against both of these beliefs [...] [S]he regards her duty as a teacher to include presenting material that is best supported by the available evidence, which clearly includes the truth of evolutionary theory. As a result, while presenting her biology lesson today, Stella asserts to her students, 'Modern day *Homo sapiens* evolved from *Homo erectus*,' though she herself neither believes nor knows this proposition. (Lackey 2007, 599)

Just as in the classical cases, Stella can be said neither to be subject to criticism nor to be blameworthy. At the same time, as a creationist, she does not believe various propositions of evolutionary theory, including the one she asserts to her students. Since knowledge entails belief, we have another apparent counterexample to KRA.

Crucially, however, there is reason to think that the blamelessness manoeuvre will not straightforwardly get off the ground here. After all, Stella not only fails to believe the relevant propositions of evolutionary theory, but she also knows that she does not believe them. In particular, she knows that she doesn't believe what she asserts. If so, she will also know that she doesn't know what she asserts. But if she knows that she doesn't know what she asserts, she reasonably believes that she doesn't know what she asserts and so she does not reasonably believe that she knows what she asserts. That is to say, she does not reasonably believe that she complies with KRA and so asserts permissibly. If so, it would seem that the blamelessness move remains ineffective here.

Let's agree that selfless assertion cases like *Creationist Teacher* cannot be dealt with by the blamelessness manoeuvre. Since we haven't offered any other account of what is going on in this case, this means that the case continues to constitute an obstacle for KRA.

2.4.3 *Assertions under Systematic Peer Disagreement*

The last problem for KRA we will look at is due to Sandy Goldberg (2015). Here goes:

1. In cases in which S believes that p in the face of (what I will call) *systematic p-relevant peer disagreement*, [...] S is not doxastically justified in believing that p.
2. If S is not doxastically justified in believing that p, then S is not warranted in asserting that p.
3. Some cases of disagreement regarding whether p are cases of systematic p-relevant peer disagreement.
4. (Therefore) In such cases, S is not warranted in asserting that p (Goldberg 2015, 226–27).

This upshot of this argument is that whenever a proposition is subject to systematic peer disagreement, no one can permissibly assert it (or its negation for that matter). The reason this is troubling is that there appear to be entire domains such that we are not in a position to permissibly assert propositions in this domain. Philosophy is among the most obvious candidates (and the one Goldberg explicitly focuses on). The result that we threaten to be stuck with is that none (or next to none) of our assertions in philosophy are permissible. And that's unacceptable.

How does this argument cause trouble for KRA? The answer is that KRA entails one of the key premises, to wit, 2. According to Goldberg, 2 is the weakest link and ultimately has to go. As a result, we have yet another argument against KRA. We will return to it in Chapter 3.

2.5 Conclusion

We have looked at a number of problems that KRA is said to encounter and have shown that KRA can avoid some of these problems. While the classical counterexamples can be dealt with by observing that it is widely agreed that blameless ignorance excuses, we also introduced a general normative framework for blamelessness and applied it to the case of assertion. In this way, we were able to offer a particularly well-motivated version of the blamelessness response to the classical counterexamples.

We also looked at a couple of attempts to turn the tables on KRA with regard to conversational patterns and argued that they remain ultimately unsuccessful. Kvanvig's argument relies on a spurious distinction between taking back the content of a speech act and taking back the speech act itself. In contrast, those who have argued that 'How do you know challenges?' really are 'What's your evidence?' challenges do not thereby show that KRA isn't really governing assertion. On the contrary, on reflection, we found that the relevant patterns do confirm KRA after all.

We then turned to Douven's argument that JRA is a priori simpler than KRA as only JRA can be derived from the zeroth law of rationality. However, it became clear that Douven's argument fails. The derivation delivers JRA only via further assumptions, which are optional. Others lead us straight to KRA.

In this way, we were able to deal with a number of important problems for KRA. That said, we also had to note that we are not quite in the clear yet. There are a number of outstanding problems the view encounters. In Part II, we will develop in some detail a view of the normativity of assertion that will also allow us to address them. First, however, we will turn to the question of whether knowledge is not only necessary for permissible assertion but also sufficient.

CHAPTER 3

KRA and Sufficiency

In the previous chapters we have made a case for KRA. More specifically, we have provided arguments for KRA, and we have responded to a number of problems KRA encounters.

Recall that, according to KRA, one must (epistemically): assert *p* only if one knows *p*, or, alternatively, it is epistemically permissible for one to assert *p* only if one knows *p*. Note that so understood, KRA states a necessary condition for epistemically permissible assertion. One might wonder, however, whether KRA's condition is also sufficient. In other words, one might wonder whether the following holds as well:

KRA-S
If one knows that *p*, then it is epistemically permissible for one to assert that *p*.

It might seem plausible that if KRA holds, then KRA-S will hold also. In fact, one might wonder whether we should not be suspicious of KRA if it turns out that KRA-S is not true.

It is of some interest, then, that KRA-S has come under serious attack in recent literature. Most notably, Jessica Brown (2010) has argued that, when the stakes are high, one may need more in the way of epistemic support than knowledge that *p* in order to permissibly assert that *p* (henceforth, the *quantitative objection*). And Jennifer Lackey (2011, 2014) has added that it's not only the *quantity* of epistemic support that might be at stake, but the *quality* too. More specifically, Lackey identifies cases in which it looks as if the *type* of source of one's knowledge that *p* might be unsuitable for permissibly asserting that *p*. Lackey argues that in some cases of expert testimony and testimony involving aesthetic judgements, isolated testimonial knowledge will not be enough to grant the speaker the right to assert (henceforth, the *qualitative objection*).

This chapter tries to defend KRA-S by arguing that the case against it fails. In order to achieve this, we will first look at the quantitative objection

(Section 3.1) and then at the qualitative objection (Section 3.2). We will show that both remain ultimately unsuccessful.

3.1 The Quantitative Objection

At first glance, KRA-S looks fairly promising. It looks as if it's perfectly fine for you, for instance, to tell us that there's a desk in front of you while reading this book, say; the reason why you can do that is because you know there's a desk in front of you, via perception. If we were to question your assertion, appealing to your knowledge would adequately meet the challenge.

According to Jessica Brown, however, knowledge is not always enough; that is, when the stakes are high, permissible assertion may require more in the way of epistemic support than knowledge. To bring this point home, she offers the following case:

> **Affair**
> A husband is berating his friend for not telling him that his wife has been having an affair even though the friend has known of the affair for weeks.
>
> HUSBAND: Why didn't you say she was having an affair? You've known for weeks.
> FRIEND: Ok, I admit I knew, but it wouldn't have been right for me to say anything before we was absolutely sure. I knew the damage it would cause to your marriage (Brown 2010, 555).

Intuitively, we find Friend is right on this one; that is, he's right to not have hasted into telling Husband about the affair before he was absolutely sure. One should definitely not rush into breaking this kind of news. Accordingly, Brown takes this case to show that, in high-stakes contexts, knowledge is not enough; one may have to be in a stronger epistemic position vis-à-vis p in order to permissibly assert that p.

3.1.1   Brown on Overriding

Recall, however, that KRA-S is supposed to be an epistemic norm, solely concerned with epistemic permissibility. As such, one might wonder whether the apparent impermissibility in the case above is not triggered by further norms stepping in and overriding the epistemic norm. After all, assertion is a type of action; as such, we should expect it to be governed both by norms governing its particular type – in particular, the epistemic norm under consideration – and by norms governing action in general, such as prudential or moral norms. Surely no amount of epistemic support will make it permissible for me to assert any proposition *p* inasmuch as, say, my assertion will trigger the death of millions. In this case, it looks as if the epistemic norm, whatever it may be, is overridden by the moral norm.

Brown acknowledges that, in some cases, other norms might override the epistemic norm, and make the assertion impermissible even though the speaker has knowledge: '[i]n many senses of propriety, that one knows that p is not sufficient for the propriety of asserting p' (2010, 550). For instance, even if one knows that one's boss is bald, it may not be polite, prudent, or relevant to point this out to him (let's dub this case *Bald*). However, Brown argues, in *Affair*, it is not the case that further norms step in and override the epistemic norm. According to her, this is evidenced by the fact that the epistemic standards themselves seem to be higher: Friend just needs to be in a better epistemic position in order to be permitted to assert. Thus, according to Brown, when the quantity of epistemic support necessary for permissible assertion is affected, what we are dealing with is an epistemic norm at work, rather than an overriding norm of a different nature. Accordingly, inasmuch as we are restricting the discussion to whether one is in a good enough epistemic position to assert, we are safe from letting our intuitions be driven by different norms than the epistemic one. Thus, Brown takes it to be the case that we can individuate the requirements of the epistemic norm we are interested in as follows:

Content Individuation
If a norm *N* affects the amount of epistemic support needed for permissible assertion, than *N* is an epistemic norm.

Furthermore, she takes the sufficiency claim of epistemic norm we are talking about to come in the following formulation:

KRA-S-Brown (KRA-S-B)
One is in a good enough epistemic position to assert p if one knows that p (2010, 550).

Importantly, in the light of all this, Brown takes KRA-S-B to be equivalent to our previous formulation of KRA-S:

So, one might instead phrase the sufficiency claim as the claim that *if one knows that p, then one is in a good enough epistemic position to assert that p*. This leaves it open that one's assertion is incorrect on grounds other than epistemic ones, for instance, that it's rude, imprudent or irrelevant etc. It merely claims that, *if one knows that p, then there is nothing epistemically wrong with asserting that p.* (Brown 2010, 550, *emphasis added*)

Thus, Brown stands behind the following equivalence thesis:

Equivalence Thesis
One is in a good enough epistemic position to assert that *p* if and only if one's assertion that *p* is epistemically permissible.

Further on, Brown finds KRA-S-B to be false, as proven by *Affair*; Friend does know that the wife is having an affair, but, intuitively, he is still not in a good enough epistemic position to assert it. If that is the case, naturally, in virtue of *Equivalence Thesis*, she concludes KRA-S is also false; knowledge is not always enough for epistemically permissible assertion.

In what follows, we will argue that Brown is right to think that KRA-S-B is false; the epistemic position a knowledgeable asserter finds himself in might not be, all-things-considered, good enough for asserting that p. However, we will also show that both *Content Individuation* and *Equivalence Thesis* are false and that, as a result, KRA-S remains unaffected by Brown's argument. Inasmuch as what we care about is *epistemic* permissibility – that is, permissibility by the epistemic norm – rather than all-things-considered permissibility, we will argue that, for all Brown has shown, KRA-S stands.

3.1.2   *Epistemic Norms and Norms with Epistemic Content*

Let us first revisit Brown's motivation for thinking that if a norm *N* affects the amount of epistemic support needed for permissible assertion, then *N* is an epistemic norm (*Content Individuation*). Recall that the thought was, roughly, that the impermissibility of my telling my boss that he was bald was plausibly due to other norms (prudential, norms of politeness etc.) stepping in and overriding the epistemic norm. As opposed to this, according to Brown, in *Affair* the epistemic support itself is insufficient.

What is it that distinguishes *Bald* from *Affair*? It looks as if, in the former, but not in the latter case, the assertion becomes altogether impermissible, no matter the amount of epistemic support enjoyed by it. That is, even if you're certain that your boss is bald, your assertion is still impermissible. As opposed to this, in *Affair*, if Friend had had more epistemic support – closer to certainty – his assertion would have been perfectly permissible. From this, Brown concludes that, in *Bald*, further norms step in and override the epistemic norm, while in *Affair* it is the epistemic norm itself that is at work.

Is it true, however, that just because the quantity of epistemic support needed for permissible assertion is affected, it follows that it is an epistemic norm that is at work?

In order to answer this question, let us look at other types of action. Consider driving. Traffic norms are specific to this kind of action; moral norms and prudential norms are not, they govern action in general. One important traffic norm is the one regulating the speed limit within city bounds. Say you are in Barcelona and you are currently driving your sister's three-year-old son to kindergarten. Your driving will be governed by a traffic norm that prohibits driving faster than 50km/h. Now, consider the following situations:

Drive 1
Say that, as it so happens, your sister's kid suffers from carsickness and asks you to stop the car. According to the traffic norms, it is perfectly permissible for you to continue driving 50km/h. However, it looks as if, all-things-considered, you ought to stop the car: the moral norm overrides the traffic norm and makes your continuing to drive impermissible altogether.

Drive 2
Say that your sister's kid suffers from carsickness at 50 km/h, and asks you to drive a bit slower. Again, it looks as if that's what, all-things-considered, you ought to do in this situation. Still, according to the traffic norm, you are permitted to go on driving 50km/h. The moral norm, however, overrides the traffic norm and requires you to drive more slowly.

Drive 3
Say that your sister's kid needs to be at the hospital as soon as possible: his life is at stake. Surely, going faster than 50km/h is all-things-considered permissible (perhaps even required), even though it is in breach of the traffic norm. Again, moral and prudential considerations step in, override the traffic norm and modify the requirements for all-things-considered permissible driving.

Thus, it looks as if there are two ways in which further norms stepping in may override the constraints of norms specific to a particular type of action: they can make the action all-things-considered impermissible altogether (*Drive 1*), although the requirements imposed by the type-specific norm are met, or they can modify the requirements for all-things-considered permissible driving (*Drives 2* and *3*), although, again, the requirements for permissible driving by the type-specific norm remain fixed.

Notice, too, that the case of driving is hardly isolated; similar examples can be construed for many types of action, provided that the type-specific norms in question regulate how much of a gradable property one's action needs to enjoy in order to be permissible. To see this, consider the following contrast cases: if social norms forbid me to wear sports shoes in restaurants, they forbid it altogether. It cannot be that they allow me to wear 'more or less' sports shoes. When there is a gradable property that is at stake – that is, roughly, when permissible action requires more or less of a gradable property x – norms regulating it can fix the threshold for permissible action lower or higher on the x spectrum: it can become permissible/required to drive faster or more slowly, to have a better or a worse grade average, to wear a lighter or a darker dress and so on.

Now, notice the analogy between *Drive 1* and *Bald* and, respectively, *Drive 2* and *3* and *Affair*. In the former pair of cases, overriding makes the action in question all-things-considered impermissible; in the latter, arguably, it only modifies the requirements for all-things-considered permissibility. Assertion is a type of action, and justification is a gradable property: one can have more or less of it. Similarly to the case of driving, then, we should expect other norms to be able to influence the permissibility of assertion in two ways: first, it might be that asserting that p becomes all-things-considered impermissible, even though the epistemic standards are reached – in much the same way as in *Drive 1* and *Bald*. Secondly, it might be that, analogously to *Drives 2* and *3*, other norms stepping in may modify the amount of epistemic support required for all-things-considered permissible assertion that p upwards – and so knowledge is not enough for all-things-considered permissible assertion – or downwards – with the result that knowledge is not even needed.

If that is the case, however, *Content Individuation* is false. Recall that Brown takes it that the fact that the quantity of epistemic support needed for permissible assertion seems to be higher in high-stakes situations shows that it is the epistemic norm that is at work. However, in line with action in general, just because a norm N affects the amount of epistemic support needed for all-things-considered permissible assertion, it need not follow that N is an epistemic norm. Just like in the case of driving, where a moral norm affects how fast one can go, further norms can override the epistemic norm and modify the amount of epistemic support needed for all-things-considered permissible assertion. *The fact that a norm has epistemic content does not imply that it is an epistemic norm.*

One objection on Brown's behalf, already voiced by Jennifer Lackey (2011), would go along the following lines: if the above distinction is correct, how is one to distinguish between the requirements pertaining to different types of norms? Here is Lackey:

> For now, whenever evidence is adduced that concerns the epistemic author-
> ity requisite for proper assertion, it may bear on the norm of assertion or it

may bear on these other [. . .] norms. [. . .] [I]t will be extremely difficult, if not impossible, to tell which is being defended. (Lackey 2011, 277)

Here is, though, a fairly straightforward and popular way to distinguish requirements associated with different norms: How a given norm is typed has to do with the value it is associated[1] with (henceforth also *Value Individuation*). For instance, prudential norms will be associated with a prudential value – maximising practical utility – moral norms will be associated with the value of maximising moral goodness. Most importantly for present purposes, epistemic norms will be associated with epistemic values.

Think again about driving your three-year-old nephew to kindergarten. The moral norm there has traffic-related content: 'Drive slower than 50 km/h because your nephew gets carsick'. This, however, in no way makes it a traffic norm. Similarly, prudential norms can have epistemic content; take, for instance, the norm: 'Do not jump in the lake unless you know how to swim'. What makes this a prudential constraint rather than an epistemic one is the value associated with it, which is life preservation.

Given that this is so, it looks as though it is on Brown's shoulders to argue that the norm asking for stronger epistemic support in *Affair* is not only a norm with epistemic content, but also an epistemic norm as such, associated with an epistemic value, and concerned with specifically epistemic permissibility. A closer look at the case makes it highly plausible, however, that it is a moral (and prudential) norm that requires a stronger epistemic support here. After all, the relevant value is protecting Husband from unnecessary hardship, as is evidenced by Brown's very own description of the case: 'Ok, we admit we knew, but it wouldn't have been right for me to say anything before we was absolutely sure. *I knew the damage it would cause to your marriage*' (Brown 2010, 555, *emphasis added*). But given that the value is a prudential one, the norm prohibiting assertion is a prudential norm, not an epistemic one.[2]

---

[1] Notice that the claim needed for this argument is of mere association between norms and values of a particular type; as such, it does not, in any way, imply any value theoretic commitments. The teleologist will explain the 'ought' in terms of the 'good'; he will say that the norm is there to guide us in realising the value. As opposed to this, the deontologist reverses the order of explanation; he would have it that what makes something valuable is the fact that the norm gives us reasons to favour it. In any case, the mere association claim holds. Thus, the above argument can be constructed in both consequentialist and deontological terms; nothing hinges on this.

[2] One way for Brown to argue that it is for the sake of realising an epistemic value that more warrant is needed in this case could go along the following lines: Friend's assertion is aimed at generating knowledge/true belief in his audience – in this case, Husband. If Friend were to assert 'Your wife is having an affair', Husband might plausibly ask 'How do you know?' In this case, Husband might fail to believe the content of Friend's assertion if the latter is not able to back his claims by serious

But what about Brown's *Equivalence Thesis*? Crucially, if *Content Individuation* fails, *Equivalence Thesis* turns out to be false too. One's assertion that *p* can be epistemically permissible without it being the case that one is in a good enough epistemic position to be all-things-considered permitted to assert that *p*. This is going to be the case when the norm that dictates how much epistemic support is needed for all-things-considered permissible assertion is not the epistemic norm, but a further norm – with epistemic content – stepping in and raising the bar, as in *Affair*.

Also, one can be in a good enough epistemic position to be all-things-considered permitted to assert that *p* without it being the case that one's assertion that *p* is epistemically permissible. This is going to be the case when further norms step in, override the epistemic norm[3], and set the threshold for being in a good enough epistemic position to be all-things-considered permitted to assert *p* lower than the epistemic norm. One example of this is Tim Williamson's (2000) train case:

> **Train**
> Suppose that you, knowing that it is urgent for us to get to our destination, shout 'That is your train' upon seeing a train approach the station.

Asserting seems to be permissible, even though you do not know that it is our train; you merely believe that it is very likely so.

To sum up, once we make the necessary distinction between epistemic norms and norms with epistemic content, *Content Individuation* and *Equivalence Thesis* both turn out to be false. If this is the case, Brown's

---

epistemic support. If Friend fails to generate belief in his audience, he also thereby fails to generate knowledge, or true belief, for that matter, so he fails to realise the epistemic value.

  Notice, however, that a norm of assertion that would be able to accommodate this case would be implausibly strong; not only would it be asking for a high quantity of warrant in high-stakes scenarios, but also for the speaker to have access to it, so that he can discursively justify his speech act. This, however, seems to over-intellectualise the practice of assertion. Children, for instance, due to lacking the cognitive sophistication to reflect on their warrant, would never be allowed to assert in high-stakes circumstances. Furthermore, consider also the fact that most of our knowledge comes from memory. Now, in most cases of memorial knowledge that p, we tend not to recall how we came to know that p in the first place. We surely know that Berlin is the capital of Germany, that we were born, respectively, in January and March, that the Petronas Towers are in Kuala Lumpur, and so on, but we have no clue as to how we came across all this knowledge. Does that mean that we are not allowed to assert any of this in high-stakes scenarios? That seems highly implausible. Or, to say the least, we believe it to be on Brown's shoulders to make the case for such a demanding norm.

[3] In this case, KRA. Notice also that no one in the literature questions the prudential explanation in *Train* (see subsequent discussion). However, *Train* is for KRA what *Affair* is for KRA-S: a case in which the quantity of epistemic support needed for prudentially permissible assertion is not the same as the one needed for epistemically permissible assertion. It is, therefore, surprising that *Affair* is seen as problematic for KRA-S, while *Train* is widely acknowledged to not put any pressure on KRA.

argument against KRA-S-B in no way affects KRA-S, which is the epistemic norm we were interested in to begin with.

3.2   The Qualitative Objection

We have seen that the quantitative case against KRA-S does not stand up
to closer value-theoretic scrutiny. That is, we have seen that further
norms – like prudential and moral norms – can override the epistemic norm
and raise the quantity of epistemic support needed for all-things-considered
permissible assertion. We have also looked at a principled way to distinguish
between the constraints imposed by the epistemic norm we are interested in
and those sourced in other types of norms, by looking at the value plausibly
associated with the requirement in question. On the face of it, at least, this
method suggested that high practical stakes cases such as Brown's are not
going to do the intended work for proving KRA-S false.

Jennifer Lackey (2011, 2014), however, argues that the quantity of
epistemic support is not all there is to it. That is, according to Lackey, the
type of epistemic support might be problematic for permissible assertion by
knowledgeable speakers also; in some contexts, Lackey argues, mere isolated
testimonial knowledge is not enough for permissible assertion.

3.2.1   *Expert Testimony*

Consider the following case:

> **Doctor**
> Matilda is an oncologist at a teaching hospital [. . .]. One of her patients,
> Derek, [. . .] has been experiencing intense abdominal pain [. . .]. After
> requesting an ultrasound and MRI, the results of the tests arrived on
> Matilda's day off [and were] reviewed by Nancy, a competent medical
> student in oncology training at her hospital. [. . .] Nancy communicated
> to Matilda simply that her diagnosis is pancreatic cancer, without offering
> any of the details of the test results [. . .]. Shortly thereafter, Matilda had her
> appointment with Derek, where she truly asserts to him purely on the basis
> of Nancy's reliable testimony, 'we am very sorry to tell you this, but you
> have pancreatic cancer'. (Lackey 2011, 254)

In this case, Matilda knows the target proposition via reliable testimony.
Even so, her assertion of it seems impermissible. According to Lackey, this
is due to the joint action of two factors: the purely testimonial source –
what Lackey dubs second-hand knowledge – and the isolated character of
the piece of knowledge – the asserter knowing nothing other than *p* about

the subject matter. It may also be worth noting that, as Lackey explicitly acknowledges, just one of the two factors (isolatedness and second-handness) would not be enough to trigger the intuition; had Nancy given Matilda more information about the test results (non-isolation), or had Matilda, say, seen the result of at least only one isolated test herself (not entirely second-hand knowledge), her assertion would have been just fine.

Consider, though, what would be the case if the source of Matilda's isolated second-hand knowledge had not been Nancy, but rather Matilda's supervisor, Dr Jones, the chief physician of the oncology ward. Surely, then, Matilda's assertion would be perfectly permissible. But this suggests that it is not the nature of the source – that is, its being isolated and second-hand – that does the trick here, but its reliability. Dr Jones is just a more reliable source than Nancy is. And while the testimony of both of them seems good enough for Matilda to gain knowledge, in the high-stakes scenario we're facing, Dr Jones's testimony would just raise the quantity of required epistemic support closer to certainty, so as to enable Matilda to make an all-things-considered permissible assertion.

In a similar vein, it is also worth noticing that, in high-stakes situations, it might be the case that even non-isolated first-hand knowledge would not be enough for assertion. That is, plausibly enough, telling Derek that he has cancer only on the basis of two blood test results, even if Matilda saw the results herself, would hardly make for a permissible assertion, given the high stakes involved.

And, finally, when the stakes are not high, it is no longer clear that isolated second-hand knowledge will not be enough for proper assertion. To see this, suppose Derek undergoes a routine blood test. Suppose Matilda evaluates it and comes to the conclusion that Derek is perfectly healthy. Given that she is very busy just now, she tells the nurse to communicate the result to Derek. When the nurse tells Derek that everything is fine, their assertion is entirely permissible. At the same time, their assertion is both second-hand and isolated. These considerations further confirm that the problem with Matilda's epistemic support for her assertion is not one of quality but one of quantity (and stakes).

Another response to Lackey's argument has recently been offered by Matt Benton. Crucially, while his approach is different than ours, the two are compatible. It may be that there is more than one way of explaining why Lackey's argument fails to make a convincing case against KRA-S. In what follows, we will first outline Benton's response and look at a recent rejoinder by Lackey. While we argue that Lackey's rejoinder can be made to work against Benton, we will show that it ultimately remains unsuccessful. Let's start with Benton, who offers two reasons for thinking that the intuitively impermissibility in Lackey's case is not epistemic but pragmatic.

First, Benton claims that there is an important difference in intuitive permissibility depending on whether we assume (i) that Derek wants any expert opinion or else (ii) that he specifically wants Matilda's expert opinion. In particular, if we assume (i), it is just not clear that Matilda's assertion is intuitively impermissible (in fact Benton describes it as 'pragmatically acceptable'), whereas if we assume (ii) it is intuitively impermissible but also pragmatically misleading. Roughly, this is because Derek seeks Matilda's expert opinion but gets Nancy's (2016, 496–97).

Key to Benton's second response is the following case:

> Matilda is an oncologist at a teaching hospital who has been diagnosing and treating various kinds of cancers for the past fifteen years. One of her patients, Derek, was recently referred to her office because he has been experiencing intense abdominal pain for a couple of weeks. Matilda requested an ultrasound and MRI, but the results of the tests arrived on her day off; consequently, all the relevant data were reviewed by Nancy, a very competent colleague in oncology at her hospital. Being able to confer for only a very brief period of time prior to Derek's appointment today, Nancy communicated to Matilda simply that her diagnosis is pancreatic cancer, without offering any of the details of the test results or the reasons underlying her conclusion. Shortly thereafter, Matilda had her appointment with Derek with Nancy in attendance, where Matilda truly asserts to Derek purely on the basis of Nancy's reliable testimony, 'I am very sorry to tell you this, but you have pancreatic cancer.' (Benton 2016, 499)

And the crucial claim is that in this version of the case, Matilda's assertion is intuitively permissible. If so, whatever explains the intuitive impermissibility in Lackey's version of the case, it cannot be Matilda's epistemic position toward the proposition asserted. After all, that is something that remains unchanged across the two cases. And, of course, what both responses point to is that the reason why, in Lackey's case, the assertion is intuitively impermissible, is not epistemic but pragmatic (2016, 499–500).

Lackey (2016) has recently offered the following rejoinder to Benton's argument. Regarding the case in which Nancy is present – Benton's second response – Lackey argues that the only way to elicit the intuition is that Nancy and Matilda are presenting the diagnosis as a group. But, of course, since the group featuring Nancy does not assert from isolated second-hand knowledge, this does little to mitigate the force of the original case against KRA-S (2016, 516).

Regarding Benton's first response, Lackey argues that, no matter what we assume, Derek will not get an expert opinion because an expert opinion is an opinion *grounded in expertise*. Crucially, grounding in expertise, according to Lackey, excludes isolated second-hand character. No matter what we assume about the case, Matilda simply fails to offer her expert opinion. As a result, her assertion is bound to remain impermissible. Moreover, this does nothing to mitigate the challenge for KRA-S, as Lackey argues in the following passage:

> The upshot of these considerations is that Matilda's assertion being pragmatically misleading does not provide an alternative explanation to its being epistemically improper. Rather, Matilda's assertion is epistemically improper because it lacks the appropriate grounding – i.e., a grounding in expertise, which requires that it not be isolated second-hand knowledge. This epistemic explanation, in turn, explains why Matilda's assertion might seem pragmatically misleading, not the other way around. (Lackey 2016, 514)

One worry one might raise for Lackey's response is that it does so very little to speak to Benton's intuition that if we assume (i) Matilda's assertion is intuitively permissible. On the contrary, it follows from her response that Matilda's assertion is equally impermissible. And, of course, if given the assumption of (i), Matilda's assertion is permissible and given assertion (ii) it isn't, it now looks eminently plausible that the problem with (ii) is pragmatic: Derek expects something he doesn't get, i.e. Matilda's expert opinion.

Now Lackey might deny the intuition that Benton registers for assumption (i). And there is something to this. After all, what Benton cannot have in mind is the perhaps most natural way of desiring any expert's opinion. Derek doesn't care who offers it, but he does care that, whoever may offer it, offer *their* expert opinion. After all, if assumption (i) is unpacked in this way, then we may still expect Matilda's assertion to come out impermissible. What Benton needs is an interpretation of (i) that allows for someone's expert opinion to be delivered by someone else. And one issue one might have this kind of interpretation is that it shouldn't really matter whether the person who delivers it is also an expert. If all you are interested in is any expert opinion in this sense, you should be fine with getting it from a graduate student or a nurse. But then it's not clear that this is right. Derek might very well resent the assertion if it's delivered by a nurse or a graduate student. Or so Lackey might argue. But if so, then Derek is equally entitled to resent the assertion if it's delivered by Matilda. So, there really is no way of interpreting (i) on which the assertion is intuitively permissible.

That said, we are unconvinced that assertion of expert opinion needs to be grounded in expertise in the way Lackey suggests. To see this, recall the variation of the case mentioned earlier in Derek undergoes a routine blood test. While Matilda evaluates it and comes to the conclusion that he is perfectly healthy, she tells the nurse to communicate the result to Derek. When the nurse tells Derek that everything is fine, she gives an opinion that is grounded in expertise in the right way. Crucially, her assertion is entirely permissible. At the same time, her assertion is both second-hand and isolated.

We take this to strongly suggest that there is indeed a pragmatic problem with Matilda's assertion in Lackey's original case. If this isn't entirely obvious, consider a variation of our case in which the evaluating doctor is Nancy and the delivering doctor is Matilda. If Matilda were to introduce herself as a doctor and simply assert that the tests are fine, Derek might take issue with her assertion. However, if Matilda were to explain that she was asked by Nancy to deliver the result, there would be no problem here. This further confirms the diagnosis in terms of a pragmatic problem. In sum, then, we agree with Benton that the intuitive impermissibility in Lackey's case can be explained in pragmatic terms.

3.2.2   Aesthetic Judgements

Consider:

Food
My neighbour Ken is a connoisseur of fine dining. As we were leaving Starbucks this afternoon, he told me that the food at a new local restaurant about which I was previously quite unfamiliar, Quince, is exquisite, though being in a hurry prevented him from offering any details or evidence on behalf of this claim. While talking to my friend Vivienne later in the day, she was fretting over where to take her boyfriend to dinner for Valentine's Day. I promptly relieved her stress by truly asserting, 'The food at Quince is exquisite'. (Lackey 2011, 260)

Now, Lackey argues that what explains the apparent impermissibility of the assertion in this case is the joint action of isolation and second-handedness.

We disagree. The reason for this is that Lackey's case can be given a straightforward Gricean treatment. Notice that there are three different things Lackey might mean when making her assertion involving an aesthetic judgement in *Food*. By uttering: 'The food at Quince's is exquisite'

Lackey might mean to say that she has tried it and liked it, or that it is generally considered good food (by experts, or most people, etc.), or both. However, the most common implicatures are the first and the third on the list. To see this, notice that if Lackey wanted to say that experts consider it good but she doesn't like it or hasn't tried it, she will not merely say 'The food is good', but qualify her statement accordingly.

As such, it is easy to see how making assertions involving aesthetic judgements based on solely second-hand knowledge in *Food* will hardly be fully permissible, unless, of course, Lackey cancels the implicature and makes it clear that it is according to experts, or most people, that the food is good, even though she hasn't tried it herself. After all, in the above case, all Lackey comes to know by testimony from her neighbour Ken is that Ken likes the food, or, at most, that it is considered good by experts in the field; this, of course, might increase the chances of her liking it too. But she surely does not acquire testimonial knowledge that *she likes the food herself.* So the implicature to the effect that she has tried the food and liked it will, of course, render her assertion impermissible, not because knowledge is not sufficient for assertion, but because it is necessary (KRA⁴).⁵

What would help with the permissibility of the assertion would be if the case stipulated that Ken and Lackey have the exact same taste in food. The implicature thus generated would not be problematic anymore. But then the same goes for the assertion. According to (KRA and) KRA-S this is exactly as it should be. After all, so modified, Lackey would come to know that she likes the food herself in this case.

So, in sum, it seems that in order to turn Lackey's assertion into a permissible one, we have to re-describe the case such that either she knows that she likes the food herself, or else she cancels the implicature to this effect. But this goes to show that the underlying problem is not that knowledge is not sufficient for epistemically permissible assertion, but

---

⁴ Weaker norms are broken too: e.g. Lackey is not even justified in believing the implicature.
⁵ For an argument against the claim that one has to know the conversational implicatures of one's assertions, see Fricker (2012); while we find Fricker's argument promising, we think that the case we are making here is not affected by it. Roughly, Fricker takes it that we might not be able to hold the speaker responsible for lack of epistemic support for the generated conversational implicatures, because in many contexts it is not clear whether the hearer gets the implicature right. However, importantly, Fricker's argument only targets (and, arguably, only goes through for) *mere* conversational implicatures. The ones we are concerned with here, however, are *conventional* conversational implicatures, that is, implicatures that are carried by the meaning with which the sentence is *conventionally* (usually) uttered (more about this below). Roughly put, it looks as if, if a sentence is *conventionally* uttered with a particular meaning, the hearer is in a better position to get the implicature right, and therefore in a better position to criticise the speaker for lack of sufficient epistemic support for it.

simply that in the original case Lackey asserts more than she actually knows, and so violates KRA.

3.2.3   Objections and Replies

OBJECTION 1.   Lackey considers a possible reply along Gricean lines, but she argues that it would not stand as, by Grice's own lights, implicatures are 'not carried by what is said, but only by the saying of what is said, or by "*putting it that way*"' (Lackey 2011, 270). In contrast, in the cases involving aesthetic judgement under consideration, it looks as if the impermissibility is linked to the content of the assertion rather than to uttering it in one context or another.

REPLY.   Grice (1989, 25, 37, 39) distinguishes between three types of implicatures:

1. *Conversational implicatures* (cancellable, and to which the quote above refers to): carried by uttering p in a specific context rather than by p itself, like in:

   'Are you going to Paul's party?'
   'I have to work.'
   (Implicature: I am not going to Paul's party.)

2. *Conventional implicatures* (non-cancellable): carried by the meaning of the sentence itself, like in:

   'He is an Englishman; he is, therefore, brave.' (Implicature: His being an Englishman implies that he is brave.)

3. *Conventional conversational implicatures* (cancellable): carried by the meaning with which the sentence is conventionally (usually) uttered:

   'Some athletes smoke.'
   (Implicature: Not all athletes smoke.)

It is easy to see that assertions involving aesthetic judgements pertain to the third category. That is, the implicature is (i) carried by the meaning conventionally associated with uttering a sentence of the type 'X is good', and (ii) cancellable.

OBJECTION 2.   Lackey argues that one can easily imagine cases when the presumed implicature is not cancellable. By way of support, she offers the following 'presumed witness'[6] scenario:

Recommendation
Josie, who was asked to support a philosophy student applying to Ph.D. programs, wrote in her letter of recommendation for his applications,

---

[6] Notice the Gricean flavour here.

"Mitchell has very polished writing skills." While Josie does indeed know this about the student, her knowledge is grounded purely in the isolated, reliable testimony of her trustworthy colleague. Josie herself has had Mitchell in class for only a few weeks, and has yet to see any of his writing. (Lackey 2011, 264)

REPLY.   In the light of the discussion in the two previous sections, it might have become transparent already that *Recommendation* is but a combination of the above: an aesthetic judgement offered in an institutional context defined by particular stakes. In virtue of being an aesthetic judgement alone, the assertion will be impermissible due to generating the false implicature that Josie likes the student's writing style herself (and thus impermissible due to being in breach of KRA). Interestingly enough, though, what happens in this particular case of aesthetic judgement is that Josie cannot even permissibly cancel the implicature as the institutional requirements in play here specifically ask for Josie's own aesthetic judgement on the matter.

Notice, however, that this, again, fails to speak against KRA-S. The institution of writing recommendation letters is so designed as to involve the writer's aesthetic judgements, if any, because it is her reputation that's at stake. Josie's addressee wants to know what Josie, the author of the letter, thinks about the student's writing style. Had Josie testified to something not involving an aesthetic judgement in her letter – say, the fact that Mitchell is a student representative the faculty's committee for gender issues – isolated second-hand knowledge would have been just fine.

To see that the implicature's non-cancellability is due to institutional norms in play, rather than to the epistemic norm we are interested in, notice the difference with testifying in court. In these cases, even testimony based on second-hand knowledge about non-aesthetic matters of fact will be problematic – and, conversely, the implicature will be non-cancellable – due to the fact that this is just how the institution is designed to work.

OBJECTION 3.   Lackey considers a possible appeal to institutional norms stepping in, but she argues that 'assertions involving isolated second-hand knowledge are not epistemically problematic because various institutions say that they are wrong; rather, the institutions say that they are wrong because such assertions are epistemically problematic' (Lackey 2011, 274).

REPLY.   Notice, first, that we do not aim to explain the impermissibility of the target assertions in terms of institutional norms, but the uncancellability of the implicatures generated.

That said, we trust that Lackey is right on the order of explanation here. Notice, however, that this suggests a quantitative picture again. Plausibly enough, we designed the institutions in line with the stakes usually implied by their target concern. When the institution is in charge of informing you that you have cancer, its representatives had better be sure about it before proceeding. Journalism students are taught to corroborate information from at least three sources before publishing a piece of news, given the large-scale impact it might have. In the case of writing recommendation letters, too, both the reputation of the writer and the student's career are at stake.

In contrast, isolated testimonial knowledge from an average source is surely pretty fine for the purpose of assertion in many low stakes environments, like, say, companies providing cleaning services. We doubt that any such service provider would have to double check before telling me that my house has been cleaned, rather than just trusting the word of her employee.

So it looks as if, again, we are just faced with a quantitative issue here; that is, the reliability of the source being in line with the stakes. If that is the case, if Lackey's argument eventually boils down to a quantitative objection, her case is open to the same worries as Brown's.

3.3   Back to Goldberg

We are now in a position to deal with the last of the outstanding problems for KRA that we first introduced at the end of Chapter 2. Here it is again:

1. In cases in which S believes that p in the face of (what I will call) *systematic p-relevant peer disagreement*, [...] S is not doxastically justified in believing that p.
2. If S is not doxastically justified in believing that p, then S is not warranted in asserting that p.
3. Some cases of disagreement regarding whether p are cases of systematic p-relevant peer disagreement.
4. (Therefore) In such cases, S is not warranted in asserting that p (Goldberg 2015, 226–27).

Recall also why, according to Goldberg, 4 is problematic. If 4 holds, there appear to be entire domains such that we are not in a position to permissibly assert propositions in this domain, including philosophy. However, the result that none (or next to none) of our assertions in philosophy are permissible is just unacceptable.

Goldberg's own way of resisting this conclusion is by giving up KRA, or at least an unrestricted version of it. While KRA does hold in ordinary contexts, in contexts in which we are talking about questions and perhaps even domains that are subject to systematic peer disagreement, the epistemic requirement on assertion is significantly weakened. In particular, according to Goldberg, what the epistemic norm of assertion requires is determined in part by what it is reasonable in context to believe is mutually believed about things like the informational needs of the parties to the conversation (2015, 273). And, most importantly for present purposes, this idea is motivated along Gricean lines. Here goes:

> [M]y main motivation is that I think it emerges naturally out of a Gricean picture of speech exchanges. Once one sees such exchanges as a rational, cooperative activity, one is already seeing these exchanges as taking place against a rich background of mutual belief and mutual expectation. [...] Cooperativeness requires that (absent overriding reason not to do so) one provide one's audience with what is wanted in the way of information, in such a way that it is clear that this is what one is doing. When it is mutually manifest that the conversation is taking place under conditions of epistemically diminished hopes, and mutually manifest as well that both parties want to continue the conversational exchange, the very picture of Gricean cooperativeness would predict that both speaker and hearer adjust their epistemic expectations accordingly. It is this that motivates the context-sensitivity in my account. That the resulting picture can accommodate the phenomenon of assertion in cases of systematic disagreement is a bonus. (Goldberg 2015, 275)

To see why Goldberg's argument does not require us to abandon KRA, note that, according to Goldberg himself, the context sensitivity of the epistemic norm of assertion is motivated by the fact that other normative requirements – in particular, the requirements of cooperativeness – step in and lower the requirements for epistemically permissible assertion.

Of course, if one individuates epistemic norms by content, and if one accepts Goldberg's picture, one will be also be committed to a contextualist epistemic norm of assertion. However, once we realise that *Content Individuation* is false and replace it by the more plausible *Value Individuation*, it is clear that the argument from the fact that other normative requirements (e.g. the requirements of cooperativeness) may step in and lower the requirements for permissible assertion to the conclusion that KRA is not the epistemic norm of assertion will simply not go through.

In fact, a very attractive alternative account of what's going on naturally suggests itself. To see how, recall that we argued earlier on in this chapter that the epistemic norm of assertion can be overridden by other normative requirements. Moreover, it can be thus overridden not only in the sense that other normative requirements make assertion impermissible altogether, but also in the sense that they may drive the epistemic requirements for all-things-considered permissible assertion up or down. Crucially, overriding normative requirements leave the epistemic norm of assertion, KRA, intact. It will not come as a surprise that, in our view, this is exactly what happens in the cases that Goldberg adduces. In fact, in the above passage Goldberg even describes just how KRA gets overridden in these cases: the requirements of cooperativeness step in and lower the epistemic requirements for all-things-considered permissible assertion. Compatibly with that, KRA remains unaffected entirely.

In sum, then, we agree with Goldberg that any commitment to the claim that none (or next to none) of our assertions in e.g. philosophy are permissible would be unacceptable. We can also agree with Goldberg that Gricean story about how the epistemic requirements for permissible assertion in e.g. philosophy are lowered. However, what we have now seen is that this does not mean we have to abandon KRA in favour of a contextualist epistemic norm of assertion. On the contrary, both of these claims are entirely compatible with KRA.

3.4   Conclusion

This chapter has argued that, given some fairly plausible assumptions regarding the characteristic epistemic purpose associated with the practice of assertion, knowledge is enough for epistemically permissible assertion.

In order to defend the view, we have argued that Brown's quantitative worries regarding the amount of epistemic support needed for permissible assertion in high-stakes contexts need not concern the epistemic norm of assertion itself. The variation in quantity of epistemic support needed for permissible assertion can be explained in terms of other, more stringent norms stepping in and overriding it – like prudential, social or moral norms. We should have expected this to be the case to begin with: permissible assertion need not mean epistemically permissible assertion.

We have also provided a quantitative explanation of Jennifer Lackey's cases. Lackey thinks that isolated second-hand knowledge will not always render assertion permissible. We have argued that, in her 'expert testimony' cases, isolated second-hand knowledge from a very reliable source does render assertion permissible, which suggests that what is at play is quantity (related to the high stakes of the featured context) rather than quality of support. We then looked at Lackey's cases involving aesthetic judgements and argued that they afford a straightforward Gricean explanation, and thus pose no problem for the sufficiency claim we are interested in.

Finally, we looked at Goldberg's argument that certain cases of peer disagreement suggest that KRA is too strong and showed that once we are clear on the distinction between epistemic norms on the one hand and norms with epistemic content on the other, the objection can be avoided along the very lines Goldberg himself suggests.

PART II

FFAA
A Function First Account of Assertion

CHAPTER 4

FFAA

Part I of the book argued that KRA is true, that there is an epistemic knowledge rule governing assertion. Note that champions of KRA typically (if not invariably) also accept, albeit implicitly, the following account of when assertions are good or proper assertions:

KRA-Good Assertion-Link
One's assertion that *p* is (epistemically) good if and only if it satisfies KRA.

It is easy to see that KRA and *KRA-Good Assertion-Link* together entail the following:

The Knowledge Account of Good Assertion
One's assertion that *p* is (epistemically) good if and only if one knows that *p*.

This chapter will take a closer look at accounts of the normativity of assertion that accept KRA as well as *KRA-Good Assertion-Link* and derive *The Knowledge Account of Good Assertion* from these two theses. Recall that any such account is *rule first* in the sense that the conditions for epistemically good assertion are derived from the epistemic rule of assertion. Recall also that we introduced the label 'rule first account of assertion' or 'RFAA' for such accounts. Our aim is to develop in some detail an alternative to RFAA and to argue that it compares favourably with RFAA. Unlike RFAA, our account derives the conditions for epistemically good assertion not from KRA but from an etiological function of assertion, which, recall, we will refer to as 'the function first account of assertion' or 'FFAA' for short.

Here is the game plan for the remainder of this chapter. We will first develop an account of etiological functions and their normative import (Section 4.1). In Section 4.2, we argue that assertion has the etiological function of generating knowledge in hearers and develop the proposed account of the normativity of assertion by unpacking the normative import of this thesis. Finally, in Section 4.3, we compare RFAA and FFAA and show that there is reason to believe that FFAA is the more attractive view.

4.1   Etiological Functions and Their Normative Import

4.1.1   Etiological Functions

We would now like to investigate the relation between etiological functions (or 'e-functions') and certain kinds of norm. To begin with, let's look at the following plausible account of e-functions:

E-Function

A token of type T has the e-function of producing effect E in system S iff

(EF1) Past tokens of T produced E in S's ancestors

(EF2) Producing E benefitted S's ancestors

(EF3) Producing E's having benefitted S's ancestors contributes to the explanation of why T exists in S.[1]

Consider your heart, which plausibly has the e-function of pumping blood. Notice that one effect that past tokens of hearts had in your ancestors was to pump blood (EF1). Moreover, this effect was beneficial to your ancestors (EF2). In fact it was of vital importance. If their hearts had not pumped blood, they would not have survived very long. Finally, that past hearts pumped blood in your ancestors contributes to the explanation of why hearts exist in present-day humans (EF3). Past hearts' pumping blood contributed to the proliferation of the genes responsible for them and in this way to the explanation of the existence of the heart in present-day humans. By *E-Function*, your heart has the e-function of pumping blood.

In contrast, while your heart also produces a certain kind of sound, producing this kind of sound is not an e-function of your heart. One reason for this is that producing the relevant kind of sound had no discernible benefit for your ancestors. (EF2) is not satisfied. Even if we assume (EF2) to be satisfied, say because the kind of sound hearts produced was pleasant to your ancestors, production of this benefit does not contribute to the explanation of why hearts exist in humans. So (EF3) is

---

[1]   Etiological accounts of functions are the most widely accepted accounts in contemporary literature. Prominent champions include David Buller (1998), Peter Godfrey-Smith (1993, 1994), Paul Griffith (1993), Ruth Millikan (1984), and Karen Neander (1991a, 1991b). That said, there are a number of noteworthy dissenters, including John Bigelow and Richard Pargetter (1987), Philip Kitcher (1994) and Denis Walsh and André Ariew (1996). For applications to epistemology see, e.g. Graham (2012, 2014a,b). In fact, *E-Function* is close to Peter Graham's (2014b) account of e-functions. It differs from Graham in explicitly opting for a weak account of e-functions along the lines of Buller (1998).

not satisfied in any case. By *E-Function*, your heart does not have the e-function of producing this kind of sound.[2]

While your heart is a paradigm case of an item with an e-function, we'd also like to look at a slightly more complex case (or, perhaps, a slightly different case with a bit more explicit structure). Consider a system that is constituted by the following types of subsystem: a type of producer, a type of product, a type of consumer, and a type of return, such that the producer produces product tokens, which may be consumed by consumers in exchange for a return. In what follows, we will refer to any such system as a *simple economic system* (SES). By way of example of an SES, consider the practice of producing and consuming cups of espresso at your local coffee shop (SES-Espresso). This practice is a system involving baristas (producers) who produce cups of espresso (product). Furthermore, the system features costumers at the coffee shop (consumers), who may purchase (return) and then consume token cups of espresso.

Tokens of the product in an SES may (and often will) have the e-function of producing a certain effect, E, in consumers. One might wonder how this could be given that, according to *E-Function*, the effect must occur in the system, i.e. the SES. Recall, however, that the consumer is a subsystem of a given SES that partly constitutes it. Since, plausibly, an effect in a system may be produced by producing it in one of its constituent subsystems, the idea that tokens of products may (and often will) have the e-function of producing E in consumers should not raise too many eyebrows.

By *E-Function*, product tokens will have the e-function of producing E in consumers if and only if past tokens of the product produced E in past consumers (EF1), E was beneficial for an ancestor (i.e. here, a past self) of the SES (EF2) and the fact that E was beneficial for an ancestor of the SES contributes to explaining why the SES continues to exist today (EF3).[3]

---

[2] We borrow this example from Graham (2012).

[3] This is a somewhat simplified formulation of EF3, which should really read as follows: the fact that E was beneficial for an ancestor of the SES contributes to explaining *why the type of product continues to exist* in the SES today. Note, however, that when the SES features only a single type of product, the SES will cease to exist when and only when the product ceases to exist in the SES. For instance, assuming that cups of espresso are the only type of product produced by baristas in SES-Espresso, SES-Espresso will cease to exist when and only when cups of espresso cease to exist at your local coffee shop. Of course, this is not the case in SESs that feature more than one type of product. Consider, for instance, the practice of producing and consuming coffee products at your local coffee shop, including espressos, cappuccinos, lattes and so on. Here the relevant SES may continue to exist even if cups of espresso don't continue to exist in it. Accordingly, EF3 cannot be simplified in the above way. Since, for the purposes of this book, we will be focusing only on SESs that feature a single

We take it that it is pretty clear how EF1 can be satisfied in an SES. For instance, in SES-Espresso, past cups of espresso may very well have generated pleasant gustatory experiences in customers. Assuming that they did, EF1 is satisfied here. The cases of EF2 and EF3 might benefit from some further commentary. EF2 may be satisfied in a given SES in virtue of the fact that E was beneficial for past consumers. In that case, the benefit for the SES resides in the benefit for consumers.[4] In SES-Espresso, for instance, it is plausible that the production of pleasant gustatory experiences in customers is beneficial for SES-Espresso in virtue of being beneficial for customers. The benefit of pleasant gustatory experiences in customers for SES-Espresso resides in the benefit of such experiences for customers here. Since we take it to be clear enough that pleasant gustatory experiences do constitute a benefit for customers, EF2 will be satisfied. Finally, EF3 will often be satisfied in a given SES because the beneficial effect produced in past consumers of past tokens of the product motivated them to continue to offer returns for tokens, which, in turn, motivated producers to continue producing tokens of the type, thus contributing to the explanation of why the SES continues to exist. For instance, in SES-Espresso, the fact that token cups of espresso generated pleasant gustatory experiences in costumers motivated costumers to continue purchasing cups of espresso, which, in turn motivated baristas to continue producing them, thus contributing to explaining why SES-Espresso continues to exist today.

4.1.2   Two Kinds of Norm

With this account of e-functions in play, we'd now like to introduce a distinction between two broad normative categories. While this distinction is widely recognised in the literature (e.g. Nolfi 2014, Smith 2005, Tappolet 2014, Thomson 2008), different contributors have used different terminology to mark it. Here we will adopt Conor McHugh's (2012) terminology, who introduces it as a distinction between *prescriptive* and *evaluative norms* and characterises it as follows:

---

type of product, the simplification is unproblematic. Accordingly, the fact that we use it frequently in what follows should not be cause for concern either.
[4] We do not mean to suggest that the benefit to the SES must always reside in the benefit for consumers. On the contrary, it seems plausible that, on occasion, there may be a benefit for the SES without there being a benefit for consumers. Conversely, it also seems plausible that a benefit for consumers may not be a benefit for the SES. All we are saying is that the benefit for the system may reside in the benefit for the consumer.

Prescriptive Norms
[Prescriptive norms] are to do with what one ought, may or ought not do: they require, permit or forbid certain pieces of conduct on the part of agents, and are apt to guide that conduct. (McHugh 2012, 9)

Evaluative Norms
[Evaluative norms] are norms primarily to do with what is good or bad, valuable or disvaluable. (McHugh 2012, 10)

Examples of prescriptive norms include many moral norms, such as the norm forbidding stealing, and traffic norms, such as the norm requiring drivers to stop for at least three seconds at a stop sign. It is clear that these norms, respectively, forbid and require certain forms of conduct and are apt to guide an agent's behaviour: they are 'ought-to-dos'. It is easy to see that what we have so far called 'rules' are prescriptive norms in this sense. Accordingly, for the sake of terminological consistency and ease of exposition, in what follows we will use 'rule' and 'prescriptive norm' interchangeably.

In contrast, evaluative norms are not prescriptive in this way. They don't tell agents what to do. Rather, they specify conditions of attributive goodness, i.e. goodness as it pertains to a certain kind. They are 'ought-to-bes' rather than 'ought-to-dos', where the ought-to-be in question specifies the conditions under which a token of type T is a good token of its type. There is such a thing as a good knife or a good sprinter. An evaluative norm specifies the conditions under which a knife is a good knife or a sprinter is a good sprinter. 'A good knife is a sharp knife' would be an example of an evaluative norm, 'a good sprinter runs fast' another. (Note that *The Knowledge Account of Good Assertion* also qualifies as an evaluative norm in this sense.)[5] Evaluative norms use 'good' in Geach's (1956) attributive sense (McHugh 2012, 22), where 'good' functions as a predicate modifier rather than as a predicate in its own right. When the evaluative norm states that good knives are sharp, it merely states that knives *qua knives* are good only if they are sharp. It does not entail that good knives are good *simpliciter*, or good for some purpose or another. Similarly, it might be true that good burglars are stealthy (stealth thus

---

[5] It may be worth noting that evaluative norms can also be expressed in terms of ought. The evaluative norm for knives can be put as follows: 'Knives ought to be sharp' and 'Sprinters ought to be fast'. Note, however, that the oughts here are *ought-to-bes*. Unlike the *ought-to-dos* at issue in prescriptive norms, they do not require, permit or forbid pieces of conduct.

being a condition on complying with the evaluative norm for burglars), but this does not entail that good burglars are good simpliciter.[6]

It's important to keep in mind that, although evaluative norms differ from prescriptive norms in that they don't prescribe a certain piece of conduct for agents, this is not to say that evaluative norms do not feature genuine oughts. On the contrary, there is a clear sense in which evaluative norms tell us something about how things ought to be. For instance, the evaluative norm for hospitals tells us that hospitals ought to be clean, the evaluative norm for knives that knives ought to be sharp and the evaluative norm for driving that driving ought to be safe. But this does not detract from the fact that such norms still do not prescribe a certain course of conduct and, as a result, are not prescriptive norms. The main difference lies in the fact that, while prescriptive norms are ought-to-dos, evaluative norms are ought-to-bes.

Evaluative and prescriptive norms can come apart. It is entirely possible for an evaluative norm to be violated without a prescriptive norm being violated. Consider for instance the following evaluative norm: good sunsets are not too cloudy. On a very cloudy evening this evaluative norm will not be satisfied. Compatibly with that, no prescriptive norm may be violated. And, conversely, it is possible to violate a prescriptive norm without violating any evaluative norm. Suppose your boss has imposed a completely pointless rule for making coffee according to which coffee powder must be scooped into the filter alternatingly with a blue and a red teaspoon. Suppose you violate this rule, say because you are only using the red spoon. You have broken a prescriptive rule for coffee making at your office. However, it seems plausible that you need not have violated some evaluative norm as well. In particular, the coffee that you are making may still be good coffee, the way in which you are making it may still be a good way of making coffee and you may still be a good barista.

While evaluative norms thus differ from prescriptive norms, the two may still be related. In particular, prescriptive norms often enough derive from evaluative norms. They serve to ensure that the evaluative norm is likely enough complied with. For instance, prescriptive norms of driving, such as the norm 'Drive no more than 50 km/h within city bounds', serve to ensure that the evaluative norm of driving, according to which good driving is safe driving, is likely enough complied with. In this way,

---

[6] Note that Geach also claims that all uses of 'good' are attributive. In particular, there is no such thing as good simpliciter, independently of a kind; we want to stay neutral on this latter issue. What matters is that there is such a thing as attributive goodness, which seems safe enough.

evaluative norms often come first and prescriptive norms are in their service.

That being said, as McHugh also points out, while there may be relations between prescriptive and evaluative norms, these are by no means straightforward or uncontroversial: to give just one example, take, for instance, the debate between consequentialists and deontologists about the direction of explanation between goods and prescriptive norms. According to consequentialism, goods explain norms; in contrast, deontological views explain 'X is good' in terms of there being a norm that gives us reason to favour X.[7] It is easy to see that what one thinks about the relationship between evaluative and prescriptive norms will depend on one's theoretical commitments, i.e. on one's favourite take on this debate.

In this chapter, we will focus exclusively on evaluative norms and their relation to e-functions. In Chapter 5, however, we want to take a closer look at one way in which e-functions, evaluative norms and prescriptive norms are related. More specifically, in this chapter we will argue that e-functions give rise to evaluative norms and in Chapter 5 that, under certain conditions, e-functions serve to generate prescriptive norms as well.

4.1.3 Etiological Functions and Evaluative Norms

In what follows we will argue that once a token of a type has an e-function, there are facts about what it is for a token to be a good token of its type. In this way, e-functions have normative import. To get there, we will first have to introduce some further conceptual machinery.

The first concept we need is the concept of *function fulfilment*. For any token that has an e-function, there is such a thing as function fulfilment. Roughly, a token with an e-function fulfils its function if and only if it produces the relevant beneficial effect. For instance, given that the e-function of a cup of espresso in SES-Espresso is to produce pleasant gustatory experiences in customers, a token cup of espresso fulfils its e-function if and only if it generates pleasant gustatory experiences in some costumer.

Second is the concept of *normal functioning*. For any token that has an e-function, there is such a thing as normal functioning. This is the way in which past tokens functioned when the type acquired its e-function. That is to say, it is the way in which past tokens of the type functioned when producing the benefit that made the contribution to the explanation of

---

[7] See Schroeder (2021) for an excellent overview.

why the type now exists in the system. In the case of SES-Espresso, it is the way past cups of espresso functioned when they generated pleasant gustatory experiences in past costumers. Let's say that this includes the stimulation of certain taste buds in the mouths of consumers, and the like.

The third and last concept is the concept of *normal conditions*. For any token that has an e-function there is such a thing as normal conditions. These are the conditions in which past tokens were situated when the e-function was acquired. That is to say, they are the conditions in which past tokens of the type produced the benefit which made the contribution to the explanation of why the type now exists in the system. Let us say that, in the case of SES-Espresso, this includes that token cups of espresso were properly consumed (drunk rather than snorted), that consumers had properly functioning taste buds, that the air was sufficiently clean and so forth.

With these points in play, here is the key thesis concerning the normative import of e-functions. E-functions give rise to evaluative norms: a token of type T with the e-function of producing E may be a good token of T. Crucially, this may be the case even if the token does not fulfil its e-function. A token of cup of espresso that is forgotten on the counter may be a good cup of espresso (at least for a while), even though it did not fulfil its function. Why is that? We would like to suggest the following answer:

The Evaluative Norm of Tokens with an E-Function.
A token of type T with the e-function of producing E is a good T if and only if it has the disposition to fulfil its e-function by functioning normally when in normal conditions.

The Evaluative Norm of Tokens with an E-Function accommodates the datum that, in the above case, the cup of espresso is a good cup of espresso. After all, even though it has been forgotten on the counter, it retains the disposition to fulfil its e-function by functioning normally when in normal conditions. That is to say, it retains the disposition to produce pleasant gustatory experiences (function fulfilment) by stimulating taste buds, and the like (normal functioning) when properly consumed, taste buds are functioning properly, the air is sufficiently clear and so forth (normal conditions).

In contrast, suppose that a token cup of espresso is spoiled by a trickster who has added salt to the espresso. In this unfortunate situation, the cup of espresso no longer has the disposition to fulfil its e-function by functioning normally when in normal conditions. *The Evaluative Norm of Tokens with an E-Function* predicts, again correctly, that the cup of espresso is not a good cup.

4.1.4   *Typing Norms*

In line with the proposal for typing norms from Chapter 3, we want to suggest that e-functions can be typed in accordance with the type of benefit that they produced in the ancestors of its possessor and that contributed to explaining why the system continued to exist. For instance, in the case of your heart, the relevant benefit is survival, i.e. a biological benefit. Accordingly, the e-function of your heart is a biological e-function. In contrast, in the case of cups of espresso in SES-Espresso, the relevant benefit is a pleasant gustatory experience, i.e. a culinary benefit.

Similarly, evaluative norms (or rules for that matter) that e-functions of a certain type give rise to can also be typed in accordance with the type of benefit they produced in the ancestors of its possessor and that contributed to explaining why the system continued to exist. For instance, in the case of your heart, the evaluative norm that derives from your heart's biological e-function of contributing to survival is a biological norm. It states what it is for your heart to be a biologically good heart. In the case of cups of espresso in SES-Espresso, the evaluative norm that derives from cups of espresso's producing pleasant gustatory experiences is a culinary norm. It states what it is for a cup of espresso to be a culinarily good cup of espresso.

A given token of a type may simultaneously possess several types of e-function. Token cups of espresso in SES-Espresso may have the culinary e-function of generating pleasant gustatory experiences in customers. However, they also have the economical e-function of making a profit for baristas.

Different types of e-function give rise to different types of function fulfilment, norm, and rule. For instance, a cup of espresso in SES-Espresso will fulfil its culinary e-function if and only if it generates pleasant gustatory experiences in some customer. It will be a culinarily good cup of espresso if and only if it has the disposition to do so. In contrast, it will fulfil its economic function if and only if it makes a profit for the local coffee shop. It will be an economically good cup of espresso if and only if it has the disposition to make a profit.

Finally, where a token has various e-functions, it can fulfil its function with respect to one of them without doing so with respect to another and satisfy the evaluative norm generated by one without satisfying the norm generated by the other. If a cup of espresso in SES-Espresso is spilled right after purchase, it fulfilled its economic but not its culinary e-function. On the other hand, a cup of espresso that has been spoiled by salt and, as a result, is not a culinarily good cup of espresso may still have the disposition to make a profit for the local coffee shop, thus being a good cup of espresso economically. And it may of course still make a profit for baristas, thus fulfilling its economic e-function.

4.2   The Normativity of Assertion

4.2.1   The E-Function of Assertion

A number of contributors to the literature (Graham 2010, Millikan 1984) have argued that assertion has the epistemic e-function of generating true belief in hearers. We disagree. We think that assertion has the e-function of generating knowledge.

In what follows, we will first reconstruct their argument in a way that lines up with some of the earlier discussion about SESs, and then proceed to argue for our favourite view.

Linguistic practices, including practices of producing and consuming linguistic devices such as assertions, can be viewed as SESs. Producers are speakers, linguistic devices such as assertions are products and consumers are hearers. This much is easy.

However, SESs also feature a type of return. What is the return in the case of linguistic practices in general and in the case of assertion in particular? To answer these questions, consider first the following passage from Millikan:

> Language devices will produce effects that interest speakers often enough to encourage continued replication only if hearers replicate hoped-for cooperative responses often enough. (Millikan 2004, 25)

What comes to light here is that linguistic practices do feature a return, viz. a *cooperative response* on the part of the hearer. Moreover, taking another leaf from Millikan and Graham, we want to suggest that, in case of the practice of producing and consuming assertions, the cooperative response is *belief* on the part of the hearer.[8]

Given that the practice of producing and consuming assertions can be viewed as an SES (henceforth also 'SES-Assertion'), we may now investigate whether the product, i.e. assertion, does indeed have the epistemic e-function of generating true belief in hearers. It will do so if and only if

---

[8] Millikan (2004, 26) and Graham (2010, Section 4). It may be worth noting that Millikan states her argument in terms of 'indicative sentences'. Even so, it is easy to see that the argument will work just as well for assertion, not in the least because we typically make assertions by means of indicative sentences.

(EF1) past assertions generated true beliefs in hearers, (EF2) this constituted a benefit for SES-Assertion and (EF3) that this constituted a benefit
for hearers contributes to the explanation of why SES-Assertion continues
to exist.

EF1 is a highly plausible empirical claim. Concerning EF2, note first
that, according to a widely accepted thesis, our epistemic aim is to amass a
large body of beliefs with a favourable truth/falsity ratio.[9] The generation
of true belief in hearers, then, means that hearers make progress in the
direction of attaining their epistemic aim. This, we take it, is a benefit for
hearers. Note also that it is an epistemic benefit. Finally, just as in SES-
Espresso earlier, it is plausible that the benefit for the system resides in the
benefit for the consumer. If so, the generation of true belief in hearers not
only constitute a benefit for hearers but also for SES-Assertion as a whole.
EF2 is satisfied also.

This leaves us with is EF3. In a nutshell, here is the Millikan/Graham
argument: speakers continue to produce a linguistic device only if this
often enough produces the cooperative response on the part of hearers.
Since, in the case of assertion, the desired hearer response is belief, hearers
will respond cooperatively to the production of an assertion only if they
benefit from responding in this way. In the case of assertion, gaining a true
belief is the main benefit for hearers. This is evidenced by the fact that if
hearers had not gained true belief sufficiently often by responding to
assertions with belief, they would before long have stopped responding
to assertion with belief. Since if they had done so, they would no longer
have produced the cooperative response, before long speakers would no
longer have been motivated to make assertions and the practice of producing and consuming assertions would have been discontinued. In this
way, the fact that past assertions generated true belief in hearers does
contribute to explaining why SES-Assertion continues to exist today.
EF3 is satisfied as well.

Since all of EF1–EF3 are satisfied, it follows that assertion has generating true belief in hearers as an e-function. Moreover, since the benefit that
contributes to explaining the continued existence of SES-Assertion is an
epistemic benefit, generating true belief in hearers is an epistemic e-
function of assertion.

---

[9] We take it that the thought here is that amassing a large body of beliefs with a favourable truth/falsity ratio
is the constitutive aim of the epistemic domain. However, for present purposes, not much hinges on
whether the aim is thus constitutive so long as it is indeed our epistemic aim in some sense.

We find the above argument by and large compelling. Our only disagreement with Millikan and Graham is that we think that the e-function of assertion is stronger than they make out. More specifically, we think it consists in generating *knowledge* in hearers,[10] not just *true belief.*

Holding on to the first part of the argument, according to which the practice of producing and consuming assertions can be viewed as an SES in which assertion is the product and belief on the part of the hearer the return, what needs to be shown is that past assertions not only generated true belief in hearers but also knowledge (EF1), that this constituted an epistemic benefit for SES-Assertion (EF2) and that the fact that it did so hearers contributes to the explanation of why SES-Assertion continues to exist (EF3).

EF1 is a highly plausible empirical claim. Since knowledge entails true belief, it would seem that EF2 remains plausible at least for the same reasons that motivated the corresponding claim about true belief. Note, however, that this consideration alone will not do by way of support for EF2. After all, if knowledge and not just true belief is to be the e-function of assertion, shouldn't the benefit at issue in EF2 be one that attaches specifically to knowledge? Fortunately, it is quite plausible that knowledge does come with specific benefits, even epistemic ones. After all, as most

---

[10] Note that Williamson (2000) considers and Turri (2016) argues that the function of assertion is to transmit knowledge from speaker to hearer and that this serves to provide a rationale for KRA. While these ideas are in the spirit of the claim we are defending here, there are nonetheless important differences. First, neither Williamson nor Turri tells us anything about what they mean by 'function' and they do not offer an argument for their claim about the function of assertion either. Second, they do not explore the normative implications of this claim in any detail. In particular, neither of them even notes the relation between an item's function and its evaluative norm. Accordingly, neither offers the kind of hearer-oriented evaluative norm of assertion that is of such central importance to our project (Section 4.2.2). Third, Turri (2016) argues that KRA serves to solve the value problem. As a result, our account of the function of assertion will not be available to him. The reason for this is that, to have the epistemic e-function of transmitting knowledge in hearers, knowledge must already be better than true belief that falls short of knowledge (see subsequent discussion). In fact, it becomes hard to see how Turri could unpack the notion of function as an e-function. Given the popularity of the etiological account of functions, this is a clear drawback. Fourth, both Williamson and Turri take the content of their function claim to be different. They take the function of assertion to consist in the *transmission* of knowledge from speaker to hearer. In contrast, we take it to consist in the *generation* of knowledge in the hearer. This difference is of crucial importance to our treatment of cases of selfless assertion (Sections 4.3.3 and 4.3.4) that will simply not be available to Williamson and Turri. Finally, while Williamson considers a transmission of knowledge-based rationale for KRA, he ultimately rejects it. Moreover, as we will argue below (in Chapter 7), it is just not clear that Williamson can have any kind of rationale for KRA given his account of the nature of assertion.

One notable account that is close in spirit, although less so in form, to ours is Ernest Sosa's epistemic teleology. There is no denial that Sosa's account and ours share in their teleological normative structure. Apart from this, however, Sosa (pc) does not subscribe to the kind of functionalist approach to the normativity of assertion that we opt for here, nor does he countenance a hearer-oriented evaluative norm of assertion.

epistemologists agree, knowledge is epistemically more valuable than true belief. Given that this is so, knowledge comes with epistemic benefits over and above the ones that attach to true belief. EF2 is plausible even if we require that the benefits at issue in EF2 attach to knowledge in particular. (Note that the question of how exactly it is that knowledge is epistemically more valuable than mere true belief is of little consequence for present purposes. After all, our argument will go through given that knowledge does have the value in question, no matter why it does so. And, again, this much is widely agreed in the literature. That said, Appendix A offers one promising way of explaing the value of knowledge in more detail.)

Again, EF3 is the hard one to justify. It may seem as though, in the present case, it is particularly tricky because it is far from clear that SES-Assertion would cease to exist altogether if assertions never produced knowledge. Suppose, for instance, that were assertion not to generate knowledge in hearers, this would be because it is common knowledge that, whenever a speaker produces an assertion, the content passes through a randomiser, which outputs the same content with a probability 0.9 and outputs a false content with a probability of 0.1. In that case, assertion never generates knowledge in hearers. Or, to be more precise, the assertion that p never generates knowledge that p in hearers. At the same time, there is little reason to think that SES-Assertion would cease to exist. Assertion is still too useful a tool to abandon it entirely in this situation.

At the same time, EF3 only requires that the benefit produced by past tokens of a type *contributes to the explanation* of why the system continues to exist. Can it be the case that such a benefit contributes to the explanation of why the system continues to exist even though it is not the case that had tokens of the type not produced the benefit, the system would not have existed? As we are about to argue the answer to this question is yes. In order to achieve this, we will argue that satisfaction of EF3 for products in an SES does not generally require the truth of a counterfactual of the form *had past tokens of the product not produced the benefit, the system would not have existed today*. We will then offer an alternative account of what it takes to satisfy EF3, and we will argue that, in SES-Assertion, knowledge does satisfy EF3.

First, let's return to SES-Espresso. Let's continue to assume that past cups of espresso produced pleasant gustatory experiences in customers and that this constituted a benefit for SES-Espresso. If so, EF1 and EF2 are satisfied. But now suppose that even if past cups of espresso had not produced pleasant gustatory experiences in customers, they would still have produced gustatory experience of mediocre quality in them. Suppose, furthermore, that, whilst constituting a lesser good for customers, experiences of this quality would nonetheless have been good enough to make them willing to pay for the provision of cups of espresso. This would have been good for the baristas and would have motivated them to continue producing cups of espresso with the result that SES-Espresso would have continued to exist anyway.

In this case, do cups of espresso in SES-Espresso have the e-function of generating pleasant gustatory experiences in customers? Since we have already seen that EF1 and EF2 are satisfied, this boils down to the question of whether EF3 is satisfied also. That is to say, it boils down to the question of whether the fact that past cups of espresso produced pleasant gustatory experiences in customers contributes to the explanation of why SES-Espresso continues to exist today. Crucially, if in order to do this it must be the case that had past cups of espresso not produced pleasant gustatory experiences in customers, SES-Espresso wouldn't have continued to exist today, the answer to this question is no. After all, in the case under consideration, this counterfactual is false.

Should we accept, then, that cups of espresso in SES-Espresso do not have any e-function at all in this case? That also seems implausible. After all, it looks as though there is some benefit that they produced in customers that contributes to explaining why SES-Espresso continues to exist today. So perhaps the thing to say is that, while cups of espresso do have an e-function in this case, it's not the e-function of producing pleasant gustatory experiences. Rather, it is some different e-function. Should we perhaps say that, in the present case, the e-function of cups of espresso consists not in producing pleasant gustatory experiences, but in producing at least mediocre ones? Before leaping to an answer, notice that it might be that had cups of espresso not even done that, SES-Espresso would still have continued to exist. This might have been because, for instance, people's habit of drinking espresso would remain socially robust in spite of espresso not being particularly tasty. What we have in the actual world in this scenario is a case of overdetermination: people keep consuming espresso because they like it, but they would continue to do so even if they didn't like it anymore. Does this now mean that in the actual world, where cups of espresso do generate pleasant gustatory experiences, their function is not to generate pleasant gustatory experiences? This seems implausible.

The problem is that once we give up on the idea that the relevant benefit produced are pleasant gustatory experiences in customers, on the grounds that it doesn't satisfy the relevant counterfactual, it is not clear that we will have any satisfactory alternative candidate left. After all, no alternative candidate that is even remotely plausible may satisfy the counterfactual either. To see this, note that the e-function in question cannot be 'social bonding' either, since, in virtue of overdetermination, this benefit will not satisfy the counterfactual either. Does this mean that cups of espresso have no function at all? That seems wrong. If anything, more plausibly, they have two functions: generating pleasant gustatory experiences and social bonding. In view of this, it seems wiser to abandon the idea that, in order to satisfy EF3, a benefit actually produced by a product in an SES must satisfy the counterfactual that had past tokens of the product not produced it, the SES would not have continued to exist today.

In a nutshell, then, what transpires is the following. Even if there is no effect such that had cups of espresso not produced it in the past, SES-Espresso would not have continued to exist, it remains plausible that cups of espresso have some e-function here. After all, it is plausible that they produced some benefit in the system that contributes to explaining why SES-Espresso continues to exist today. As a result, the fact that had cups of espresso not produced pleasant gustatory experiences in the past, SES-Espresso would have continued to exist does not mean that producing pleasant gustatory experience isn't an e-function of SES-Espresso.

Let's move on to the question of what it takes for a product in an SES to satisfy EF3, i.e. what it takes for a certain benefit of past tokens of a type to contribute to the explanation of why the SES continues to exist. We would like to suggest the following answer: EF3 is satisfied if the benefit was actually produced and actually was part of the instantiation of the causal structure in virtue of which the explanation of why the SES continues to exist comes out true. If so, it is easy to see that the benefit of producing pleasant gustatory experiences in customers does contribute to the explanation of why SES-Espresso continues to exist today: the benefit was actually produced by past cups of espresso and is part of the instantiation of the causal structure in virtue of which the explanation comes out true. That's why past cups of espresso contribute to the explanation of why SES-Espresso continues to exist today. On this account, then, present cups of espresso have generating pleasant gustatory experiences as an e-function in SES-Espresso.

Now, we want to suggest that, just as in SES-Espresso cups of espresso have the e-function of producing pleasant gustatory experiences in customers even if SES-Espresso would have existed had they not produced this benefit, so in SES-Assertion assertions can have the e-function of generating knowledge in hearers even on the assumption that SES-Assertion would have existed today had they not generated knowledge in hearers. What matters to whether EF3 is satisfied is whether the relevant benefit was actually produced by the product and that it is actually part of the instantiation of the causal structure in virtue of which the explanation comes out true. And this is the case in both SES-Espresso and SES-Assertion. Just as past cups of espresso actually produced pleasant gustatory experiences in customers, so past assertions actually generated knowledge in hearers.[11] Moreover, just as the benefit of pleasant gustatory experiences is actually part of the instantiation of the causal structure in virtue of which the explanation of why SES-Espresso continues to exist today comes out true, so the benefit of generating knowledge in hearers is actually part of the instantiation of the causal structure in virtue of which the explanation of why SES-Assertion continues to exist today comes out true. Since this suffices for cups of espresso to satisfy EF3 in SES-Espresso, the same goes for assertion in the case of SES-Assertion. If so, assertion does have generating knowledge in hearers as an epistemic e-function.[12]

4.2.2   The Evaluative Norm of Assertion

Given that assertion has the epistemic e-function of generating knowledge in hearers, we get the corresponding accounts of what counts as function fulfilment, normal functioning and normal conditions.

---

[11] Say that we are right that the actual benefits of a product fix that product's e-function. If that is the case, one could worry that it is not clear that there is one single un-gendered, un-racialised act, 'assertion' that we all participate in (many thanks to an anonymous referee for pointing this out). After all, one might think, often enough and in many contexts, the act did not produce the benefit of being believed for women or people of colour. Might there be an individuation problem, here? Can white-assertion, black-assertion, woman-assertion and the like all have different etiological profiles and functions? While we think this is an extremely interesting hypothesis that deserves empirical investigation, at least from the armchair, we find it plausible that the relevant instances of disbelief are not widespread enough to bring the assertions in question – or assertion in general – below the reliability threshold for function acquisition. In particular, we find it plausible that on everyday matters – such as whether there is milk in the fridge and whether it's raining outside – assertion is neither gendered nor racialised. If so, and if assertions on everyday matters constitute the bulk of the practice, the individuation problem does not arise.

[12] Are there further epistemic e-functions of assertion, besides this one? We are not sure. That said, we will not attempt to answer this question in any detail here. Rather, we simply assume that generating knowledge in hearers is the only epistemic e-function of assertion. While we agree that this is a substantive assumption, it is at least not evident that it will be of much consequence for our purposes here. That is to say, it is not clear that, even if there turned out to be further epistemic e-functions besides this one, our central argument will not go through. For that reason, we will leave it to those who want to criticise FFAA on the grounds that it countenances only one epistemic e-function of assertion to establish that assertion has further epistemic e-functions and to show that this compromises FFAA.

In the case of assertions' e-function of generating knowledge in hearers function fulfilment will of course consist in generating knowledge in some hearer.

Normal functioning and normal conditions are defined as expected in terms of, respectively, the way assertion functioned back when it acquired its e-function and the conditions that obtained back then.

Most importantly for present purposes, however, we also get the following evaluative norm:

> **The Evaluative Norm of Assertion.**
> One's assertion that p is (epistemically) good if and only if it has the disposition to generate knowledge that p in one's hearer(s) (function fulfilment) by functioning normally when in normal conditions.

4.3 Function First or Rule First?

The account we propose, FFAA, explains the evaluative norm of assertion in terms of its function, or, to be more precise, in terms of its epistemic e-function of generating knowledge in hearers.[13] In this way, FFAA places function first. It differs from standard rule first accounts, which take the evaluative norm of assertion to derive from a rule or prescriptive norm of assertion, to wit, KRA.

One question that arises at this stage is which of the two accounts of the normativity of assertion is preferable: the function first account we developed above or its standard rule first competitor. In what follows, we will offer the first part of our case that the balance tips in favour of FFAA.

4.3.1 Assertions of Moorean and Lottery Propositions

Recall that RFAA was said to receive support from the fact that, intuitively, assertions of Moorean conjunctions aren't good assertions. The same goes

---

[13] Some have proposed norms that are somewhat similar to FFAA, in that they are hearer-oriented (Garcia-Carpintero 2004, Hinchman 2013 and Pelling 2013b). The account that we are most sympathetic to is Garcia-Carpintero's. This is because Garcia-Carpintero explicitly defends his view on function-theoretic grounds. More specifically, he suggests that his norm is preferable to Williamson's because it brings out the social, communicative function of language (2004, 157). The main differences from our proposed account are (1) champions of all three view endorse a rule-first view and (2) they explain the hearer-oriented condition in terms of *transmission* of knowledge to the hearer, rather than in terms of generating knowledge in hearers and (3) they do not offer any form of explicit functionalist framework in support of the relevant views. Moreover, Garcia-Carpintero frames his account in a strong, Williamsonian constitutivity framework that we discuss and reject in Chapter 7.

for assertions of lottery propositions, at least when the only evidence available is the probabilistic evidence against winning. RFAA could easily accommodate these intuitions. Speakers don't know lottery and Moorean conjunctions. Since an assertion is an epistemically good one only if the speaker knows it to be true, RFAA predicts that assertions of lottery and Moorean conjunctions aren't epistemically good thus accommodating the intuition that such assertions aren't good ones.

The question that arises, then, is whether these cases allow RFAA to score against FFAA. Unfortunately for RFAA, there is reason to believe that the answer here is no. This is beccause assertions of lottery and Moorean conjunctions come out not good on FFAA, too.

Consider lottery propositions first. When the only evidence available for a certain lottery proposition, p_l, is the relevant probabilistic evidence, no one is in a position to know that p_l. If so, an assertion of p_l could not generate knowledge that p_l in hearers either. If so, the assertion is guaranteed not to have the disposition at issue in *The Evaluative Norm of Assertion* and so is bound not to be an epistemically good assertion.

FFAA can also secure the result that assertions of Moorean conjunctions aren't epistemically good. Or to be more precise, it can do so given the plausible assumption that knowledge of the second conjunct of an asserted Moorean conjunction – the speaker doesn't know that p – provides hearers with enough reason to distrust the first conjunct – p – that they cannot come to know that the first conjunct is true. When a speaker asserts a Moorean conjunction, either hearers come to know the second conjunct or they don't. Suppose they don't. Since knowledge of a conjunction requires knowledge of each conjunct, it follows that they do not come to know the conjunction. Suppose, next, they do. By the above assumption, in that case they don't come to know the first conjunct. And since, again, knowledge of a conjunction requires knowledge of each conjunct, it follows that they do not come to know the conjunction. Either way, then, assertions of Moorean conjunctions could not generate knowledge of the Moorean conjunction in the hearer. Any such assertion is guaranteed not to have the disposition at issue in *The Evaluative Norm of Assertion* and so is bound not to be an epistemically good assertion.[14]

---

[14] But wasn't one of the main points about assertions of Moorean conjunctions that we didn't only have to explain why they aren't good assertion, but also why they sound paradoxical? And won't we still need KRA for this explanation? Even if we do need KRA to explain why Moorean assertions sound paradoxical, this is no problem for us. The reason for this is that we do not mean to replace KRA by *The Evaluative Norm of Assertion*. Rather, we want to hold on to KRA and, as we will argue in more detail in Chapter 4, there is excellent reason to believe that KRA actually fits quite nicely

FFAA and RFAA do equally well when it comes to explaining the intuition that assertions of lottery and Moorean conjunctions aren't good ones. There are no points to be scored by RFAA here.[15]

4.3.2 *Theoretical Motivations*

We take it that one of the major attractions of FFAA is the theoretical motivation it can offer for its account of the normativity of assertion. First, the account is backed by a plausible general account of the normativity of tokens with an e-function. This account distinguishes clearly between evaluative and prescriptive norms and offers an independently motivated story of how evaluative norms are generated for items with an e-function. FFAA also offers independent arguments to the effect that assertions do have an e-function, to wit, the e-function of generating knowledge in hearers and that, as a result, the general account of the normativity of tokens with an e-function does apply to the case of assertion. In sum, according to FFAA, the (evaluative) normativity of assertion turns out to be but one instance of a familiar and more general kind of normativity that is associated with tokens with an e-function and offers a detailed and independently motivated account of this normativity.

In contrast, champions of RFAA have spent a lot of time and energy on defending KRA. However, there is little to no explicit recognition of the distinction between evaluative and prescriptive norms. Unsurprisingly, then, it is simply assumed, and typically (if not invariably) only implicitly, that a good assertion is an assertion that satisfies KRA, an idea that is captured in RFAA's second key thesis *KRA-Good Assertion-Link*. This means that champions of RFAA have simply assumed one out of two key theses of their account, rather than supported it by independent argument. Once we are clear on the distinction between evaluative and

---

into FFAA. If so, we will of course be free to use KRA to explain why Moorean conjunctions sound paradoxical. Of course, the question remains as to whether assertions of Moorean conjunctions are good assertions. If the answer here is no and the evaluative norm proposed by RFAA but not FFAA can explain why, this will be evidence in favour of RFAA. That's why it's important to establish what the above argument shows, to wit, that the evaluative norm proposed by FFAA can also explain why assertions of Moorean conjunctions aren't good assertions.

[15] It may also be worth noting that *The Evaluative Norm of Assertion* predicts that assertions of false propositions are bound not to be epistemically good. Given that knowledge is factive, a false assertion that p simply could not generate knowledge that p in any hearer. If so, the assertion is guaranteed not to have the disposition at issue in *The Evaluative Norm of Assertion* and so is bound not to be an epistemically good assertion. FFAA can thus also explain another datum Williamson adduces in his discussion of the so-called RBK account, to wit, that 'we regard the false assertion itself . . . as faulty' (Williamson 2000, 262).

prescriptive norms and once we acknowledge that they need not be related in the way champions of RFAA have assumed, it should also be clear that it won't do to just assume that the conditions for satisfying the evaluative norm coincide with the conditions required for satisfying the prescriptive norm. If they do, this point affords independent argument. Since champions of RFAA have not produced any such argument, there is an important lacuna in their account.

In fact, things may be worse than this. After all, FFAA not only clearly distinguishes between the evaluative and the prescriptive norm of assertion. it also offers independent support for its proposed evaluative norm which derives from the general account of the normativity of tokens with an e-function and the argument that assertion has an e-function. Given that this is so, if it can be shown that FFAA's and RFAA's evaluative norms come apart, this will serve to exert pressure on RFAA. After all, there is independent theoretical reason to believe that FFAA's norm is true, whereas there is no such reason to believe that RFAA's norm is true. If so, there is some theoretical reason to believe that, in cases in which the two come apart, FFAA's verdict is the correct one. In what follows, we will look at one case that fits the bill and argue that it serves to establish a further advantage for FFAA.

4.3.3   Cases of Selfless Assertion: Theoretical Considerations

At this stage, we'd like to return to one of the unresolved problems for KRA from Chapter 2, that is, Lackey's cases of selfless assertion. As a reminder, here is the famous case of the creationist teacher once more:

Creationist Teacher.
Stella is a teacher who, whilst herself being a creationist, recognises that the scientific evidence strongly supports evolutionary theory. Since she takes it to be her duty as a teacher to present the view that is supported by scientific evidence, she asserts to her students various truths of evolutionary theory, including that modern-day Homo sapiens evolved from Homo erectus.[16]

Recall that Lackey takes this case to constitute a counterexample to KRA. Being a creationist, Stella does not believe and hence does not know that *Homo sapiens* evolved from *Homo erectus*. Hence her assertion violates KRA. At the same time, intuitively, her assertion is good. So, KRA is in trouble.

---

[16] Lackey (2007, 599). Note that Douven (2006) also offers a similar kind of case although he does not explicitly use it to target KRA.

With Lackey's assessment of the case on the table, we'd like to set it aside for now. We will return to it in due course (Section 4.3.4).

What we would like to focus on instead is what FFAA and RFAA have to say about this case. Let's start with RFAA. Recall RFAA's key evaluative norm of assertion, *The Knowledge Account of Good Assertion*: one's assertion that *p* is (epistemically) good if and only if one knows that *p*. Since it is undeniable that Stella does not know that Homo sapiens evolved from Homo erectus, *The Knowledge Account of Good Assertion* delivers the result that Stella's assertion is not an epistemically good one.

Let's now take a look at FFAA. Recall that FFAA's key evaluative norm of assertion is *The Evaluative Norm of Assertion*: one's assertion that *p* is (epistemically) good if and only if it has the disposition to generate knowledge in hearers by functioning normally when in normal conditions. Crucially, there is reason to believe that Stella's assertion does have this disposition. After all, when Stella's students acquire the corresponding beliefs about the evolution of Homo sapiens, their beliefs will qualify as knowledge. That is to say, in this case, Stella's assertion does generate the relevant knowledge in her students. If so, in this case, there is reason to believe that Stella's assertion manifests the disposition to generate knowledge in students. What's more, it does so in just the same way as the assertions of a knowledgeable speaker would in the same conditions. If so, it is plausible that her assertion manifests the disposition by functioning normally in normal conditions. Since her assertion can manifest only dispositions it also has, there is reason to believe that Stella's assertion does have the disposition to generate knowledge in hearers by functioning normally when in normal conditions. According to *The Evaluative Norm of Assertion*, her assertion is an epistemically good one.

It comes to light that FFAA and RFAA do come apart in the sense that they make diverging predictions about *Creationist Teacher*: FFAA predicts that Stella's assertion is good, whereas, according to RFAA, it isn't. Since as we saw above, FFAA's evaluative norm is independently motivated, whereas RFAA's is simply assumed to be true, there is independent theoretical reason to think that FFAA's prediction is the right one here.

Moreover, according to FFAA, *Creationist Teacher* is but one instance of a more general phenomenon that arises for tokens with an e-function. There are other non-epistemic cases in which product tokens with an e-function satisfy the relevant evaluative norm, and may do so even if production of such tokens is governed by a rule and this rule has been violated. By way of illustration, let's return once more to SES-Espresso. Note that a cup of espresso may satisfy the evaluative culinary norm of being a good cup of espresso: it does have the disposition to generate pleasant gustatory experiences in consumers by functioning normally when in normal conditions. At the same time, the barista who made it may have done just about everything wrong when making it. That is to say, he may have broken just about any rule of espresso making there is, including the rule operative at the local coffee shop. What we have is a case of a cup of espresso that is good despite the fact that it was produced in violation of the rule for making good cups of espresso. The fact that, according to FFAA, *Creationist Teacher* turns out to be but another instance of a general phenomenon adds to making FFAA's analysis a theoretically appealing one.[17]

4.3.4   Cases of Selfless Assertion: Intuitive Considerations

With these theoretical considerations in play, we would now like to return to Lackey's analysis of cases of selfless assertion. Recall that we said that

---

[17] Even if FFAA gets *Creationist Teacher* right, it might be thought that there are cases in the vicinity the view will struggle with. Consider, for instance, the following case due to McKinnon:

Stepping-Stone Physics.

Jenny is teaching a grade 10 science class. She wants to explain the structure of an atom and, more specifically, the electron configuration of different elements. Jenny is well aware that an early model of the electron structure of atoms, the Bohr model, is no longer considered accurate [...] More recently, though, the Bohr model has been replaced with the *valence* model [...] Jenny also knows that her students aren't yet able to understand the valence model, but they are able to understand the Bohr model. Students of this age [...] need to learn concepts such as the Bohr model as a stepping-stone. So when it's time to teach her students about the electron structure of atoms, she asserts, 'Electrons behave according to the Bohr model'. (McKinnon 2015, 61)

According to McKinnon, Jenny's assertion is intuitively good. Crucially, there is reason to think that FFAA's story about *Creationist Teacher* won't work here. The reason for this is that, in *Stepping-Stone Physics*, Jenny's assertion is false. As a result, by FFAA's *Evaluative Norm of Assertion*, it simply won't qualify as a good assertion. In this way, the case causes trouble for FFAA. Or so it might be thought.

We agree that our account of *Creationist Teacher* can't be extended to *Stepping-Stone Physics*. Fortunately, it need not be. The reason for this is that there is an attractive alternative account of the case in terms of overriding norms. More specifically, practical pedagogical norms, pertaining to easiness of content delivery, override KRA and render Jenny's assertion all-things-considered permissible. That is why it seems good intuitively. In fact, McKinnon herself effectively suggests this treatment when she writes that Jenny's assertion 'will best meet her pedagogical obligations' (2015, 204). It may also be worth noting that Jenny's assertion in contrast to Stella's, is intuitively good only in very specific contexts. To see this consider a different context in which the audience is able to understand the valence model. Or consider a default context in which someone of whom Jenny doesn't know whether they are able to understand the valence model asks Jenny how atoms behave. If she asserts that electrons behave according to the Bohr's model, her assertion will not be intuitively good. This provides excellent evidence that what's going on in *Stepping-Stone Physics* is that pedagogical norms override KRA.

Lackey takes these cases to constitute counterexamples to KRA as the speakers' assertions are good and yet they violate KRA. Recall also that cases of selfless assertion are not taken to be just any old problem for KRA. Rather, they are thought to be a particularly difficult problem for the view. The reason for this is that other apparent problem cases – such as intuitively good assertions in Gettier cases and in cases in which the speaker has a justified false belief – can be explained by champions of KRA in terms of blamelessness. Clearly, however, this will not work for cases of selfless assertion. Selfless asserters such as Stella may be well aware that they are violating KRA, their assertions may be fully under their control and there may be no other norms overriding KRA.[18] As a result, the intuitive goodness of selfless assertions cannot be explained in terms of blamelessness. That's why cases of selfless assertions pose a particularly hard problem for KRA.[19]

Do cases of selfless assertion refute KRA? Unsurprisingly, we think the answer to this question is no. To see this, note that if a student of Stella's were to know that Stella does not believe that Homo sapiens evolved from Homo erectus, she may prima facie legitimately criticise Stella for her assertion, for instance by saying: 'You don't believe that yourself!' Moreover, this criticism would call for or make appropriate an excuse, explanation etc. on the part of Stella. A rebuttal of the criticism as misplaced or irrelevant would not be prima facie legitimate. For instance, 'So what?' is not a prima facie legitimate response. As we have already seen, these considerations suggest that KRA is in full force here.

But then what exactly is going on in Lackey's argument? Let's first take another look at it. There are two important claims here. First, Stella's assertion violates KRA. This much is hard to deny. Second, intuitively, Stella's assertion is good. Now, we have just seen that the case does not serve to refute KRA. Even so, we still need an account of the intuitive goodness of Stella's assertion. It is here that FFAA can again score points. After all, according to FFAA, Stella's assertion is actually an epistemically

---

[18] If this isn't immediately obvious, just note that we can describe the case such that making the selfless assertion will have disastrous moral, practical and the like consequences. For instance, we may suppose that, Stella's assertion causes some hearer in the audience to detonate a bomb killing everyone in the room (perhaps because he was counting on Stella to publicly denounce evolutionary theory). In that case, her assertion is still an (epistemically) good assertion. However, she will not be blameless due to overriding by (non-overridden) moral, practical and so foth norms.

[19] Note, furthermore, that the perhaps most obvious alternative response to the case, to wit, that selfless asserters don't assert in their own names but in accordance with the requirements of a social role, does not appear to work. Lackey (2008) and Douven and Kelp (2012) both offer examples of cases of selfless assertion in which the speaker does not occupy a certain social role when asserting.

good one. In this way, FFAA can accommodate the intuition that Stella's assertion is good in a straightforward way. As a result, FFAA can offer an appealing account of a kind of case that has long been a thorn is the side of KRA: FFAA can allow (i) that KRA is violated in this case, whilst (ii) plausibly resisting the idea that this provides convincing reason to think that KRA is not in force. Finally, (iii) FFAA can also accommodate the intuition that assertions like Stella's are epistemically good in a straightforward way.

Of course, this kind of account is not available to champions of RFAA. After all, according to RFAA, the conditions for epistemically good assertion are satisfied if and only if the speaker satisfies KRA. Given that selfless assertions clearly don't satisfy KRA, according to RFAA, these assertions are bound not to be epistemically good. FFAA's appealing account of cases of selfless assertion is not available to RFAA. What transpires, then, is that cases of selfless assertion serve to give FFAA an advantage over RFAA when it comes to not only theoretical considerations, but also intuitive ones.

Before moving on, we would like to briefly offer a diagnosis of what went wrong with RFAA here. The discussion of theoretical considerations indicated that one of RFAA's key theses, *KRA-Good Assertion-Link*, is simply assumed to be true rather than independently motivated. In addition, the discussion of intuitive considerations showed that RFAA's evaluative norm, *The Knowledge Account of Good Assertion*, comes under pressure by cases of selfless assertion. But now recall that *The Knowledge Account of Good Assertion* is entailed by KRA and *KRA-Good Assertion-Link*. Since KRA is independently plausible and, as we have just seen, not impugned by *Creationist Teacher*, this means that the intuitive pressure exerted by cases of selfless assertion on *The Knowledge Account of Good Assertion* transmits to *KRA-Good Assertion-Link*. What comes to light, then, is that *KRA-Good Assertion-Link* is not only wanting independent support, but also comes under intuitive pressure. It is thus tempting to think that RFAA fails because *KRA-Good Assertion-Link* is false.

4.4 Conclusion

Standard accounts of the normativity of assertion are rule first accounts (RFAA). Given the truth of KRA, RFAA accepts that assertion is governed by KRA and that whether or not a particular assertion is a good one depends on whether the speaker satisfies KRA.

This chapter has developed an alternative to RFAA, which explains good assertion in terms of assertion's e-function (FFAA). In particular, we have offered an independently plausible account of e-functions. With this account in play we have argued that e-functions give rise to evaluative norms. Since assertion has the epistemic e-function of generating knowledge in hearers, we were able to derive an evaluative norm of assertion according to which, roughly, a good assertion is one that has the disposition to generate knowledge in hearers.

Finally, we have argued that FFAA compares favourably with RFAA. First, FFAA can offer an equally plausible account of why assertions of lottery and Moorean conjunctions aren't good ones, which means that there is no advantage to be gained for RFAA here. Second, FFAA offers an independently motivated account of the normativity of assertion that distinguishes clearly between evaluative and prescriptive norms. In contrast, champions of RFAA do not distinguish explicitly between these two kinds of norms. As a result, their evaluative norm remains without independent support. Third, this means that there is theoretical reason to favour FFAA's account in cases in which FFAA and RFAA make diverging predictions such as cases of selfless assertion. Fourth, this theoretical reason is confirmed by the intuitive verdicts in such cases. FFAA can offer an appealing account of the intuition of the goodness of selfless assertions whilst holding on to KRA, thus offering an appealing solution to a particularly difficult problem for champions of KRA.

CHAPTER 5

FFAA and KRA

Chapter 4 has developed the first part of a functionalist account of the normativity of assertion. We developed a general account of one way in which e-functions have normative import: they give rise to evaluative norms. Then we argued that assertion has the epistemic e-function of generating knowledge in hearers and derived the corresponding evaluative norm of assertion, thus arriving at a function first account of good assertion. We also argued that this account compares favourably with the standard rule first account, which derives the evaluative norm of assertion from KRA.

Recall that we do not take this argument to show that KRA is false. On the contrary, KRA is correct. To see why this is possible, recall also that we introduced a distinction between two kinds of norm, evaluative and prescriptive. KRA is a prescriptive norm. The mere fact that our evaluative norm does not derive from KRA does not show that KRA does not in fact govern assertion.

However, the question arises as to how KRA fits into the functionalist account of assertion. One aim of this chapter is to address just this question. More specifically, we will argue that in SESs, with certain features, it makes sense to govern production of product tokens with an e-function by a rule and that SES-Assertion has the relevant features. The resulting account will explain the status of KRA as derivative from its function. It will also offer a rationale for KRA, that is an explanation of why KRA should govern assertion in the first place.

The questions of status and rationale for KRA are of independent interest. At the same time, they have received little attention, certainly in comparison with the debate over the content of the norm of assertion. Even so, there are a couple of relevant proposals in the literature, all of them congenial to the rule first approach. One is due to Bach and Hindriks, the other adapted from Douven. Both venture to derive KRA from other norms. Another aim of this chapter is to take a closer look at these alternatives from the rule first camp. In particular, we aim to show that none of these proposals are ultimately satisfactory. As a result, the functionalist account will score further points against its rule first competitor.

We will start our discussion by looking at extant accounts of the status and rationale of KRA that can be found in the rule first literature.

5.1 Extant Accounts

5.1.1 *Bach and Hindriks*

One important proposal here is due to Kent Bach (2008) and Frank Hindriks (2007). Roughly, their key idea is that KRA can be derived from the idea that assertion is the linguistic expression of belief, which gives rise to a belief rule on assertion, as well as a knowledge rule on belief. This idea has subsequently been developed in more detail by Frank Hindriks. He starts from the following idea:

(1) To assert that p is to utter a sentence that means that p and thereby expresses the belief that p.

Hindriks goes on to argue that, in situations of normal trust, which obtain unless it is permissible to lie, assertion is governed by a sincerity rule to the effect that one must express an attitude only if one has it. This gives us:

(2) In situations of normal trust, one must: express the belief that p only if one believes that p.

(1) and (2) imply

(3) In situations of normal trust, one must: assert that p only if one believes that p.

Note that (3) is a restricted belief rule on assertion. The final premise in the argument is the knowledge rule of belief:

(4) One must: believe that p only if one knows that p.[1]

---

[1] We'd like to flag that neither of us accepts the knowledge rule of belief and have argued against it in (e.g. Kelp 2011, 2016 and Simion, Kelp and Ghijsen 2016). As far as we are concerned, Hindriks's derivation fails at the very least at this step. However, since we do not want to embark on a debate over the norm(s) of belief, we will set this point aside for the time being. On behalf of Hindriks, we'd also like to point out that (4) is unexceptional given Hindriks's argumentative aim, which is to offer view that compares favourably Williamson's. After all, Williamson also accepts (4).

Hindriks claims that the following can be derived from (3) and (4):

> (5) In situations of normal trust, one must: assert that p only if one knows that p.

And, of course, (5) looks just like a version of KRA, albeit a restricted one (Hindriks 2007). (In what follows we will also refer to (5) as HKRA.)

Let's take a closer look at the remainder of Hindriks's derivation. The derivation has been discussed in some detail in recent exchange between Brian Ball (2014a,b) on the one hand and Hindriks and Barteld Kooi (2014) on the other. Since we believe that Ball makes a number of plausible points against Hindriks's derivation, in what follows we will briefly outline selected parts of the exchange and provide further support for Ball's side of the divide.

Ball's (2014a) main objection to Hindriks's derivation is that it falls foul of a fallacy of equivocation. In particular, Ball points out that (2) and hence (3) express moral rules, whereas (4) expresses an epistemic rule. Given that this is so, (5) no more follows from (3) and (4) than (8) follows from (6) and (7) in the following argument:

> (6) You own a Jaguar.
> (7) Jaguars are animals.
> (8) You own an animal.

Ball backs up his claim by sketching a semantics for deontic expressions such as 'must'. According to this semantics,

Semantics for 'Must'
'one must φ' is true at a world W if and only if, at all possible worlds accessible from W, one does φ.

Moreover, Ball notes that one can account for different kinds of rule in terms of different in accessibility relations. For instance, one 'must (morally) φ' is true at a world W if and only if one does φ at all worlds morally accessible from W. He offers the following accounts of moral and epistemic accessibility:

Moral Accessibility
[A] world $w2$ is *morally accessible* (or *permissible*) from the point of view of $w1$, for a subject S, if and only if it contains no violations of S's moral obligations in $w1$ .... (Ball 2014a, 78)

Normative Epistemic Accessibility
[A world $w2$] is *(normatively) epistemically accessible* ... from the point of view of $w1$, for a subject S, if and only if it contains no violations of S's epistemic obligations in $w1$. (Ibid.)

Given this semantics for deontic expressions, it is easy to see that Hindriks's derivation will go through if and only if the set of morally accessible worlds is a subset of the set of epistemically accessible worlds. However, as Ball also points out, Hindriks provides no reason to think that this should be so. As a result, his derivation remains unsuccessful.

Let's now look Hindriks and Kooi's response. They first point out that not every ambiguity is tantamount to an equivocation and that the onus is on those pressing the charge to prove that the fallacy has been committed.

That said, they make a more constructive point:

> Suppose, for instance, that one distinguishes empirical knowledge from conceptual knowledge. Now consider the following argument: one knows that Socrates was not a bachelor because one knows that he was married and because one knows that all bachelors are unmarried. Someone could criticize this inference by saying that it constitutes a fallacy of equivocation, since two senses of 'know' are used. However, this would be rather uncharitable. Admittedly, the knowledge mentioned in one premise is empirical whereas the knowledge in the other premise is conceptual. In spite of this, the argument is unproblematic as it stands and does not lead to misunderstandings, even though we derive empirical knowledge on the grounds of both empirical and conceptual knowledge. (Hindriks and Kooi 2014, 90)

They go on to claim that the case of 'must' in the derivation is analogous to the case of 'knows' in the above case. What's going on in the case of 'knows' is that there is only one kind of knowledge albeit with different sources (a priori/a posteriori). Similarly, in the case of obligations, there is only kind of obligation with different sources (moral/epistemic). Hence the derivation avoids the charge of equivocation (Ibid.).

There are a number of difficulties with this response. For present purposes, we will focus on only one. To see this, consider first the following standard semantics for 'knows':

Semantics for Knows'
'One knows that p' is true if and only if p is true in all epistemically accessible possible worlds.

We can now define empirical and conceptual knowledge in terms of different accessibility relations. A straightforward adaptation from the standard proposal will give us the following accounts of conceptual and empirical accessibility:

Conceptual Accessibility
A world $w2$ is *conceptually accessible* from another world $w1$, for a subject S, if and only if it is compatible with what S knows conceptually at $w1$.

Empirical Accessibility
A world $w2$ is *empirically accessible* from another world $w1$, for a subject S, if and only if it is compatible with what S knows empirically at $w1$.

Now, given that conceptual truths are necessary truths, conceptual knowledge is restricted to knowledge of necessary truths. It follows that *all* possible worlds are conceptually accessible. Given that this is so, the set of empirically accessible worlds is a subset of the set of conceptually accessible worlds. The derivation of further knowledge from conceptual and empirical knowledge is borne out by the semantics of 'knows'. In fact, the semantics sheds light on one further fact about such derivations, to wit, that the knowledge one arrives at will always be empirical, never conceptual. While the conceptual and empirical knowledge of the premises guarantees that the conclusion will be true at all worlds compatible with what one knows empirically, it will not generally be the case that it will be true at all worlds compatible with what one knows conceptually. For instance, one's empirical knowledge that Socrates is married and one's conceptual knowledge that all bachelors are unmarried together guarantee that at all worlds compatible with what one knows empirically, Socrates is a not bachelor. It does not guarantee that this is so at all worlds compatible with what one knows conceptually. After all, at some such worlds, Socrates is an unmarried man.

What about Hindriks's derivation? One problem we already saw is that Hindriks provides no parallel reason to believe that the set of morally accessible worlds is a subset of the set of (normatively) epistemically accessible worlds here.

However, things are worse for Hindriks. To see this, consider a case in which a friend of yours has been diagnosed with cancer. You have no evidence that he will survive the cancer (and no evidence against it). In order to stand any chance of surviving, he must remain confident that he will survive. In order to remain confident, he needs your moral support. You will have the strength to provide the needed moral support only if you believe that he will survive. Suppose, then, in this situation, you believe that your friend will survive. During one of your visits, your friend asks you: 'Tell me the truth, will I survive this?' to which you answer, sincerely: 'Yes, you will.'

We take it (i) that you believe that your friend will survive the cancer, (ii) that this belief is morally permissible as is (iii) your corresponding assertion, and, finally, (iv) you don't know that your friend will survive the cancer. (i) is ex hypothesi true. (ii) is plausible in view of the fact that you don't appear to violate any moral obligation in holding your belief (note, in particular, that the knowledge rule of belief is not a moral rule). Moreover, you have excellent moral reason to believe that your friend will survive the cancer and no reason not to do so. (iii) is plausible in view of the fact that you do not violate the sincerity rule of assertion and that you have excellent independent moral reason for making the assertion (i.e. providing moral support for your friend) and no independent reason not to. (iv) is plausible in view of the fact that you have no evidence whatsoever in support of the proposition that your friend will survive the cancer and the fact that you are in a position to know this proposition only if you have evidence for it.

Notice that, if (i)–(iv) and the knowledge rule of belief are true, then the set of morally accessible is not a subset of the (normatively) epistemically accessible worlds. Given (ii) and (iii), the world you inhabit contains no violations of your moral obligations (or so we may assume) and so is morally accessible. Given (i), (vi) and the knowledge rule of belief, you violate an epistemic obligation at the world you inhabit. As a result, this world is not (normatively) epistemically accessible from itself. The world you inhabit is a morally accessible but epistemically inaccessible world.

Given that, in this case, the relevant world is morally but not epistemically accessible, we would expect it to be a world at which the combination of the relevant instance of moral and epistemic rules at issue in (1)–(4) fail to generate the instance of the rule at issue in (5). And, indeed, this is exactly what happens.

To see this, notice first that all the relevant instances of (1)–(4) are plausibly true of this case. That is to say, it is the case that in asserting that your friend will survive the cancer you express the corresponding belief (instance of (1)); that, in situations of normal trust, you must: express the belief that your friend will survive the cancer only if he has that belief (instance of (2)); that hence, in situations of normal trust, you must: assert that your friend has the cancer only if you have the corresponding belief; and, finally, that you must: believe that your friend has the cancer only if you know it (instance of (4)). Of course, you violate the relevant instance of (4) in this case. However, that is not to say that it is not true of the case. The case is not a counterexample to the knowledge rule of belief.

At the same time, (5) is plausibly false. We have already seen that it is plausible that, in this case, your assertion that your friend will survive the cancer is morally permissible and that you don't know that he will survive it. Moreover, it is plausible that the situation is one of normal trust. After all, it satisfies the characterisation of situations of normal trust provided by Hindriks. According to Hindriks, situations of normal trust are situations in which 'circumstances that are presupposed by cooperative communication' (2007, 401) obtain. Hindriks also says that '[t]he qualification "in situations of normal trust" serves to allow for permissible lies' (2007, 402). The situation described is one in which the relevant circumstances obtain and in which you (permissibly) don't lie. The situation is just not one that needs to accommodate the possibility of permissible lies and so qualifies as one of normal trust.[2] Since the situation at issue in the case is one of normal trust, it is morally permissible for you to assert that your friend will survive the cancer and yet you don't know this, (5) is false. Hindriks's derivation is does not go through.

Even so, it may yet be possible to rescue Hindriks's argument. Why exactly should a moral sincerity rule govern assertion in the first place? Why should we find it morally objectionable to make insincere assertions? One plausible answer is that insincere assertions are prone to induce false beliefs in others and that's something bad. But now notice that false beliefs are in the first instance an *epistemic* bad. One might think, then, that the moral sincerity rule is ultimately grounded in an epistemic sincerity rule, which, in turn, exists in order to minimise the epistemic bad of false belief. Perhaps, then, an additional moral injunction against insincere assertions will give speakers an even stronger incentive not to make insincere assertion. On this picture, the epistemic sincerity norm gives us:

(3') In situations of normal trust, one must (epistemically): assert that p only if one believes that p.

If we combine this with the knowledge rule of belief, i.e.

(4') One must (epistemically): believe that p only if one knows that p
we would appear to get:

(5') In situations of normal trust, one must (epistemically): assert that p only if one knows that p

This appears to be as straightforward a derivation of KRA as one may hope for. Unfortunately, even now there remains a fly in the ointment. Rules are not transitive in the sense that if there is a rule to the effect that one must: φ only if condition C obtains, and a rule to the effect that one

---

[2] But isn't the situation such that you would be permitted to lie, for instance, if you were to believe that your friend is not going to survive? First, it's not clear to us that this means that now that you do not lie (and permissibly so), the situation is not one of normal trust. More importantly, it is easy to see that the case can be set up such that it would not be permissible for you to lie, say because this would be even worse for your friend than knowing the truth.

must: ψ (where ψ-ing entails that condition C obtains) only if condition D obtains, then there is also a rule to the effect that one must: φ only if condition D obtains.

To see this, suppose that there is a rule to the effect that one must: admit a student to the university only if she has been issued a high school diploma. Suppose that there is another rule to the effect that one must: issue a high school diploma to a student only if she has paid her high school tuition fees. It simply does not follow that there is a rule to the effect that one must: admit a student to the university only if she has paid her high school tuition fees. If such a rule exists, it must have been introduced separately.

By way of evidence, note that if we were to criticise someone for admitting a student even though she hasn't paid her tuition fees, for instance, by saying: 'The student has not paid her tuition fees!', our criticism would be prima facie illegitimate, even if we know that she hasn't paid and can provide reason in support of it. The agent criticised may prima facie legitimately rebut our criticism as misplaced, perhaps by telling us to direct it at the person who issued the diploma. (And even if the person who grants admission is the same person as the one who issued the diploma, that person may point out that the problem is a different one, pertaining to the issuing of the diploma rather than the admission to university.) If we want it to be the case that the person admitting the student can be prima facie legitimately criticised for admitting the student despite not having paid the high school tuition fees, we need to introduce a separate rule to this effect. Note, also, that this is exactly as *Legitimate Criticisms*, *Appropriate Responses*, *Illegitimate Criticisms* and *Legitimate Rebuttals* from Chapter 1 would have it.

Here is, more formally, what is going on: according to the Bach–Hindriks line,

(3") In normal trust situations, it is permissible to assert p only if you believe p.
(4") It is permissible to believe p only if you know p,
(5") Therefore, in normal trust situations, it is permissible to assert p only if you know p.

It is easy to see that, since the first premise features belief, while the second stipulates necessary conditions for *permissible* belief, and since belief does not imply permissible belief, the Bach–Hindriks line fails: deontic 'possible' does not work like this.[3] There will be worlds where you believe

---

[3] Note that, although the structure of the Bach–Hindriks line closely resembles the so-called deontic transmission principle (DT), the appearance is misleading; here is DT: If one ought to X in order to Y and Z in order to X, then one ought to Z in order to Y. Again, in virtue of moving from discussing

impermissibly, but you still do, therefore you can permissibly assert. Obligation just does not transmit like the Bach–Hindriks line needs it to transmit. The lesson to take home, then, is the following: you might be criticisable for your beliefs, for breaking the norm of belief (say, for believing non-knowledgeably). However, insofar as you keep with the norm of assertion – in our case, the sincerity norm requiring you not to say things you don't believe yourself – your assertions will be just fine.

One way to save the Bach–Hindriks argument that readily comes to mind, then, is to modify the second premise as to feature permissible belief:

(3''') In normal trust situations, it is permissible to assert p only if you permissibly believe p.
(4''') It is permissible to believe p only if you know p,
(5''') Therefore, in situations of normal trust, it is permissible to assert p only if you know p.

However, while this revamped version of the Bach–Hindriks argument is, indeed, valid, it is not clear what in the Bach–Hindriks story can be taken to offer support to premise (3'''). To see this recall that, in the original argument, (3) is derived from a thesis about the nature of assertion – (1) that assertion is the expression of belief – and a sincerity norm on assertion – (2) that, in situations of normal trust, one must express a belief only if one has it. While (1) and (2) entail (3), they don't entail (3'''). To get (3'''), Bach and Hindriks would either have to hold that assertion is the expression not only of belief but of permissible belief, or else that the sincerity norm amounts to the idea that, in situations of normal trust, one must express a belief only if one has it permissibly. However, neither option seems very promising. The first option deviates from the popular view of assertion in speech act theory that Bach and Hindriks appeal to. The second deviates from the standard account of sincerity. As a result either would mean a significant setback for the Bach–Hindriks line.[4]

---

belief in the first premise to permissible belief in the second, the Bach–Hindriks line fails to instantiate DT.

[4] Martin Montminy (2013) also notes the normative transmission failure in the Bach–Hindriks derivation and offers an alternative derivation, relying on the knowledge norm for action: (1) One must act on the belief that *p* only if that belief counts as knowledge; (2) One must assert that *p* only if one's assertion manifests one's belief that *p*. (KRA) One must assert that *p* only if one's assertion manifests one's knowledge that *p*. We agree with Montminy that his derivation works. We worry, however, that the knowledge norm for action is not more plausible than the knowledge norm for assertion to begin with. As a side note, we also think that, once we assume the knowledge norm for action, an even more straightforward derivation becomes available: (1) one must act on the belief that *p* only if that belief counts as knowledge; (2) assertion is a species of action; (3) KRA.

5.1.2 *Douven*

Yet another way of tackling the rationale question for KRA has been pursued by Igor Douven (2006). In fact, we have already encountered Douven's derivation in Chapter 1. Recall that the rule Douven aims to derive is actually not KRA. Rather, it is the rational credibility rule. However, we have also seen that Douven's derivation might still enable us to derive KRA, to wit, if rational credibility entails knowledge. So, let's take another look at Douven's derivation, this time with an eye to the prospects of deriving KRA.

(1) One must: XY only if it is rational for one to XY. (Zeroth law of rationality)

(2) One must: assert that *p* only if it rational for one to assert that *p*. (1)

(3) Belief is assertion to oneself. (Belief–assertion parallel)

(4) If it is rational for one to assert that *p*, then it is rational for one to assert *p* to oneself. (Assumption)

(5) One must: assert *p* only if it is rational for one to believe that *p*, i.e. only if *p* is rationally credible for one. (2–4)

(6) It is rational for one to believe *p* only if one knows that *p*.

(7) One must: assert *p* only if one knows *p*. (5,6)

With this Douven-style derivation of KRA in play let's ask whether it is satisfactory. Unfortunately, there is reason to think that, at the end of the day, the answer is no. First, perhaps the most natural way of interpreting Douven's fundamental rule of rationality is as a rule concerning *all-things-considered* rationality. On this interpretation, the argument takes the following shape:

(1') One must (all-things-considered): XY only if it is all-things-considered rational for one to XY. (Zeroth law of rationality)

(2') One must (all-things-considered): assert that *p* only if it all-things-considered rational for one to assert that *p*. (1')

(3') Belief is assertion to oneself. (Belief–assertion parallel)

(4') If it is all-things-considered rational for one to assert that *p*, then it is all-things-considered rational for one to assert *p* to oneself (Assumption)

(5') One must (all-things-considered): assert *p* only if it is all-things-considered rational for one to believe that *p*. (2' – 4')

(6') It is all-things-considered rational for one to believe that *p* only if one knows that *p*.

(7') One must (all-things-considered): assert *p* only if one knows *p*. (5',6')

Unfortunately, there is reason to think that this argument is unsound. In a nutshell, the reason is that all-things-considered permissibility and all-things-considered rationality allow for trade-offs of trivial bads for great goods. To see this, consider a case in which you are offered a million Euros for asserting that two plus two equals five in a desert with no one around. In this case, it may well be all-things-considered permissible as well as all-things-considered rational for you to assert this. At the same time, you know for certain that two plus two is four, not five. As a result, $(7')$ comes out false. Something must have gone wrong. It is fairly easy to show that $(4')$ is false, at least on the assumption that the belief–assertion parallel holds. To see this, note that we can easily describe the case in such a way that the great benefit for asserting is tied directly to what's rational for you to believe, or rather what isn't. You are offered a million Euros for asserting something that it is not rational for you to believe, e.g. that 2+2=5. It may very well be all-things-considered rational for you to assert that 2+2=5 even though it is not all-things-considered rational for you to believe it. Since according to the belief–assertion parallel belief just is assertion to oneself, it may well be all-things-considered rational for you to assert that 2+2=5, even though it is not all-things-considered rational for you to assert it to yourself.

Douven may try to solve this problem by taking the relevant type of rationality at issue in his argument to be *epistemic* rationality rather than all-things-considered rationality.[5]

(3") One must (epistemically): XY only if it is epistemically rational for one to XY. (Zeroth Law of Rationality)

(4") One must (epistemically): assert that p only if it is epistemically rational for one to assert that p. (1")

(5") Belief is assertion to oneself. (Belief–Assertion Parallel)

(6") If it is epistemically rational for one to assert that p, then it is epistemically rational for one to assert p to oneself. (Assumption)

(7") One must (epistemically): assert p only if it is epistemically rational for one to believe that p. (2"–4")

(8") It is epistemically rational for one to believe that p only if one knows that p.

(9") One must (epistemically): assert p only if one knows p. (5",6")

Unfortunately, it is not clear that the restriction to the epistemic domain will do the trick here. To begin with, note that there is a sense of 'epistemically rational' according to which epistemic trade-offs can be epistemically rational. For instance, in this sense of 'epistemically rational',

---

[5] In fact, Douven and Kelp (2012) offers a response to an objection by Casalegno that (1) must be understood as concerning practical rationality along exactly these lines.

it may well be epistemically rational to assert something that it is not epistemically rational for one to believe, say that there are fewer than 100 grains of sand in the Sahara desert, in exchange for the gift of logical omniscience, say. It is easy to see that, given this sense of 'epistemically rational', (4") meets with the same fate as (4') did earlier (again, given that the belief–assertion parallel holds).

In fact, things are worse than this. When 'epistemically rational' is so understood, (6") also appears to come out false. After all, we might be offered the gift of logical omniscience for believing a proposition that we do not know. In this case, it may well be epistemically rational in the relevant sense for us to believe this proposition even though we don't know it.

One way to avoid this difficulty is by interpreting 'epistemically rational' in such a way that it doesn't allow for the kinds of epistemic trade-offs that caused the trouble with the derivation. In fact, ideally, the relevant sense would vindicate both (4") and (6"). One proposal that would do the trick here is the following:

The Knowledge Account of Epistemic Rationality
It is epistemically rational for one to $X(p)$ only if one knows that p.

Here 'X' is a variable for operations on p, where p is a proposition. On this account, it is epistemically rational for one to assert p only if one knows that p and to believe that p only if one knows that p. Given the plausible assumption that one knows that p only if p is epistemically rational for one to believe p, it follows that it is epistemically rational to assert something only if it is epistemically rational for one to believe. Thus (4") is vindicated. And since it is epistemically rational for one to believe that p only if one knows that p, (6") is vindicated also.

The obvious difficulty with this proposal lies with the resulting version of the zeroth law of rationality. Far from being an obvious truth, the principle looks very implausible. Here it is:

(3''') One must (epistemically): X(p) only if one knows that p

To see just how bad (1''') is, consider: one must (epistemically): conjecture that p only if one knows that p, hope that p only if one knows that p, suspend judgement on whether p only if one knows that p, and the like. All of these are highly implausible.

Champions of the Douven line will thus face the task of identifying a sense of 'epistemically rational' that strikes the rather delicate balance of vindicating (4") and (6") – or, at the very least not allowing for the kinds of trade-offs incompatible with (4") and (6") – and still yielding a plausible version of (1"). As we have just seen, it is far from obvious that this task can successfully completed.

Finally, we'd like to point out that it is far from clear that the resulting version of (1") can plausibly be regarded as a version of the zeroth law of rationality in the first place. The reason for this is that this version of (1") will be violated in the trade-off cases. However, it strikes us as rather implausible that when we decide to assert an obvious falsehood such as that 2+2=5 in exchange for the gift of logical omniscience, for instance, we are violating a version of the zeroth law of rationality. By the same token, there is reason to believe that any principle that could get a Douven-style derivation off the ground is not as fundamental a principle of rationality as Douven makes out. In view of these considerations, we also think that the prospects for a derivation of KRA from Douven's zeroth law of rationality are not altogether bright.

5.2 The Status and Rationale for KRA: A Function First Account

It comes to light that extant attempts to answer the question about the status and rationale of KRA from the rule first camp remain unsuccessful. In this section, we will show that the function first account can do better: it can offer an attractive account of the status and rationale of KRA.

5.2.1 E-Functions and Prescriptive Norms

How do prescriptive norms or rules fit in the functionalist framework? To answer this question, we will now look at a certain kind of situation in which it makes sense to govern the production of tokens with an e-function by rules.

To get started, let's suppose that tokens of a certain type have a certain e-function. Now suppose that, in addition, the following conditions obtain:

Reliability
It matters that tokens of the type fulfil their e-function reliably.

Variation
There are a number of ways of producing tokens of the type which differ in the degree of reliability with which the tokens produced fulfil their e-function.

Humanity
Tokens of the type are produced by human agents who are criticism-averse.

In situations with these features, it makes sense to regulate the production of tokens with an e-functional type by *rules* that prescribe the use of ways of producing tokens of the relevant types that reliably lead to the fulfilment of the relevant e-function. Since tokens are produced by criticism-averse human agents and since violating the rules will make producers liable to criticism, regulating production by such rules will lead producers to favour using prescribed ways of producing tokens, at least given that all else is equal. Given that prescribed ways reliably lead to the fulfilment of the relevant e-function, this in turn, will increase (or sustain) the ratio of tokens that fulfil their relevant e-functions to those that don't. In this way, regulating production of e-functional tokens by a rule will contribute to ensuring that tokens reliably fulfil the relevant e-function. Since this is something of value, it makes sense to regulate production of tokens with an e-function in situations with the above features by rules.

By way of illustration, consider once again our toy case of SES-Espresso. Let us suppose that it matters that cups of espresso produce pleasant gustatory experiences reliably here (*Reliability*), because, otherwise, the local coffee shop will no longer make a profit off them and will stop producing them. There are many ways of producing cups of espresso, which differ in the degree of reliability with which cups of espresso produced by them produce pleasant gustatory experiences in costumers (*Variation*). One may produce them by filling the portafilter with unground coffee beans, the espresso machine with juice and the cup with exactly three millilitres of liquid and so on (W1). Alternatively, one may produce them by filling the portafilter with ground coffee, the espresso machine with water and the cup with approximately 25 millilitres of liquid (W2) and so on. It is not hard to see that producing cups of espresso via W1 will yield cups of espresso that produce pleasant gustatory experiences in customers with a very low degree of reliability, whereas W2 achieves a considerably higher degree of reliability. Cups of espresso at the local coffee shop are produced by baristas, that is, by human employees who are criticism-averse and so will, all else equal, seek to avoid ways of producing cups of espresso that make them liable to criticism (*Humanity*).

In this case, it makes sense to regulate production of cups of espresso at the local coffee shop by a set of rules, including a rule that requires employees to produce espressos via W2. Once the rule is in place, any way of producing espressos other than W2 will make employees liable to criticism. Since employees are human agents and so criticism-averse, the rule will lead employees to favour producing cups of espresso via W2 over other ways of producing espressos, including W1. This, in turn, will increase (or sustain) the ratio of token cups of espresso that are produced by W2, a reliable way of producing cups of espresso that produce pleasant gustatory experiences in customers, and so contribute to ensuring that cups of espresso reliably produce pleasant gustatory experiences in customers at the coffee shop. Since it matters that cups of espresso produce pleasant gustatory experiences in customers reliably, it makes sense to regulate production of them by the rule in question.

Finally, suppose that, in some case in which it makes sense to govern production of tokens with an e-function by a rule because it matters that product tokens fulfil their e-function reliably, we also have independent reason to believe that production of tokens of a certain type of product is actually governed by a particular rule. For instance, suppose that, in SES-Espresso, there actually is a rule that requires producers to produce cups of espresso via W2. If it can be shown that governing production of the relevant tokens by the particular rule does actually contribute to ensuring that they reliably fulfil their e-function, then we will have a rationale for this rule. For instance, if it can be shown that regulating production of cups of espresso in SES-Espresso by a rule that requires producers to produce them via W2 does contribute to ensuring that cups of espresso reliably produce pleasant gustatory experiences in customers, then we will have a rationale for this rule. It makes sense not only to govern production of cups of espresso by some rule, it makes sense to govern it by *this rule in particular*.[6]

5.2.2   The Case of Assertion

We have seen that, when *Reliability*, *Variation* and *Humanity* are satisfied, it makes sense to govern production of tokens with an e-function by a rule. SES-Espresso was one case in point. What we will argue now is that assertion in SES-Assertion is another. Here goes. First, in the case of assertion, it matters that token assertions fulfil their e-function of generating knowledge in hearers reliably (*Reliability*). If they didn't, say because

---

[6] This is of course not to say that the rule we have thus provide a rationale for is the best rule we could operate. There may well be room for improvement. For instance, there may be alternative rules that will do an even better job at ensuring that product tokens fulfil their e-function reliably. In this case, we may have reason for changing rules. While such reason may in certain cases defeat the rationale, it needn't always do so. It won't when we (non-culpably) fail to know of the existence of any better rules, when the costs associated with implementing a change of rules do not match the benefits that arise from increase in reliability and so on. We take these considerations to show that the kind rationale for an existing rule sketched above really is a prima facie rationale.

more often than not assertion produced beliefs in hearers that are either unjustified, false or gettiered, it is hard to see how assertion could continue to be a source of knowledge at all. Even if this doesn't mean that assertion will cease to exist altogether, at the very least SES-Assertion will undergo a significant transformation: its e-function will change. Moreover, there are many ways of producing assertions which differ in the degree of reliability with which assertions produced by them generate knowledge in hearers (*Variation*). One may assert that p based on a mere guess that p (W1), an educated guess that p (W2), an unjustified belief that p (W3), the fact that one has justification for p (W4), knowledge that p (W5), a priori certainty that p (W6) and so on. It is easy to see that there is a significant difference in the degree of reliability with which assertions produced in these ways generate knowledge in hearers. In particular, W4–W6 achieve a much higher degree of reliability than W1–W3. Finally, assertions are produced by human agents who are criticism-averse and so will, all else equal, seek to avoid producing assertions in ways that make them liable to criticism (*Humanity*).

As a result, it makes sense to regulate the production of assertions in SES-Assertion by rules that prescribe using ways of producing assertions that are reliable in generating knowledge in hearers. So doing will lead criticism-averse asserters to favour producing assertions in ways that don't make them liable to criticism to ways that do. This will increase (or sustain) the ratio of assertions produced in reliable ways compared to assertions produced in unreliable ways and so contribute to ensuring that assertions reliably generate knowledge in hearers.

Recall that we argued that (i) when it makes sense to govern production of tokens with an e-function by a rule because all of *Reliability, Variation* and *Humanity* are satisfied; (ii) when we have independent reason to believe that production of the relevant tokens actually is governed by a certain rule; and (iii) when it can be shown that governing production of the relevant tokens by this rule does actually contribute to ensuring that they fulfil their e-function reliably, then it makes sense to govern production of these tokens by this rule in particular. In other words, we will have a rationale for the particular rule.

Now, note that we have just seen that, in the case of assertion, (i) holds. Moreover, Chapters 1 and 2 made a case for a relevant instance of (ii), to wit, that KRA actually governs assertion. This means that if it can be shown that the relevant instance of (iii) is true as well, i.e. that governing production of assertions in SES-Assertion by KRA contributes to ensuring that assertions fulfil their e-function of generating knowledge in hearers reliably, we have reason to believe that it makes sense to govern production of assertion by KRA in particular. In other words, we will have a rationale for KRA.

So does operating KRA contribute to ensuring that assertions in SES-Assertion reliably generate knowledge in hearers? As we are about to argue the answer to this question is yes. To see why, note first that it is plausible that, in the vast majority of cases, a hearer acquires testimonial knowledge that p only if the speaker knows that p also. That is to say, cases in which testimony transmits knowledge predominate and cases in which testimony generates knowledge are rare exceptions. Moreover, second, absence of knowledge is often enough detectable as such by one's audience and so, if assertion is regulated by KRA, one's audience may often enough criticise one for asserting without knowledge. Given that this is so, regulating assertion by KRA arguably contributes to ensuring the reliability of assertion's fulfilling its e-function of generating knowledge in hearers. It does so in at least the following ways.

First, it will prevent third parties to the conversation from acquiring testimonial beliefs that fall short of knowledge. Let S be any speaker, H_1 and H_2 any two hearers and p any proposition. When S asserts that p and H_1 criticises S by saying: 'You don't know that!', H_2 will, typically at least, not acquire the belief that p based on S's testimony. Since, in the vast majority of cases in which S doesn't know that p if H_2 does acquire a belief that p based on S's testimony, H_2's belief will not qualify as knowledge, H_1's intervention will very likely have contributed to improving the ratio of assertions that generate knowledge in hearers compared to assertions that don't. In this way, KRA contributes towards ensuring the reliability of assertion's fulfilling its e-function.

Second, it will lead speakers to refrain from asserting unknown propositions in the long run. Let S be any speaker, R a range of propositions such that (i) S's beliefs about propositions in R tend to fall short of knowledge and (ii) S is disposed to assert propositions in R. If S is often enough criticised for asserting propositions in R, S's criticism-aversion will lead S to favour refraining from asserting propositions in R in the long run. Since, in the vast majority of cases in which S doesn't know what she asserts, her hearers won't acquire knowledge based on her testimony, S's refraining from asserting propositions in R will have the effect that future hearers won't acquire testimonial beliefs from S that fall short of knowledge. Given the plausible assumption that some of these hearers would have acquired beliefs based on S's say-so, criticisms contribute to improving the ratio of assertions that generate knowledge in hearers compared to assertions that don't. KRA contributes towards ensuring the reliability of assertion's ful-filling its e-function once again.

It comes to light that, in SES-Assertion, all three conditions for a successful rationale for the rule that actually governs assertion are satisfied. If so, it not only makes sense to govern assertion by some rule or other, but it also makes sense to govern it by KRA in particular.[7]

5.2.3   *Goals and Norms Again*

Now that our function first account of the normativity of assertion is in clear view, it is a good moment to return to another of the problems that we left hanging at the end of Chapter 2, to wit, McKinnon's worry about the relation between goals and norms. Recall that McKinnon observed that the norms of a given practice must be distinct from its goals. However, on KRA, expressing knowledge is both the norm and the goal of assertion. Hence, KRA must be false.

It is easy to see that this argument will not get traction against FFAA. According to FFAA, the goal (function) of assertion is the hearer-oriented goal of generating knowledge in hearers. The norm of assertion, in con-trast, is the speaker-oriented norm of asserting only what one knows. While goal and norm of assertion both feature knowledge, they are nonetheless distinct. McKinnon may well be right in claiming that the goals and norms of a practice must be distinct. Even so, her argument does not serve to disconfirm KRA, at least not in our distinctively functionalist account of the normativity of assertion.

5.3   Conclusion

This chapter has investigated the status of KRA as well as ways of providing a rationale for it. We have argued that our functionalist account offers an attractive account of both KRA's status and its rationale. According to our proposal, KRA derives from assertion's epistemic e-function of generating knowledge in hearers. The reason it exists is that it contributes to ensuring that assertion fulfils this e-function reliably.

We also looked at a couple of alternative approaches to the status and rationale for KRA, which are congenial to FFAA's a rule first rivals, and

---

[7] Again, the rationale really is a prima facie one. That said, we take it that there is no alternative rule we might use to govern assertion such that our failure to use it instead of KRA defeats the rationality of governing assertion by KRA. If so, KRA will also have an ultima facie rationale.

found all of them wanting. The first, due to Hindriks and Bach, ventures to derive KRA from a moral sincerity rule of assertion and an epistemic knowledge rule of belief. Aside from the fact that we find the knowledge rule of belief highly unattractive, we have argued that the envisaged derivation does not work. Ball's charge that this amounts to a fallacy of equivocation turns out to be correct. The reply by Hindriks and Kooi that there is just a difference in sources in much the same way as with deriving a piece of empirical knowledge from one piece of conceptual knowledge and another piece of empirical knowledge did not stand up to scrutiny. A closer look at the relevant semantics shows that the derivation is arguably fine in the case of empirical/conceptual knowledge, but arguably problematic in the case of moral/epistemic norms. Finally, we argued that rules are not transitive and so the derivation is bound to fail in any case.

The second approach we looked at was a KRA-friendly version of Douven's derivation from the zeroth law of rationality. Crucially, Douven's derivation fails for any notion of rationality/epistemic rationality such that trade-off between trivial bads and great goods can be rational/ epistemically rational. If the notion of rationality/epistemic rationality is unpacked such that it does not admit of such trade-offs, it is far from obvious that the relevant version of the zeroth law of rationality continues to be true. At any rate, it is clear that it does not have the kind of fundamental status Douven seems to think it has.

It might be thought that there are two further candidate rationales that have not been discussed in this chapter. One takes its cue from the Gricean pragmatics and aims to provide a rationale for KRA by deriving it from the cooperative principle.[8] The reason we skip this rationale is that we believe that the relevant work has already been done in a recent paper by Benton (2016a) which argues that KRA is independent of the cooperative princi- ple. The other rationale is due to McKinnon, who argues that 'the norms of betting, and the relationship between the norms and goals of betting provide a perfect analogy for how we ought to think about [. . .] the norms of assertion' (2015, 176). While we believe that McKinnon is wrong to think that the norms of assertion are analogous to the norms of betting, we won't stop to argue the point in detail here. To see why, note that (i) we have already made a case for KRA and (ii) we have developed a workable rationale for it. As a result, any viable competitor to FFAA's rationale must, at the very least, be able to serve as a rationale for KRA. However, that's

---

[8] Of course, any such rationale will work only if Grice's maxim of quality is understood as requiring knowledge. This point has been argued in Benton (2016a) and Gazdar (1979).

just not something that McKinnon's proposal can do. In view of this, McKinnon's alternative isn't viable competition to FFAA's rationale, at least not at this stage of the dialectic.

In sum, since our functionalist account offers not only an attractive account of the status of KRA but also an appealing rationale for it, while the proposals offered by the rule first competition remain unsatisfactory, it comes to light that there is even further reason to favour FFAA over RFAA.

CHAPTER 6

FFAA and the Duty to Believe

Chapter 5 defended a distinctively functionalist account of the status and rationale for KRA. In a nutshell, the idea was that KRA serves to ensure that assertion fulfils its function of generating knowledge reliably. We also saw that this approach fares better than two prominent alternatives in the literature, due to Bach and Hindriks on the one hand, and Douven on the other.

While Chapter 5 discussed a rule of assertion on the speaker side, in this chapter we will turn to rules of assertion on the hearer side. One of the central aims of this chapter is to argue for one specific such rule which requires hearers to believe what is asserted. Or, in other words, hearers have an epistemic duty to believe what they are told. To this end, we will first take a closer look at an important phenomenon in recent epistemology, to wit, testimonial injustice. We will argue that in order to make proper sense of this phenomenon, we must countenance an epistemic duty to believe on the part of the hearer.

With the epistemic duty to believe in play, we will once again turn to the corresponding rationale question, i.e. the question of why it is that there should be a duty to believe for hearers. Again, this duty has received little attention in the literature so far. That said, there has been some discussion of conversational pressure on hearers. Since the duty to believe is a form of conversational pressure, we will look at a couple of different types of accounts of this phenomenon. One is associated with the 'assurance view' of testimony, the other has been developed in a recent book by Sandy Goldberg (2020). We will argue that neither camp provides a satisfactory answer to the rationale question for the duty to believe. Finally, we will show that FFAA can once again excel where its competition struggles in that it can offer an attractive rationale for the duty to believe.

6.1 Testimonial Injustice and the Duty to Believe

6.1.1 Fricker on Testimonial Injustice

A phenomenon that has received an increasing amount of attention in recent literature is epistemic injustice. In a nutshell, to say that someone is done an epistemic injustice is to say that they are wronged in their capacity as a knower (Fricker 2007, 20). While a variety of species of epistemic injustice have been investigated, it is fair to say that the one that has received the most attention is a distinctively testimonial form of epistemic injustice.[1]

To get the phenomenon into sharp relief, let's take a look at it in action. One of Fricker's famous examples features a woman who knows that the death of her fiancée was not suicide based on excellent evidence. When she asserts that her fiancée's death was not a suicide to a male interlocutor, her assertion is dismissed on the grounds that 'there's female intuitions, and there are facts' (Fricker 2007, 9). What's most important about this case is that the female speaker is not believed as a result of sexist prejudice on the part of her male interlocutor. In this way, she is wronged in her capacity as a knower and thereby done an epistemic injustice.

While in this particular case, the woman is wronged in her capacity as a knower in virtue of not being believed by her interlocutor, it is important to note that the lack of belief is not an essential feature of the case. The interlocutor would have committed an epistemic injustice of exactly the same kind if they had believed the female speaker whilst, as a result of sexist prejudice, giving her less credibility than she is due. Similarly, the fact that it is a woman who is wronged in virtue of sexist prejudice is also an inessential feature of the case. The interlocutor would have committed the same kind of epistemic injustice if the case had featured a black person and the prejudice would have been racist, a disabled person and the prejudice would have been ableist, and so on. Generally speaking, what matters to the kind of epistemic injustice under consideration is that it is committed out of an identity prejudice.

With these points in play, here the definition of the distinctively testimonial kind of epistemic injustice that Fricker offers:

---

[1] For excellent discussion see e.g. Lackey (2018) and Luzzi (2016).

> [A] speaker sustains . . . a testimonial injustice if and only if she receives
> a credibility deficit owing to identity prejudice in the hearer. (Fricker
> 2007, 28)

Fricker adds a number of further details to this definition. For instance, she allows for testimonial injustice owing to credibility excess. However, she thinks that credibility excess can lead to testimonial injustice only cumulatively. The individual instances of credibility excess that eventually lead to the injustice are not themselves instances of injustices. Since she is interested in testimonial injustices that manifest in individual instances, she sets injustices owing to credibility excess aside (Fricker 2007, 21).

Moreover, Fricker distinguishes between two species of testimonial injustice. Incidental testimonial injustices have highly localised effects, while their systematic counterparts '"track" the subject through different dimensions of social activity' (Fricker 2007, 27). While Fricker does countenance both types, she focuses on the systematic type as the central case. The reason for this is that Fricker's interest lies with testimonial injustice as an ethical and social justice phenomenon. This comes out nicely when she explains why she focuses on systematic testimonial injustice: 'it [i.e. systematic testimonial injustice] is central from the point of view of a guiding interest in how epistemic injustice fits into a broader pattern of social justice' (Fricker 2007, 27).[2]

Finally, Fricker takes it that cases in which a speaker receives a credibility deficit as a result of non-culpable error are not real cases of testimonial injustice. Again, the reason for this is once again her interest in the distinctively ethical dimension of testimonial injustice. This becomes clear when she allows that cases of innocent mistake may still constitute a 'weak form of testimonial injustice' that she sets aside because of an interest in

---

[2] On a similar note, the extensive literature discussing the phenomenon of silencing (e.g. Langton 1993) also focuses on the ethically significant instances of epistemically unjust disbelief, as a failure to reciprocate in the testimonial exchange (Hornsby 1995), or as an instance of epistemic violence (Dotson 2011). According to Hornsby, for instance, speakers exhibit a particular type of vulnerability in testimonial exchanges: the success of a speaker's attempt to communicate ultimately depends upon audiences. Speakers require audiences to 'meet' their effort 'halfway' in a linguistic exchange. Hearer's prejudicial refusal to do so, according to Hornsby, harms the speaker by denying them the satisfaction of a need that they have in communication: 'The existence of reciprocity is actually a perfectly ordinary fact, consisting in speakers' being able not only to voice meaningful thoughts but also to be heard' (Hornsby 1995, 134). In a similar vein, Kristie Dotson characterizes hearers' denying speakers the satisfaction of this need they exhibit in testimonial exchanges as an instance of violence; according to her, when an audience refuses, intentionally or not, to communicatively reciprocate a linguistic exchange due to harmful ignorance, the speaker is the victim of epistemic violence (2011, 238).

'cases in which there is something ethically bad about the hearer's mis-judgement' (Fricker 2007, 22).

6.1.2   To Each Their Due

We think that Fricker's account of testimonial injustice is perfectly appropriate given her interest in testimonial injustice as an ethical and social justice phenomenon first and foremost. That said, we think that there is room if not for improvement on Fricker's account, then at least for recognition of a broader genus of injustice against speakers, of which Fricker's testimonial injustice is a species. This is mostly for theoretical reason, as we will explain now.

To begin with, we want to suggest a lightweight account according to which injustices are failures to render to each their due.[3] Suppose that you are convicted for a crime without a fair trial. Or suppose that your employer fails to pay you your salary at the end of a month of hard work. These are cases in which you suffer an injustice. On the present proposal, this is because in each case, you are not being rendered your due. When we say that this account is lightweight, we mean that it should be widely accepted. More substantive accounts of injustice can be seen as competing accounts of what a failure to render each to their due amounts to.

It is easy enough to see that the lightweight account confirms Fricker's claim that cases in which speakers receive a credibility deficit owing to identity prejudice in the hearer are cases of injustice. After all, in these cases, speakers who receive a credibility deficit owing to identity prejudice in the hearer are precisely not rendered their due. As a result, they suffer an injustice. So far, so good.

The most important point that we want to make is that the lightweight account of injustice provides reason to believe that the category of testimonial injustice is broader than Fricker's account suggests, or, at the very least, that testimonial injustice is a species of a broader genus of injustices against speakers. To see this, note that if cases of credibility deficit which is owed to identity prejudice are cases in which the speaker suffers an injustice, then the same goes for cases in which the speaker receives a credibility deficit but not because of an identity prejudice. After all, in both

---

[3] Note that this tallies nicely with David Miller's claim in the SEP entry on justice that the most plausible option for a core definition of justice is in terms of rendering each to their due, which dates back all the way to antiquity (Miller 2017, §1).

cases the speaker does not receive the credibility they are due and thus is not rendered their due.

Another point that it may be worth noting is that the lightweight account of injustice provides reason to believe that the issues of injustice and culpability are separate. In particular, it is entirely possible that one fails to give someone else their due in a perfectly non-culpable manner. To illustrate this point, consider another example from Fricker. Suppose, as a result of misleading evidence, you come to falsely believe of a fellow philosopher that they are a medic. In a conversation about a philosophical topic you dismiss their views unduly quickly (Fricker 2007, 22). In this case, you do not give them the credibility that they are due. Given the lightweight account of injustice, it follows that they suffer a testimonial injustice at your hands. Compatibly with that, you are entirely blameless for perpetrating this injustice.[4]

Again, we'd like to emphasise that we take this to be compatible with Fricker's project. In fact, we think that Fricker is right in that cases of testimonial injustice featuring a credibility deficit owing to identity prejudice deserve special ethical consideration, in particular due to their ubiquity and centrality to the phenomenon: indeed, if any cases of testimonial injustice are plausibly paradigmatic, cases of testimonial injustice due to prejudice are. In comparison, the vast majority of cases of injustices in the broader category are going to be rather mundane and of no special ethical interest. And the same goes for cases in which testimonial injustices are perpetrated non-culpably. Even so, we take the above considerations to show that there is theoretical reason to think that there is a broader genus of injustices against speakers. To count as a case of this broader kind of injustice it will suffice that a speaker does not receive the credibility they are due.

6.1.3   Injustices, Rights, and Duties

Here is another claim that we take to enjoy widespread consensus: we have the right not to be done injustices. More specifically, we take this right to

---

[4] It may be worth noting that cases of credibility excess are a little trickier. The reason for this is that while it is pretty clear that the lightweight account militates against rendering people less than their due, it's not quite clear what it says about cases in which they are rendered more than their due. Questions about testimonial injustice and credibility excess are fascinating and have rightly received a growing amount of attention in recent literature (e.g. Davis 2016, Lackey 2018, 2020). At the same time, they are of comparatively little interest for the purposes of this book. That's why we will set them aside here.

be a Hohfeldian (1919) claim right that each of us has on every one of us. You have a claim right that I don't do you injustices, I have a claim right that you don't do me injustices, and so on. Most importantly for present purposes, it follows from the right not to be done injustices that speakers have a claim right that hearers don't do them testimonial injustices, i.e. that they don't give them less credibility than they are due.

Now, Hohfeldian claim rights correspond to directed duties in the following way:

A has a claim right that *B* φ if and only if *B* has a duty to *A* to φ.

Given that this is so, the claim right that speakers have against hearers corresponds to a duty that hearers have to speakers. In particular, the result that we get is that hearers have a duty not to give speakers less credibility than they are due. But now note that this is a substantive claim about the normativity of testimony. After all, it states a duty that hearers must comply with in testimonial exchanges with speakers. By the same token, it constrains theories of the normativity of testimony in that any adequate such theory must accommodate this duty.

6.1.4 Two Kinds of Testimonial Injustice

Recall that we led with an example from Fricker in which a male hearer does a female speaker a testimonial injustice because, as a result of sexist prejudice, he doesn't believe what she says. We then followed Fricker in moving quickly to the observation that it is entirely possible to do someone a testimonial injustice even if one does believe what they say, to wit, if one does not give them the credibility they are due. And we have effectively been focusing on testimonial injustice as credibility deficit ever since.

Now, we do not mean to deny that it is natural to do so. After all, it is quite natural to think that the move to testimonial injustice as credibility deficits is just a generalisation of the phenomenon of testimonial injustice as lack of belief that we originally found in Fricker's case. However, now we do want to insist that this is a mistake. Testimonial injustice as credibility deficits and testimonial injustice as lack of belief are separate phenomena. To see this, note that it is entirely possible to assign a speaker exactly the degree of credibility that they are due. What's more, we may assume that this degree is as high as you like. Even so, it may be that – for one reason or another that has nothing to do with perceived speaker credibility – one does not form the belief in what the speaker says. In this case, the speaker is being done an injustice. They do not get their due, which is to be believed. It follows that there is reason to countenance testimonial injustice as lack of belief as a separate kind of testimonial injustice, alongside testimonial injustice as credibility deficit.

One crucial consequence of this is that given the claim right not to be done injustices and the relation between claim rights and duties, we can derive the following central duty on hearers: *hearers have an epistemic duty to believe what they are told*. Again, this is another substantive claim about the normativity of testimony. As a result, it also constrains theories of the normativity of testimony in that any adequate such theory must accommodate this duty.[5]

To be clear, we take the duty in question to be distinctively epistemic: prudentially, if I don't care at all about your stamp collection, I don't have a duty to form beliefs about your stamp collection based on your tellings. However, epistemically speaking, I do have to accord my beliefs to the extant evidence. Since you told me that you just got a new stamp, and I heard it loud and clear, we hold that I have an epistemic duty to believe that you just got a new stamp (absent defeat).

6.2   Extant Accounts

The main point of our discussion of testimonial injustice, at least for the purposes of this book, is this: In order to make proper sense of the

---

[5] We'd like to emphasise again that this point leaves the bulk of Fricker's project unaffected. The reason for separating the two kinds of testimonial injustice is theoretical. In the kind of case that Fricker is most interested in and that she rightly takes to deserve special ethical consideration, the two kinds of testimonial injustice don't come apart.

That said, there is noteworthy point of (possible) contention. It concerns the relation between the two kinds of testimonial injustice and, more specifically, the duties that they give rise to. The question we want to ask is whether the two duties are on equal footing or whether one is more fundamental than the other. Since Fricker develops an epistemology of testimony in which (capacities to make) credibility judgements play a central role, we take it that she takes the duty that corresponds to the right against testimonial injustice as credibility deficit to be at least on equal footing, if not the more fundamental one.

In contrast, in our view, it is the duty that corresponds to the right against testimonial injustice as lack of belief that is fundamental. To see why, note that by complying with this duty one can avoid doing speakers testimonial injustices without even making a credibility judgement. It thus allows for the possibility that credibility judgements enter the picture only when the duty to respond with belief is defeated. We take this to be a desirable consequence. After all, there is excellent reason to think that we are pretty bad doing the sorts of thing that, according to Fricker, we are doing when making credibility judgements. Perhaps most noteworthy is recent empirical literature suggesting that we are quite bad at gauging deception. What's more, there is a growing body of literature that suggests that we are quite bad at overcoming bias even when we are aware of it, which flies in the face of the more optimistic picture that Fricker paints in her discussion.

While we do think that there is reason to part ways with Fricker here, for present purposes, the relation between the two duties it is of little consequence. Having noted our preference and briefly gestured at our reasons for them, we will set them aside in what follows.

phenomenon of testimonial injustice, we must countenance a duty to believe what speakers tell us. What's more, any adequate theory of the normativity of testimony will have to accommodate this duty to believe. Note that what we are interested in here is a rationale for this duty to believe, an explanation of why there should be a duty to believe in the first place. The question about a rationale for the duty to believe will be on the agenda for the remainder of this chapter.

The vast majority of the epistemological literature on testimony has focused on explaining testimonial entitlement or justification. As a first observation, we would like to point out that insofar as we are interested in accommodating a duty to believe, turning to this debate will be of little help. The reason for this is that the task of explaining testimonial entitlement/justification is the task of explaining under exactly what conditions it is permissible for receivers of testimony to believe what they are told. But, of course, explaining what a *permission* to believe amounts to is one thing, accommodating a *duty* to believe is quite another. If this isn't immediately obvious, note that even if we accomplish the former task, the question of whether there even exists a duty to believe what we are told remains wide open.

That said, there has been some discussion of conversational pressure in recent literature. This is the issue of what exactly hearers owe to speakers when they tell them that p. Since what hearers owe to speakers corresponds to what directed duties hearers have to speakers, and since the discussion of conversational pressure has aimed not only to answer the question of what it is that hearers owe to speakers but also on why it is that they do, contributions to this discussion may just help us with the question about a rationale for the duty to believe.

In a recent book, Sandy Goldberg (2020) has usefully distinguished between two general accounts of what it is that hearers owe to speakers and why: presumption-based accounts and purport-based accounts. In what follows we will look at both kinds of account in turn.

6.2.1 *Presumption-Based Accounts*

Presumption-based accounts are perhaps most closely associated with the assurance view of testimony (Hinchman 2005, Moran 2006).[6] The good

---

[6] While Hinchman and Moran defend presumption-based accounts based on the assurance view, there have been defences that are independent of the assurance view (e.g. Gibbard (1990), Ridge (2014)).

news for presumption-based accounts is that they have the resources not only to deliver the duty to believe we are after, but also to do so in a way that offers an answer to the rationale question. To see this, note first how presumption-based accounts arrive at the presumption to believe speakers to be trustworthy. While there are differences in detail, the core idea is that when a speaker, S, tells a hearer, H, that p, say, S incurs certain responsibilities for the truth of p. Crucially, H, in virtue of recognising what S is doing, thereby acquires a reason for presuming S to be trustworthy in their assertion that p. But since anyone who is to be presumed trustworthy in asserting that p ought to be believed, we get exactly what we were looking for: a duty to believe alongside an answer to the rationale question.

Of course, the question remains whether the rationale provided is ultimately convincing. Goldberg argues that the answer is no. To see what he takes to be the most important reason for this, let's first look at a distinction Goldberg introduces between a practical entitlement to *hold* someone responsible and an epistemic entitlement to *believe that they are* responsible. Crucially, one can have the former without the latter. For instance, if your teenager tells you that they will be home by midnight and they are not, you will have a practical entitlement to hold them responsible even though you don't have an epistemic entitlement to believe that they are responsible. And, finally and importantly, to establish a presumption of trustworthiness, you need to make a case for an epistemic entitlement to believe. A case for a practical entitlement to hold responsible won't be enough. Again, the case of the teenager provides evidence for this point. When you do not have an entitlement to believe that they are responsible, you cannot presume them to be trustworthy, even if you can hold them responsible.

The trouble for the rationale offered the presumption-based accounts starts coming into view once we take on board Goldberg's claim that presumption-based accounts only deliver an entitlement to hold speakers responsible for their assertions, not an entitlement to believe that they are responsible. That is to say, when S tells H that p and thereby incurs certain responsibilities for the truth of p and when H recognises that this is what S is doing, H comes by an entitlement to hold S responsible for the truth of p. Crucially, to get to the presumption of trustworthiness we need more than this, as the case of the teenager clearly indicates. But presumption-based accounts do not offer more. Rather, they fail to recognise the distinction between entitlements to hold responsible and entitlement to believe responsible. As a result, their derivation of the presumption of trustworthiness rests on an illicit conflation. The rationale for the duty to believe remains ultimately unsatisfactory (Goldberg 2020, chapter 4).

While we agree with Goldberg that the presumption-based views in the literature remain ultimately unsatisfactory, we think that this particular problem can be solved. To see why, note that, as Goldberg also grants, speakers have a moral obligation to live up to their responsibilities for the truth of p. It is the recognition of this moral obligation that provides hearers with a distinctively epistemic entitlement for believing that they will live up to this moral duty. But, of course, this epistemic entitlement is an epistemic entitlement to think that they will live up to their responsibilities for the truth of p. After all, that's precisely the content of the moral duty in question. And an epistemic entitlement to think that speakers will live up to their responsibilities for the truth of p is just what is needed to get to the presumption of trustworthiness that, in turn, will give us the duty to believe that we are after.

Now, Goldberg may respond that rather than rescuing presumption-based accounts, the above argument simply identifies the precise point of their illicit conflation. The key move in the argument proceeds from a moral obligation to an epistemic entitlement. This is exactly where the illicit conflation occurs. What the moral obligation really gives us is an entitlement to hold responsible, not an entitlement to believe responsible. Or so Goldberg may argue.

We disagree. In fact, there are two ways to argue that the moral obligation supports a genuinely epistemic entitlement to believe. The key premise of the first argument is that, due to the prudential incentive associated with norm compliance, we reliably comply with the vast majority of obligations we have in general and that speakers reliably comply with the obligation they have towards living up to the responsibilities for the truth of p in particular. But, of course, this means that the presence of the moral obligation in question on the part of speakers is a reliable indicator that speakers live up to the responsibilities they have for the truth of p. When hearers recognise the moral obligation in question on the part of speakers, what they recognise is a reliable indicator that speakers live up to the responsibilities they have for the truth of p. And now we are pretty close to the claim that hearers have a distinctively epistemic entitlement for believing that speakers live up to the responsibilities they have for the truth of p. All that's missing is the claim that hearers are appropriately attuned to the indication relation. And it is plausible enough that they are. In this way, it can be argued that that hearers have a distinctively epistemic entitlement for believing that speakers live up to the responsibilities they have for the truth of p and hence a distinctively epistemic entitlement for presuming speakers to be trustworthy.

Key to the second argument is the fact that norm compliance has default status (Bolton 1991, Ochs and Roth 1989). This is because the existence of a norm affects the utility profile of a particular context. There is future gain to be had from conforming with the norm – in terms of good reputation, social approval, decreasing risk of being subject to sanctioning. In a nutshell, norm compliance is its own reward in a way in which norm violation isn't: all else absent (absent incentives to defect), in the presence of a norm N, the utility profile of the state of affairs supports N-compliance (Simion 2020). But if norm compliance has default status, since we have an epistemic entitlement to believe that the default obtains unless we have stronger reason against so believing, it is plausible that the existence of the moral obligation in question on the part of speakers provides hearers with an epistemic entitlement for believing that speakers live up to the responsibilities they have for the truth of p. Again, champions of presumption-based accounts can argue that hearers have a distinctively epistemic entitlement for presuming speakers to be trustworthy.

What comes to light is this. Even if Goldberg is right and there is an important gap in the argument for a presumption of trustworthiness, this gap can be filled. By the same token, the rationale for the presumption of trustworthiness and the corresponding duty to believe can be made to work. Goldberg's central concern with presumption-based accounts can be laid to rest.

Recall that we mentioned that, nevertheless, we agree with Goldberg that presumption-based accounts are not the way to go. In fact, we think that Goldberg identifies at least one excellent reason against adopting any of the extant versions of presumption-based accounts. To get this reason into clear view, it is important to note that extant presumption-based accounts are distinctively second personal. This can be seen once we take into account exactly how speakers' responsibilities to the truth of p are incurred, to wit, by a certain operation on their addressees. The precise nature of this operation makes the difference between the specific accounts. Various proposals have been made, including invitations to trust, demands, promises, guarantees, among others. But all accounts share the idea that in telling an addressee that p speakers perform this further operation *on them* and that it is this further operation that generates the responsibilities to the truth that get the presumption-based account's answer to the rationale question off the ground. In this these views are second personal: they take it that, in telling H that p, S performs a particular action on H – one invites H to trust, or promises to H that p is true and the like – and thus H ends up with a duty to believe what is being told.

The key reason why presumption-based accounts remain in trouble is that the presumption of trustworthiness they deliver is too limited. As Goldberg rightly points out, the operation that generates it is an operation that is performed specifically on the addressee of their tellings. By the same token, the presumption of trustworthiness and the duty to believe extends only to these addressees. However, this is too limited in scope as Goldberg convincingly argues in the following passage:

> Recall Miranda Fricker's notion of an epistemic injustice. It seems strange to think that epistemic injustices can be perpetrated *only by those whom the speaker addressed.* Suppose Janice writes a report addressed exclusively to her boss. If the claims in her report are summarily dismissed by someone else out of misogyny, would we say that Janice is not the victim of an epistemic injustice since, after all, that reader wasn't the addressed audience? Or suppose that Joanne (an African-American woman) is speaking before a crowd of a dozen people, but is addressing only one of them, and tells him that p. If the other 11 people summarily dismiss her claim owing to a mixture of racism and misogyny, do we really want to say that she is not the victim of an epistemic injustice since, after all, none of these 11 were being addressed by her? Presumably not. (Goldberg 2020, chapter 5)

What Goldberg's cases establish beyond doubt is that in order to perpetrate an epistemic injustice against a speaker, one need not be addressed by them. Given the above result that, in order to make proper sense of the phenomenon of testimonial injustice, we must countenance a duty to believe what speakers tell us, the result that we get is that the duty to believe must extend to all hearers, not just the ones that the speakers happen to address. The trouble with extant presumption-based accounts is that they do not deliver this result. Since their derivation of the presumption to trust rests on an operation on the addressee, the presumption of trust and hence the duty to believe will extend only to the addressees of their tellings. Even though extant presumption-based accounts can give us a rationale for a duty to believe, they remain ultimately unsuccessful because the duty they can give us is too narrow in scope.

6.2.2 *Goldberg's Purport-based Account*

Goldberg not only takes issue with extant presumption-based accounts of conversational pressure, but he also offers a positive proposal. Like presumption-based accounts, Goldberg's account ventures to explain conversational pressure in terms of what speakers do when they perform their speech acts. There are two key differences between presumption-based accounts and Goldberg's alternative. First, while the former's account of what explains conversational pressure on the hearer rests on an operation of speakers on their addressees, Goldberg's explanation proceeds from what speakers purport to do when they assert. Second, while presumption-based views unpack the conversational pressure at stake in terms of a duty to believe on the hearer's side, Goldberg's view has more modest aims: according to him, the pressure on the hearer is merely to make credibility assessments.

Here is the view. According to Goldberg, assertion has a job description which is to

> present a content as true in such a way that, were the audience to accept it on the basis of accepting the speaker's speech contribution, the resulting belief would be a candidate for knowledge. (Goldberg 2020, chapter 5)

Since assertion has this job description, when speakers make assertions, they purport to achieve exactly what the job description says. Moreover, it is common knowledge that this is what speakers purport to do. But since assertion will achieve its job description only if the speaker meets certain epistemic standards and since this is also common knowledge, the audience will recognise that the speech act performed achieves its aim only if the relevant epistemic standards are met. While Goldberg recognises that there are a variety of ways of unpacking these epistemic standards, he himself settles for KRA. Given that this is so, when speakers make assertions, it is common knowledge they represent themselves as meeting KRA, i.e. as knowers. Finally, this exerts normative pressure on hearers. To be more precise, hearers owe it to speakers to recognise them as agents who purport to be knowers and to treat them accordingly.

As a first observation, note that Goldberg's purport-based account avoids the problem that he identifies for presumption-based accounts. After all, the normative pressure is generated by the fact that it is common knowledge that in asserting speakers represent themselves as knowing. In this way, the normative pressure is on anyone who happens to listen in on the conversation, not just on the direct addressees of the speech act. What's more, Goldberg will also be able to explain certain cases of testimonial injustice, including paradigm cases in which the speaker's assertion is dismissed summarily such as the example by Fricker that we started out with. After all, in these cases it is even their purport to be knowers that is disrespected.

That said, the question remains whether Goldberg's account can provide a rationale for the duty to believe. Unfortunately, the answer here is no. The mere purport of knowledge isn't enough to support a duty to believe, just as the mere purport of authority in general isn't enough to support a duty to submit to it. For instance, suppose I purport to be the emperor of the country you are currently visiting and command you to kneel before me. While actually being the emperor does of course support a duty for you to submit and kneel before me, the mere purport of being the emperor doesn't. Since Goldberg cannot provide a rationale for the duty to believe, his purport-based account remains ultimately unsatisfactory as well.

But perhaps this is too quick. Goldberg actually considers the possibility of a duty to believe and adduces an argument that there is no such duty:

> But what, precisely, is owed to the speaker ... ? In the typical case of testimony, others do not have access to a speaker's reasons, nor do they have access to her deliberations about those reasons (if indeed she did deliberate). So it would be too much if, on the basis of the injunction to respect other subjects, the interpersonal pressure on an audience were pressure to accept what a speaker says whenever *in fact* her say-so is backed by proper epistemic authority. (Goldberg 2020, chapter 5)

Before responding to Goldberg's argument, it may be instructive to look at what he actually takes the relevant duty to be. This becomes clear in the passage immediately following the above:

> Rather, what a speaker's audience "owes" her is to acknowledge the speaker's conveyed claim of relevant authority, and to factor this appropriately into their doxastic response to her testimony. More explicitly, I submit that proper treatment comes to this: *the audience should adjust their doxastic reaction to a proper (epistemic) assessment of the speaker's epistemic authority*, since in doing so they are adjusting their doxastic reaction to a proper (epistemic) assessment of the act in which she conveyed having such authority. Audiences are thus under normative pressure to assess the speaker's act *epistemically*. (Goldberg 2020, chapter 5)

It is worth noting that Goldberg clearly recognises the distinction between the two duties we countenanced above, i.e. the duty to believe and the duty to make credibility assessments. However, he thinks hearers only have a duty to make credibility assessments, not a duty to believe.[7]

With this point in play, let's return to Goldberg's argument that there is no duty to believe. According to Goldberg, this is because hearers don't have access to speakers' reasons and their deliberations. One question is

---

[7] Recall that we disagree (fn.73).

why exactly this should matter. Perhaps the idea is a general evidentialist one that, if hearers have duties to believe at all, what they have a duty to believe is what they have sufficient reason to believe. However, the fact that the speaker asserted that p provides them with sufficient reason to believe that p (absent defeat, of course). That the assertion doesn't also give hearers access to the speakers' reasons and their deliberations does nothing to detract from this. This means that the evidentialist idea does not help Goldberg get the argument off the ground. Other than dramatically strong versions of reductionism about testimony, which we are certain Goldberg himself would not want to endorse, it is hard to see why we should think that the fact that assertions don't afford hearers access to speakers' reason and their deliberations provides reason to believe that there is no duty to believe on the part of the hearer.

What's more, the positive argument for the duty to believe that we developed in Section 6.1.3, starting from the right not to be done injustices, remains entirely unaffected by the recognition of Goldberg's point that assertions don't afford hearers access to speakers' reasons and their deliberations. After all, the fact that there are cases in which speakers suffer an injustice at the hands of hearers who don't believe their assertions (even when they are given the credibility they are due) stands, as does the fact that speakers have a right not to be done injustices, and the fact that this right corresponds to a directed duty on hearers not to do speakers said injustices.

It comes to light that Goldberg's point about access to speakers' reasons and deliberations does not provide reason to think that there is no duty to believe. And it doesn't provide reason to think that our argument for the existence of a duty to believe does not go through either. Our argument stands. But since Goldberg's purport-based account of conversational pressures does not support a duty to believe, there is reason to think that, just as presumption-based accounts, Goldberg's account remains ultimately unsuccessful.

6.3   The Duty to Believe: A Function First Account

To get our own account into clear view, we'd like to return once more to SESs. Recall that SESs feature a type of producer, a type of product, a type of consumer and a type of return such that the producer produces a product token which may be consumed by a consumer in exchange for a return. Recall also that product token in SESs often have the e-function of producing a certain effect in consumers. Now, consider an SES in which product tokens have the e-function of producing a certain functional effect in consumers. Suppose that the following conditions are fulfilled:

Reliability*
It matters that consumers offer the type of return at issue in the SES reliably.

Humanity*
Returns are offered by criticism-averse human agents.[8]

In situations with these features, it makes sense to have a *rule* that requires consumers to offer returns for consumed product. Since returns are offered by criticism-averse human agents and since violating this rule will make consumers liable to criticism, regulating consumption by this rule will lead consumers to avoid not offering the return, at least given that all else is equal. In this way, regulating consumption of product tokens by this rule will contribute to ensuring that returns are offered reliably. Since this is something of value, it makes sense to regulate consumption of product tokens with an e-function in situations with the above features by the rule under consideration.

Now, we take it to be pretty clear that Reliability* and Humanity* are features that SESs typically have. However, it may still be useful to see how the above line of thought plays out in a more concrete case. To this end, consider once again our toy case of SES-Espresso. Let us suppose that it matters that customers pay the designated price for their cups of espresso reliably (*Reliability**), because, otherwise, the local coffee shop will no longer make a profit off them and will stop producing them. Customers are human beings who are criticism-averse and so will, all else equal, seek to avoid ways of behaving that make them liable to criticism (*Humanity**). In this case, it makes sense to operate a rule that requires customers to pay for their cups of espresso. Since customers are criticism-averse, this rule will lead them to avoid not paying for their cups of espresso, at least all else equal. This, in turn, will contribute to ensuring that customers pay for their cups of espresso reliably. Since this matters, it makes sense to operate the rule in question.

---

[8] Recall that our rationale for KRA in Chapter 5 proceeded from three features, Reliability, Humanity and Variation. The reason for this is that our rationale for KRA is based on an account of which of a number of possible ways of producing the product in an SES is permissible. It is easy to see that, as a result, the existence of a number of ways of producing assertion, i.e. Variation, matters. In contrast, our rationale for the duty to believe is a duty is based on an account of whether consumers need to offer a return in exchange for a product. It is easy to see that, as a result, Variation is of little consequence.

Finally, let's turn to assertion. Here is how we can get a rationale for the duty to believe out of our account. Recall that the practice of producing and consuming assertions is an SES (SES-Assertion) in which producers are speakers, assertion is the product, consumers are hearers and belief is the return. Crucially, there is reason to think that both Reliability* and Humanity* are satisfied. Regarding Reliability*, several people have argued that it matters that hearers respond to assertions with belief reliably. If not, speakers will lose their motivation to make assertions and the practice of making and consuming assertions will be in jeopardy. Dan Sperber puts this point succinctly: 'From the point of view of receivers, communication, and testimony in particular, is beneficial only to the extent that it is a source of genuine [. . .] information' (2001, 404). However, if the practice stops being beneficial to the hearers, it will plausibly be discontinued. Here is, also, Peter Graham:

> Speakers and hearers both need some reason (motive) to participate. Speakers, presumably, benefit in some way by affecting hearers. If hearers receive no benefit from being so affected, they will probably stop responding in the desired way. So unless hearers get something out of accepting reports, they will not accept them. And if they will not accept them, speakers will not benefit by making them. Then they will not get made. Hearer benefits (partly) explain speaker production (Graham 2010, 161).

What's more, it is no less plausible that consumers are criticism-averse human beings here than in SES-Espresso. This means that Humanity* is also satisfied. Finally, it is easy to see that, since both Reliability* and Humanity* are satisfied, it makes sense to have a rule in SES-Assertion that requires hearers to respond with belief to assertions. Since hearers are criticism-averse, this rule will lead them to avoid not responding to assertions with belief, at least all else equal. This, in turn, will contribute to ensuring that hearers respond to assertions reliably. Since this matters, it makes sense to have a rule that requires hearers to respond to assertion with belief. Our account provides an explanation of why there should be a duty to believe and thus an attractive answer to the rationale question we were looking for.

Before moving on, we'd like to address a potential worry that one might have for this account. We emphasised on a number of occasions that the phenomenon Fricker is targeting is a distinctively ethical phenomenon. This is because the cases in which it manifests, i.e. paradigmatic cases of testimonial injustice that involve credibility deficit due to identity preju- dice, are also cases of moral failure on top of epistemic failure. In fact, the moral failure is severe enough to warrant special ethical consideration. Now, we have granted Fricker this last point. At the same time, we have insisted that testimonial injustice is a broader phenomenon, one that has a wide range of more mundane manifestations, alongside the ones that are of special ethical interest. Even so, it is plausible that the more mundane cases are still cases of moral failure, albeit of a less severe type and ones for which perpetrators may have a legitimate excuse. This means that moral norms too, on top of epistemic norms, must have been are violated in these cases.

This is where the worry rears its head. After all, if moral norms are violated in cases of testimonial injustice, what we may expect from a successful explanation of why there should be a duty to believe is a successful explanation of why there should be a distinctively moral duty to believe. However, our account does not achieve this. Even if it explains why there is an epistemic duty to believe, it is not very plausible that this duty is a distinctively moral duty. In other words, our account does not offer a rationale for the distinctively moral duty to believe. As a result, our account doesn't provide a rationale for the right kind of duty.

Fortunately, this worry can be allayed. Recall that we pointed out earlier that we have a claim right not to be done injustices. We take it that this is right is a moral right: injustices are morally wrong. But given that this is so, any violation of the duty to believe on the part of the hearer that our account provides a rationale for will be an infringement of the right not to be done injustices on the part of the speaker. Since this right is a moral right, the duty to believe on the part of the hearer must at least also be a moral duty. Our account may not provide a rationale for the moral duty to believe directly. However, it can do so indirectly, thanks to the fact that injustices are morally wrong and the right protecting us against them is a distinctively moral right.

6.4 Conclusion

This chapter has argued that in order to properly understand cases of testimonial injustice we must countenance a duty to believe on the part of hearers. As Fricker argues convincingly, in cases in which hearers do not believe what speakers tell them as a result of identity prejudice, speakers suffer an injustice. We argued that it is plausible that this injustice extends to cases in which the failure to believe is not due to an identity prejudice. Since we have a claim right not to be done injustices, it follows that speakers have a claim right to be believed. And since claim rights are associated with directed duties, we get the result that hearers have a duty to believe what speakers assert.

With the duty to believe in play, we moved on to the question of why we should think that there is such a duty in the first place, i.e. to another rationale question. We looked at two types of account in the literature. One is associated with the assurance view of testimony. While it promises to give us a rationale for a duty to believe, the account remains problematic. This is because the relevant duty extends only to the addressees of the speech act. The other view is due to Goldberg who focuses on what speakers purport to do in asserting. While Goldberg can avoid the above problem of scope, his account simply does not support the duty to believe and so falls short as well.

Finally, we introduced our own distinctively functionalist approach to the rationale question. We showed that in SESs with certain features, it makes sense to have a rule that requires consumers to offer the relevant return in exchange for products. Since, on our view, the practice of making and consuming assertions is an SES and since it has the relevant features, it follows that it makes sense to have a rule that requires hearers to offer the relevant return when speakers tell them things. Since the return is belief, we get the result that it makes sense to have a rule that requires to respond to assertion with belief. In this way, our functionalist account can once again provide an attractive answer to the rationale question.

PART III

Knowledge and Language

CHAPTER 7

KRA and Constitutivity

In the final part of this book we will look at a couple of broader issues about the relation between knowledge and language. To begin with, in this chapter we will turn to the questions of whether KRA is also *constitutive* of assertion and so whether it can shed light on the very nature of the speech act of assertion. In particular, we will focus on Williamson's (1996, 2000) influential Knowledge Account of Assertion (KAA), which offers the most detailed positive answer on the market.

To lay our hand right on the table: our functionalist account of assertion does imply a constitutivity claim for KRA: since, on FFAA, the very continuous existence of the practice of assertion is explained by its having generated knowledge in hearers, and since the latter is ensured via regulating the speech act of assertion with KRA, it will follow that KRA explains the very existence of the practice. In this way, the practice of making and consuming assertions is constituted at least in part by KRA.

However, the constitutivity model above, which we embrace, is much lighter than the one proposed and defended by Williamson. According to Williamson's KAA, KRA is constitutive of assertion in much the same way as rules of games are constitutive of games. Since the constitutive rules of a given game are essential to it, KAA entails that it is essential to assertion that it is governed by KRA. In fact, according to KAA, KRA is not only a constitutive rule of assertion, but it is the *unique* constitutive rule of assertion. Moreover, assertion is the *only speech act* whose unique constitutive rule is KRA (Williamson 2000). In other words, KAA entails all of the following:

Essentiality
The speech act of assertion is essentially governed by KRA.

Uniqueness
KRA is the only constitutive norm governing assertion.

Individuation
Assertion is the only speech act the unique constitutive rule of which
is KRA.

The question of whether KAA is true is, of course, of independent interest
for a project that investigates the normativity of assertion. In fact, there is a
specific reason why this question is pressing for present purposes. This is
because there is a case to be made that KAA is actually incompatible with
FFAA. Or, to be more precise, there is reason to think that KAA is
incompatible with FFAA's distinctive answer to the rationale question that
we have developed and defended in the last chapter. To see why, recall that
KAA assimilates the normativity of KRA to the normativity of rules of
games. With this point in play, consider the case of games and the
corresponding rationale question of why a certain game should be governed by one set of rules rather than another. To make things a bit more
concrete, let's take chess as an example. Why should chess be governed by
one set of rules rather than another? For instance, why should chess be
governed by a rule according to which the pawn can move two squares
forward if it has not yet been moved, but only one square if it has already
been moved (R1), rather than by a rule according to which it can always
only move one square (R2)? One would not expect questions like this one
to have deep answers. We might easily have come to play a game that is
governed by R2 rather than R1. Of course, in that case, we would not have
played chess, but some different game. While, in this particular case, the
game we might have played is still quite similar to chess, there is not even
special reason to believe that we should not have played an entirely
different game instead. That certain games, including chess, became
popular, whilst others didn't, is plausibly an historical contingency.
Given that rules of assertion are constitutive of assertion in an analogous
manner, there is reason to believe that the same goes for assertion. In this
way, KAA seems to commit us to a deflationary answer to the rationale
question: we should not expect there to be a deep answer to this question
in the first place. At the same time, the distinctively functionalist answer to
the rationale question we developed in the previous chapter is everything
but deflationary.

What comes to light is that there is reason to think that KAA is
incompatible with FFAA. Accordingly, in the remainder of this chapter,
we will mount a case against KAA, thus providing independent reason for
rejecting the view. To this end, we will first review a number of extant
arguments against KAA in the literature and find them wanting

(Section 7.1). After that we will develop a new and more promising argument against KAA (Section 7.2). Finally, in Section 7.3, we consider some objections to our argument and offer replies.

7.1 Extant Arguments against KAA

Let's begin by following Williamson in distinguishing two questions that one can ask about activities that are governed by constitutive rules. The first is what the rules governing the activity actually are, the second concerns the conditions that people must satisfy in order to engage in the activity. While Williamson's main concern is with the first of these two questions and, in particular, with mounting a case for KRA, he does make two points about the second question.

First, 'constitutive rules do not lay down necessary conditions for performing the constituted act' (Williamson 2000, 240). That is to say, one can break a constitutive rule and still continue to engage in the constituted activity. For instance, it's possible to cheat in a game of draughts without thereby ceasing to play draughts. Williamson even grants that one may break constitutive rules often.[1]

Second, Williamson acknowledges that 'some sensitivity to the difference – in both oneself and others – between conforming to the rule and breaking it presumably is a necessary condition of playing the game, speaking the language, or performing the speech act' (Ibid.). In the case of draughts, for instance, if one is completely insensitive to the fact that players who move pieces diagonally conform with the rules and players who move them vertically don't, then one won't be playing draughts, even if one happens to move pieces only diagonally. Let us grant Williamson both of these claims.[2]

The issues the two questions touch upon are indeed different. Crucially, however, they are not unrelated. To see this, consider once more

---

[1] It may be worth noting that this is entirely compatible with KAA, including *Essentiality*. After all, all that *Essentiality* claims is that the constituted type of act is essentially governed by the constitutive rule, which means that every token of the act is criticisable for violating the rule when it does. It does not mean that one cannot break constitutive rules, nor even that one cannot break them frequently.

[2] For the record, the second claim seems implausibly strong: it looks as though one can engage in an activity that is constituted by rule R even though one is entirely insensitive to the difference between conforming to R and breaking it. For instance, one may speak English even though one is entirely unaware of the rule that requires one to add 's'/'es' to present tense verbs in the third-person singular. That said, there is a true claim in the vicinity of Williamson's second claim: one cannot be insensitive to the difference between conforming and breaking too many of the rules constitutive of an activity. Since, however, this issue is of little consequence for the purposes of this section, we will set it aside.

Williamson's proposed condition according to which engaging in an activity governed by a constitutive rule requires some sensitivity to the difference between conforming to a constitutive rule and breaking it. Suppose for some rule putatively constitutive of some activity, it can be shown that one can engage in the activity whilst being completely insensitive to the difference between conforming to the rule and breaking it. Given that Williamson's condition holds, it follows that the rule cannot be constitutive of the activity. For instance, suppose one can make assertions, whilst being completely insensitive to the difference between conforming to KRA and breaking KRA. If so, and if Williamson is right and that making assertions requires a sensitivity to the difference conforming with and breaking any constitutive rules governing assertion, then KRA cannot be constitutive of assertion.

A number of critics of the Williamsonian picture have ventured to use this relation between constitutive rules and engagement conditions in an effort to show that Williamson must be mistaken and KRA is not constitutive of assertion. More specifically, they have argued along the lines just suggested – that one can make assertions without satisfying the proposed condition – to show that KRA cannot be constitutive of assertion. In what follows, we will look at the main proposals in the literature in turn.

7.1.1 Pagin

Pagin (2016) argues that if KRA is indeed constitutive of assertion, then in order to make assertions, one must know that assertion is governed by KRA.[3] With his engagement condition in play, Pagin goes on to note that there is widespread disagreement in the literature on what the rule of assertion is: several people think KRA governs assertion. Others disagree and impose weaker conditions such as justification or truth, or stronger conditions such as certainty. Yet others opt for contextually variant

[3] A more precise characterisation of Pagin's thought might be the following: To fully take part in assertoric practice, one must understand what assertion is well enough. But if assertion is governed by some rule, especially a constitutive one, one cannot understand what assertion is well enough unless one knows that the rule in question governs it. This gives us the result that, if KRA governs assertion, to fully take part in assertoric practice, one must know that KRA governs assertion. The above cuts out the detour via understanding. Moreover, we are setting aside a possibility Pagin countenances of partial participation in the practice of assertion. Neither is of central importance for our purposes.

conditions on permissible assertion. Of course, it cannot be that all these people are right. But given that the issue is so hotly disputed, Pagin argues,

> it is most plausible that nobody possesses this knowledge [i.e. of what rule governs assertion] at all, even among those who happen to be right, if some are. (Pagin 2016, 189).

Now we have all the ingredients for an argument against KAA. According to Pagin's engagement condition, if some rule is constitutive of assertion, one can make assertions only if one knows that this rule governs assertion. But since there is widespread disagreement about the rule of assertion, no one knows of any rule that it governs assertion. Hence, there is no constitutive rule of assertion and KAA must be false.

We have worries about both key premises of this argument. We'll start with the second according to which widespread disagreement about which rule governs assertion precludes knowledge of what the rule is. The obvious response here that even if Pagin is right and no one has philosophical knowledge of the rule of assertion, ordinary folk may well have ordinary knowledge of it. Of course, this response will work only if widespread disagreement among philosophers leaves this ordinary folk knowledge intact. Fortunately, there is every reason to think it does. To see this, let's first ask just why one should think that widespread disagreement about the norm is incompatible with knowledge of the norm. The obvious answer is that the disagreement constitutes a defeater for any particular belief about the norm of assertion. The trouble is, however, that it is just not clear that disagreement among philosophers ipso facto constitutes a defeater for ordinary folk knowledge. If this isn't immediately obvious note that, for centuries, philosophers have been disagreeing about things like the existence of the external world and the very possibility of knowledge and so on; surely, though, this disagreement failed to defeat ordinary knowledge about these matters.[4]

What's more, it is not clear why we should buy into Pagin's engagement condition in the first place. The reason for this is that the proposal fails to generalise in the right way. Take, for instance, rules of grammar: the ordinary speaker is not explicitly aware of the grammatical rules she obeys. While some of us learn grammar in school, others never do. Why couldn't the same go for the rules of assertion? Why can't it be that, even though

---

[4] What's more, it's not even clear that the disagreement constitutes a defeater for philosophers. It doesn't if a steadfast response to the disagreement is permissible here. And, it seems, this case is as good a candidate for this as any.

speakers don't explicitly know that KRA governs assertion – assuming that it does – they are aware of it implicitly, enough to turn them into proficient practitioners? Pagin considers this option and rejects it:

> This would have been an option, had the parallel worked, but it doesn't. In the case of syntax, speakers might disagree about generalizations, but they will typically agree on judgments in particular cases. It is only the pattern itself that is hard to identify. By contrast, in the case of norms of assertion, theorists disagree not only about the generalizations, i.e. the norms, but also about the cases. A belief norm theorist will not think that a false or badly justified assertion is improper, provided it is sincere (although the belief itself might be improper in that case), while adherents of knowledge or justification norms disagree. (Pagin 2016, 190)

We believe the relevant distinction to be drawn here is not the one Pagin suggests, i.e. between generalisations and particular cases. Rather, what seems to be at stake in the case of grammar is that everyone – laymen and specialists – is in agreement about intuitive permissibility/impermissibility of particular grammatical constructions, but the former, as opposed to the latter, don't know the underlying rules that explain the intuitive data. If that is the case, however, the parallel with assertion holds: after all, the intuitions triggered by the data employed in the debate are shared by the vast majority of assertion theorists, if not by all. What they disagree about – and, thereby, if Pagin is right, don't know – is the general principle explaining the intuitive data.

Take, for instance, cases of contextual variance (low-high stakes cases): Of course, the explanations of these data differ here: contextualists invoke a shifty semantics for 'know', pragmatic encroachers take knowledge itself to be sensitive to practical stakes and champions of warranted assertability manoeuvres believe that the amount/kind of warrant needed for permissible assertion varies with context. At the same time, all sides agree on the intuitive data in these particular cases. Crucially, the same goes, mutatis mutandis, for the debate on norms of assertion. Most philosophers agree that, in cases of gettiered assertions or assertions of justified false beliefs, the assertions are intuitively proper. What they disagree about are the explanations of these data. Champions of KRA take these cases to be cases of impermissible but blameless assertion and hold that intuition does not distinguish between the two, whereas champions of the justification norm, say, take these cases to be cases of permissible assertion.

What comes to light, then, is that there is reason believe that Pagin does not offer a genuine requirement on engaging in activities that are constituted by rules. It is possible to engage in such a practice without knowing the relevant constitutive rules. As a result, even if Pagin is right and widespread disagreement about the rule of assertion signals widespread lack of knowledge of it, this will fail to speak against KAA.

7.1.2   *Cappelen*

Recall that, according to the Essentiality Claim, the constitutive rule of assertion is essential to assertion. This means that nothing that isn't governed by the target constitutive rule could be an assertion. Cappelen notices the strength of this claim and points out that all that needs to be done in order to show that KAA is false is to adduce a *possible* case in which someone makes an assertion but the assertion is not governed by KRA. Moreover, it looks as though there are possible such cases. To see this, consider any act that, according to champions of KAA, qualifies as a paradigm case of assertion. To take Cappelen's own case, consider 'Mia saying that Mandy forgot to pay her cell phone bill last week.' Now, ask whether Mia's speech act could have been governed by a different norm than KRA. If the answer to this key question is yes, this means that KRA doesn't govern this act essentially. Since the act is a paradigmatic assertion, there is reason to think that KRA doesn't govern assertion essentially. Given *Essentiality*, it follows that KAA must be false.

Unsurprisingly, Cappelen wants to argue that the answer to the key question is indeed yes. One guiding thought here is that whatever rule governs a given speech act is associated with a default assumption about that speech act. For instance, if KRA holds, assertion is associated with the default assumption that one will assert p only if one knows p. To mount a case against KAA, Cappelen now invites us to consider the question whether Mia could have performed the speech act in question if the default assumption concerning that speech act was that she perform it only if p is true or perhaps only if she believes that p. Cappelen argues that champions of KAA will have to say no. After all, since KRA is constitutive of assertion and so assertion is necessarily associated with the default assumption that one will assert p only if one knows p. Assertion doesn't allow for different default assumptions to be in play. At the same time, Cappelen claims that the plausible answer is yes. Mia could have performed the speech act in question even if a different default assumption had been in play. KAA thus makes the wrong predictions about this case and so there is reason to think that it is false.

What's worse, assertion differs importantly from other games in this respect. To drive this point home, Cappelen invites us to consider an analogous question about paradigmatic games, such as tennis:

> Could [Mia] have played tennis, if serves were thrown by hand, without a racket, and no ball could be hit by a player unless she had a foot on one of the lines? (Cappelen 2011, 31)

Unlike in the case of assertion, here the plausible answer is clearly no. This further confirms the above point against KAA.

Note that the key target of Cappelen's case against KAA is *Essentiality*. Of course, since Williamson accepts *Essentiality*, Cappelen's argument promises to identify a key weakness in Williamson's proposal. The question we want to raise is whether champions of KAA must and indeed whether they even should embrace *Essentiality*. Perhaps somewhat surprisingly, there is reason to think that champions of KAA will do well to abandon *Essentiality*. To see why, think again about games and languages. Note that both evolve over time: some rules get lost in the process, new ones come into play. At the same time, it is highly plausible that games and languages can survive these changes in rules. For instance, it is highly plausible that the game of tennis survived the introduction of the tiebreak rules in 1970. Even more dramatically, consider the case of natural languages which continuously change their rules over time and do so without losing their identity. If that is so, there is independent reason for thinking that *Essentiality* is too strong: constitutive norms do not essentially govern the activities they constitute.

Of course, this is not to say that anything goes. If we change the rules too dramatically, we'll end up with a different game as is nicely illustrated by Cappelen's tennis case. Compatibly with that, however, as the tiebreak case indicates, the game may also survive changes provided that they are sufficiently moderate. What's more there is reason for thinking that the changes to the rules of assertion that Cappelen considers fall on the sufficiently moderate side of the divide. To see this, let's look at some more drastic changes and ask whether assertion could survive them. For instance, could assertion be governed by a norm according to which one must assert p only if one is wondering whether p or that one must assert p only if one has an occurent desire for ice cream? It's pretty clear that it couldn't.

What transpires, then, is that there is independent reason to think that games can survive changes to their constitutive rules with the result that there is independent reason to give up *Essentiality*. And while these changes must indeed not be too dramatic, we have also seen that there is reason to think assertion fits the bill. So, while Cappelen's argument against *Essentiality* is indeed successful, it carries little weight against KAA, properly understood.[5]

7.1.3 Maitra

The next argument we will consider is due to Ishani Maitra (2011). Her crucial condition on engaging in activities that are constituted by rules is that constitutive rules cannot be broken flagrantly. And a violation is flagrant in the relevant sense 'if it is intentional and sufficiently marked' (2011, 283). It's easy to see that if Maitra is right, knowledge based versions of KAA are in trouble. After all, it is clearly possible to flagrantly violate KRA, for instance, when one asserts a blatant falsehood that one doesn't believe and doesn't have any reason to believe.

Unfortunately, there is reason for thinking that Maitra's condition is not really a necessary condition for engaging in activities constituted by rules. To see why, consider the case of English once more. It is clear that

---

[5] Incidentally, this may help champions of *Essentiality* to a comeback. One key thought here is that names of games such as 'tennis' and 'football' do not denote games but families of games, where membership is (in part) determined by sufficient similarity in rules. This would be motivated by the idea that we are willing to classify a certain game as tennis even if it has a rule that only permits red rackets, say, whilst being unwilling to classify the kind of game envisaged by Cappelen as tennis. At the same time, another key thought is that individual members of game families do have constitutive rules, that they have them essentially and that they are individuated by them. As a result, we are playing a slightly different game when we add the rule about racket colour, even though both are correctly classifiable as tennis. More generally, what really happens when we change the rules of games and languages is that we move through a sequence of playing slightly different games, speaking slightly different languages, though they belong to the same family.

If this view is correct, champions of KAA may just be able to hold on to *Essentiality*. After all, assertion behaves like games in that we are willing to classify a certain speech act as an assertion even if it's governed by a slightly different rule but not when the change is too dramatic. Here, too, this motivates the idea that 'assertion' really denotes a family of speech acts where membership is (partly) determined by sufficient similarity in rules. And if the view that members of game families have constitutive rules, that they have them essentially and that they are individuated by them is correct and if it is also correct that we are playing a slightly different game when we change the rules, then there is reason to think that the same goes, mutatis mutandis, for members of the assertion family.

Of course, a lot turns on whether this picture is correct. Williamson thinks that at least the part that construes changes in rules as playing slightly different games is on grounds of theoretical fruitfulness (2000, 239). Since settling this issue would take us too far afield, we will not attempt to do so here. However, we would like to note that this view would help Williamson respond to another worry by Cappelen, which is that none of the arguments Williamson offers for KRA are modal (2011, 31). To see why, note that the modality drops out of the background theory about families of games/speech acts and their members. All that Williamson will need to make his point is that the member of the assertion we are using is governed by KRA. The fact that if it is, it's governed by it essentially follows is given by the background theory.

one may flagrantly violate a constitutive rule of English, without thereby ceasing to speak English. For instance, were we to say 'Maitra's argument just don't work', we would have flagrantly violated the rule that requires us to add 's'/'es' to present tense verbs in the third person singular. While we'd be speaking bad English, we would not thereby cease to speak English altogether. Similarly, by intentionally committing an obvious foul, a football player may flagrantly violate the constitutive rule of football that prohibits fouls. However, he doesn't thereby stop playing football. (In fact, the game may not even be stopped as the referee may call an advantage for the fouled team.) As a result, Maitra's argument remains unsuccessful as well.

7.2 A New Argument against KAA

7.2.1 Another Engagement Condition

As we already acknowledged, we are granting Williamson that conforming with a constitutive rule is not a necessary condition for engaging in the constituted activity and that it may even be possible to break constitutive rules frequently.

Even so, we want to insist that there are limits to how persistently and systematically one can break the constitutive rules of an activity and still engage in the constituted activity. To see why, suppose you are playing a game of draughts with a friend. It may be that your friend cheats, perhaps even often. But now suppose you are attempting to play a game of draughts with a friend only to find that she persistently and systematically moves the pieces horizontally and vertically rather than diagonally. In this case, your friend is not really playing draughts. Alternatively, suppose you wanted to strike up a conversation in English with her. It may be that she breaks the rules of English and perhaps she does so frequently. But now consider a case in which she persistently and systematically utters only strings of the phoneme 'ka'. When you ask her how she is doing she responds: 'Kakaka', when you ask her whether she has gone mad her answer is: 'Kaka kakaka ka', and so on. If she persists in this behaviour too systematically, she is not speaking English.

We take these considerations to motivate the following condition on engaging in activities that are constituted by constitutive rules:

Engagement Condition
If some activity A is constituted by a set of constitutive rules, R, then one cannot violate too many members of R too systematically without ceasing to engage in A.

Two comments by way of clarification: First, we may want to allow for variation in what counts as violating too many members of a set of constitutive rules and what counts as violating them too systematically. In the draughts case, your friend is not playing even though she violates only one rule, albeit with near maximum systematicity. (Note that maximum systematicity is not required. If your friend were to move the pieces vertically and horizontally nearly all of the time, she'd still not be playing.) In contrast, in the English case, your friend violates many rules with a very high degree of systematicity. Here, we may want to allow that systematically violating a single rule does not mean that one ceases to speak English. If your friend were to systematically fail to add an 's' to present tense verbs in the third person singular, we may want to allow that she still speaks English.

Second, *Engagement Condition* is plausible even when your friend breaks the rules non-deliberately or otherwise blamelessly, when she tries to follow the rules or when she thinks she is following the rules. Suppose, in the draughts case, your friend is misinformed about the rules of draughts, say because she was told that pieces move horizontally and vertically. When, in this case, she systematically moves the pieces in these ways, she will systematically break the rules of draughts whilst doing so non-deliberately and blamelessly, whilst trying to follow them and thinking that she is following them. Even so, she is not playing draughts. The same goes for the case of speaking English. Even if your friend were not to blame, and the like for violating nearly all the rules of English with near maximum systematicity, say because she had been told that 'ka' is the only phoneme in English, she would still not be speaking English.

If *Engagement Condition* is plausible, then so is the following:

Engagement Condition'
If activity, *A*, is constituted by only a single constitutive rule, *r*, and if one violates *r* with near maximum systematicity, then one does not engage in *A*.

Consider, for instance, a card game, call it 'Ace of Spades' in which the only constitutive rule is that one must continue to turn over cards from a standard deck until one turns over the ace of spades. If you violate this rule with near maximum systematicity, say because you regularly stop turning over cards when and only when you turn over the three of hearts, you are not playing Ace of Spades.

It is easy to see that we can run an argument parallel to the one featuring Williamson's proposed condition above to establish a relation between *Engagement Condition'* and the issue of which constitutive rules, if any, govern a given activity. Again, (i*) let *A* be arbitrary activity (putatively) governed by constitutive rules, (ii*) let *r* be arbitrary rule that (putatively) is the only constitutive rule governing *A*. Suppose, furthermore, (iii*) that one can engage in *A* even though one violates *r* with near maximum systematicity. From *Engagement Condition'* in conjunction with (i*) and (ii*) it follows that engaging in *A* requires not breaking *r* with near maximum systematicity. However, this evidently contradicts (iii*). This means that if for any *A* such that (iii*) holds for *A*, it follows from *Engagement Condition'* that either (i*) is false and *A* is not governed by constitutive rules at all, or else (ii*) is false and *r* is not the only constitutive rule governing *A*. Crucially, either way, it cannot be the case that *r* is the only constitutive rule governing *A*. As a result, for any *A*, establishing (iii*) will be sufficient to show that the relevant *r* is not the only constitutive rule governing *A*.

In what follows, we will make a case that instances of (iii*) are true of KRA. As a result, KRA cannot be the only constitutive rule governing assertion. KAA is false.

7.2.2   Some Cases Involving Assertions

In what follows, we'd like to consider a couple of cases. Here is the first:

Case 1
A has been in causal contact with physical objects long enough for his thoughts to have the same contents as the thoughts of inhabitants of Earth. Shortly after the contents of his thoughts were fixed, *A* came under the spell of an evil demon, who sees to it that nearly all of *A*'s beliefs are false. *A* is a member of a very small set of unfortunate individuals who, shortly after the contents of their thoughts were fixed, came under the spell of an evil demon, who sees to it that nearly all their beliefs are false.

Whatever else we may think about this, at least the following is plausible about *Case 1*:

Possible Assertion 1
It is possible for *A* to assert a wide range of propositions. (For instance, *A* may assert that it is raining outside, that there is coffee in his mug, etc. even though *A* is merely deceived into believing this and, as a matter of fact, it's not raining outside, there is no coffee in his mug, etc.)

We take *Possible Assertion 1* to be eminently plausible. However, for those in doubt, there is independent reason to think that it is true. After all, *A*'s relevant speech acts may have a number of hallmark features of assertions, including the following: they present their contents as true, they furnish others with a prima facie[6] entitlement to believe their contents, and we will hold A accountable for the truth of their contents.[7]

Second, A can assert propositions to other members of his society. He may assert that he will respond to some emails before having a coffee break to his friend at work (whilst believing that he is asserting that he will first have a coffee break before responding to some emails to his wife at home). Let us assume, as we may, that A happens to be both an exceptionally sincere and rather chatty person. Of course, since nearly all of A's beliefs are false, this gives us:

Systematic Falsity
A makes assertions that, with near maximum systematicity, are false.

With these points about the first case in play, we'd now like to move on to the second case. Here goes:

Case 2
B is a compulsive liar: B is strongly disposed – perhaps even hard-wired – to assert p only when he believes p to be false.

Again, at least the following is plausible about B about *Case 2*:

Possible Assertion 2
It is possible for B to assert a wide range propositions. (For instance, B may assert that it is raining outside, that there is coffee in his mug, etc., even though he is lying about this: B really believes that it isn't raining outside, that there is no coffee in his mug, and the like.)

We also take *Possible Assertion 2* to be eminently plausible. Those in doubt may note that the considerations adduced in support of *Possible Assertion 1* will work here just as well.

Let us assume, as we may, that B happens to be not only rather chatty but also an exceptionally reliable cognitive agent who lives in an

---

[6] This is an important proviso, especially in the present case. After all, it may well become widely known that A's assertions are with near maximum systematicity false. In that case, there will be a widely available defeater for believing A's assertions. However, this is compatible with the thesis the assertion furnishes a prima facie entitlement.

[7] *Possible Assertion 1* receives further support by a popular view in recent epistemology according to which some kind of doxastic attitude – such as belief/occurrent belief/judgement – is identified with some kind of assertion – such as subvocalised assertion or assertion to oneself (Adler 2002, Douven 2006, Sosa 2011, Williamson 2000). If this view is correct, then since A can form a wide range of (occurrent) beliefs about the external world/can pass a wide range of judgements about the external world, *Possible Assertion 1* will be true also.

exceptionally hospitable epistemic environment with the result that nearly all of his beliefs qualify as knowledge. We then get:

Systematic Counter-Knowledge
B makes assertions that, with near maximum systematicity, are false and run counter to what *B* knows.

7.2.3   KAA: A Negative Result

We now have motivated a couple of conditions on engaging in activities that are constituted by rules – to wit, *Engagement Condition* and *Engagement Condition'* – and a few theses about a couple of cases involving assertions – to wit, *Possible Assertion 1* and *2* as well as *Systematic Falsity* and *Systematic Counter-Knowledge*. This is all we need for our argument against KAA. Here goes.

By *Systematic Falsity* (alternatively: *Systematic Counter-Knowledge*), *A* (*B*) makes assertions that, with near maximum systematicity, are false (run counter to what S knows). Since knowledge is factive, *A* (*B*) violates KRA with near maximum systematicity. It follows that *A* (*B*) makes assertions that, with near maximum systematicity, violate KRA. We thus have our relevant instance of (iii*) – that one can engage in *A* even though one violates *r* with near maximum systematicity – for assertion and KRA. Recall that establishing an instance of (iii*) is enough to show the falsity of the thesis that *r* is the only constitutive rule governing *A* for any putative constitutive rule *r* and any *A*. Since according to KAA, KRA is the only constitutive rule of assertion, this means that KAA is false.

7.3   Objections and Replies

Isn't it the case that even if an individual can violate a certain rule governing an activity with near maximum systematicity without thereby ceasing to engage in the activity, the same could not be true of the entire population? For instance, while an individual can systematically move draughts pieces vertically and horizontally without compromising the practice of engaging in the activity of the population, if the entire population started behaving in this way, wouldn't that just mean that the practice of playing draughts is discontinued? Isn't, mutatis mutandis, the same true of the practice of making assertions? And, finally, isn't that the important fact about constitutive rules that vindicates KAA?

By way of response, even if we grant that this is one important fact about constitutive rules and one that tallies nicely with KAA, it is certainly not the only important fact about constitutive rules there is to capture. In particular, what the objector develops here is at the very best an important fact about constitutive rules in the sense that it captures a necessary condition on engaging in activities with constitutive rules. It is entirely compatible with this that there are other important facts about constitutive rules, including that *Engagement Condition* and *Engagement Condition'* are also necessary conditions on engaging in activities constituted by constitutive rules. As a result, these points do very little to block the above argument against KAA.

But perhaps the thought is not that these considerations rescue KAA but rather that what Williamson is best understood as advancing is not a thesis about the constitutive rules of assertion, but a thesis about the constitute rules of the practice of making assertions. Moreover, so understood, an argument similar to the above serves to confirm this very thesis. After all, if the practice of assertion were to be constituted by KRA and KRA only, we would expect that if an entire population of speakers were to systematically violate KRA, the practice of assertion would at some point no longer be continued, for reasons similar to the above. And since this is just what we would find, the thesis about the practice of assertion is at any rate confirmed.

Unfortunately, there is reason to believe that KAA is false even when understood as a thesis about the practice of making assertions. Let's grant the objector (i) that practices of engaging in activities can be constituted by rules and (ii) that an important necessary condition on operating such a practice is:

Engagement Condition*
If a population's practice, *P*, of engaging in an activity, *A*, is constituted by a set of constitutive rules, *R*, and if too many members of the population violate too many members of *R* too systematically, then the population does not operate *P*.

If *Engagement Condition** is plausible, then so is:

Engagement Condition**
If a population's practice, *P*, of engaging in a rule governed activity, *A*, is constituted by only a single constitutive rule, *r*, and if nearly all members of the population violate *r* with near maximum systematicity, then the population does not operate *P*.

KAA understood as a thesis about the practice of making assertions and *Engagement Condition*** does indeed entail:

No Practice
If too many members of a population of speakers violate KRA with near maximum systematicity, then the population does not operate a practice of making assertions.

What's not so clear to us is that *No Practice* is really correct. To see why not, consider:

Case 3
φ is a population of agents such that (i) all its members only ever say what they believe to be false, (ii) this is common knowledge and, consequently, (iii) whenever a member of the population says that *p*, members of the audience will infer and thereupon come to believe that not-*p*.[8]

It seems to us that the following is plausible about *Case 3*:

Possible Assertion 3
It is possible for the members of φ to assert a wide range propositions.

Let us assume, as we may, that the members of φ happen to be not only very chatty but also otherwise exceptionally reliable cognitive agents who live in an exceptionally hospitable epistemic environment with the result that nearly all of their beliefs qualify as knowledge. We then get:

Systematic Counter-Knowledge*
The members of φ make assertions that, with near maximum systematicity, are false and run counter to what they know.

It is easy to see that our argument from Section 7.2.4, with *Engagement Condition*** in place of *Engagement Condition'* and *Systematic Counter-Knowledge** in place of *Systematic Counter-Knowledge*, will serve to show that *No Practice* is incompatible with KAA. If so, *pace* our objector, KAA understood as a thesis about the practice of making assertions is disconfirmed also.

Here is one final objection we'd like to consider. Doesn't Williamson offer an account of constitutive rules according to which constitutive rules are essential to the constituted act in the sense that it 'necessarily, the rule

---

[8] One might wonder why we shouldn't say that when a member of the population says '*p*' what he really asserts is that not-*p*. After all, if the connection between what we say and what we thereby assert is conventional, it seems possible that the community has the convention of assertion that not-*p* by saying '*p*'.

    While we would agree that it is *possible* that some such community could have the convention of asserting not-*p* by saying '*p*', we also believe that it is *not necessary*. That is to say, we believe that it is also possible for such a community to have the familiar convention of asserting *p* by saying '*p*'. Crucially, this is all we need to get the argument off the ground. After all, the constitutivity claim under consideration is necessarily true if true at all. As a result, all we need to mount a case against it is one possible case in which it doesn't hold.

    In fact, there is at least some reason to think that, in the above case, the convention is the familiar one of asserting *p* by saying '*p*'. After all, it is explicitly stated that hearers form beliefs based on these assertions by *inferring* not-*p*. This is just what we'd expect if by saying '*p*' one asserts *p* here. If, on the other hand, the case were one in which members of the community really asserted that not-*p* by saying '*p*', we would expect hearers not to form their beliefs by inference. Rather, we'd expect them to respond to the assertions by forming the relevant belief (that not-p) *non-inferentially*.

governs every performance of the act' (Williamson 2000)? And doesn't KRA come out to be a constitutive rule on this account?

By way of response, note that while Williamson does claim that the rule governing every performance of the act is a necessary condition on constitutive rules, he once again does not claim that it is also sufficient. Note, furthermore, that Williamson will do well not to strengthen this necessary condition into a sufficient condition. After all, moral and practical norms also govern every performance of a given act with necessity. However, we take it that it would be rather implausible to say that moral and practical norms qualify as constitutive rules of say, moves in draughts, utterances in English or assertions.⁹ Williamson's necessity claim is thus only plausible if it is taken to be a necessary condition on constitutive rules. As a result, it is compatible with further necessary conditions on constitutive rules as well as necessary conditions on what it takes to engage in acts constituted by constitutive rules. In particular, it is compatible with *Engagement Condition* and *Engagement Condition'*. Since we have seen these conditions are independently plausible, the prospects of blocking the argument by appeal to the necessity claim are also dim.¹⁰

7.4 Constitutivity without KAA

It has come to light that there is excellent reason to think that KAA is false. Of course, this is not quite the same as showing that KRA is not constitutive of

---

⁹ In fact, it seems to us that one very plausible way of distinguishing between constitutive rules and other norms that govern acts necessarily, such as moral and practical norms, is that constitutive rules come with conditions on what it takes to engage in the constituted act like the one Williamson mentions and the one we defended above. While constitutive rules are like moral and practical norms in that they are not contingent, they differ from the latter in that one cannot engage in a constituted act unless, for instance, one is sensitive to what counts as conforming to the constitutive rule and breaking it. In contrast, in the case of moral and practical norms, such insensitivity does not prevent one from engaging in the constituted act.

¹⁰ Goldberg (2015) also develops an extensive abductive argument that aims to show that assertion is governed by a constitutive epistemic norm. Doesn't that provide us overriding reason for thinking that KRA is constitutive after all? No. To see why not, note that none of Goldberg's insightful explanations in terms of a rule of assertion require that assertion be governed by a *constitutive* rule. Rather, all that's needed is that assertion be governed by an *epistemic* rule. Goldberg's argument will only serve to make a case for a distinctively constitutive epistemic rule of assertion on the assumption that if assertion is governed by an epistemic rule at all, then this rule must be constitutive of assertion. Given that the aim of the book is to argue that the constitutive rule account is better than the alternatives on the market – i.e. the attitudinal account, the common ground account and the commitment account – this assumption may be just fine. That said, there can be no question that, in the present context, it isn't. After all, we have not seen that it makes sense for there to be an epistemic rule of assertion on independent grounds; that is, even if this rule isn't also constitutive.

assertion in the same way in which rules of games are constitutive. After all, for all we have argued, it might still be the case that KRA is one constitutive norm of assertion among others. In that case, even if we are in agreement that engaging in an activity with constitutive rules requires one not to violate *too many* constitutive rules of assertion too systematically without ceasing to make assertion, it may still be that one violates KRA with near maximum systematicity without ceasing to make assertions.

We do believe, however, that our argument serves to generate a pretty serious challenge for those who want to argue that KRA is constitutive of assertion in the same way in which rules of games are constitutive. Note first that, at least as far as we are aware, no one has defended a view of assertion according to which KRA is one constitutive rule among others. In other words, KAA's key thesis that there is only one constitutive rule of assertion is the only game in town, at least at present. Second, it is also far from clear that, once we have some proposals for further constitutive norms of assertion on the table, our argument will not generalise. Third, recall KAA's games model committed us to a distinctively deflationary answer to the question of the rationale for KRA. This commitment will remain even if it can be shown that KRA is one constitutive rule of assertion among others. Crucially, however, this commitment is problematic on independent grounds. To see why, recall that according to the deflationary answer, it is an historical contingency that a speech act governed by KRA, say, came to be widely used, just as it is an historical contingency that we started playing a game with one particular set of rules (e.g. chess) rather than a slightly different game with slightly different rule (e.g. a game just like chess except that the pawn can only ever move one square). At the same time, it seems somewhat less plausible that, in the case of rules of assertion, it is a mere historical contingency that a speech act governed by KRA, say, came to be widely used. Supposing that assertion really is governed by KRA, it is somewhat less plausible to think that we might as well have ended up using a speech act that is governed by a different rule instead, especially when this rule is quite different than the rule that actually governs assertion. For instance, it is rather implausible that we might as well have ended up using a speech act governed by e.g. a pleasure rule of assertion according to which one must: assert p only if p pleases one. By the same token, it seems that there should be a deeper answer to the question of why assertion should be governed by KRA.

One prominent defender of the constitutivity claim that attempts to answer this question is Manuel Garcia-Carpintero (2004). While, Garcia-Carpintero agrees that assertion is governed by a unique constitutive rule, he parts ways with Williamson in that he denies that the relevant rule is KRA. Instead, Garcia-Carpintero proposes the following rule: one must (assert *p* only if one's audience comes thereby to be in a position to know that *p*). He argues that his norm is preferable to Williamson's KRA because it brings out the social, communicative function of language (Garcia-Carpintero 2004, 157).

We agree with Garcia-Carpintero's function–theoretic rationale; that being said, Garcia-Carpintero's view is explicitly construed within a strong, Williamsonian constitutivity framework that we have just rejected, i.e. the games model. It is easy enough to see that our case against Williamson's version of KAA extends to a version of KAA that replaces KRA with Garcia-Carpintero's norm.[11] After all, in both of our key cases, just as the agents' assertions violate KRA with near maximum systematicity, they violate Garcia-Carpintero's norm with near maximum systematicity also. If this isn't immediately obvious, note that, in these cases, it is not only the case that the agents make assertions that, with near maximum systematicity, run counter to what they know, but it is also the case that they make assertions that, with near maximum systematicity, don't put their audiences in a position to know what they assert. Finally, note that, by the same token, our case against KAA will also extend to a view that abandons Uniqueness and takes both KRA and Garcia-Carpintero's norm to be constitutive of assertion.

In sum: in order to defend the thesis that, despite our argument against KAA, assertion is governed by a set of rules that are constitutive in the same way in which rules of games are constitutive, its champions must not only identify some plausible candidates for other constitutive rules of assertion, mount a case that these candidates are indeed constitutive and show that our argument against KAA does not generalise to their proposal, but they must also give us a new model for these constitutive norms, i.e. one that improves on the games model in that it does not commit them to the problematic deflationary answer to the rationale question. In this way, champions of the view that KRA is constitutive of assertion do face quite a formidable task which sends them pretty much back to square one. While we suspect that it won't be accomplished, we will not stop to argue this point here. Instead, we will rest content with leaving it to those who want to pursue this route to do the relevant work, at least for the time being.

7.5   Conclusion

This chapter has taken up the question of whether KRA is in addition a constitutive rule of assertion in the way in which rules of games are

---

[11]   In addition, pace Garcia-Carpintero, we also take knowledge *generation* rather than transmission to be the relevant function (for the reasons outlined in Chapter 4).

constitutive. To this end, we have looked at KAA, which offers the most detailed positive answer to this question. While KAA had already come under attack in recent literature, we believe that extant arguments have remained unsuccessful. The key contribution of this chapter has been to develop a better argument against KAA. The key idea here was that engaging in an activity with constitutive rules does require one not to violate too many of the activity's constitutive rules too systematically. And since one can make assertions whilst violating KRA with near maximum systematicity, KAA must be false.

Importantly, this is not to say that we believe that the constitutivity claim is false about KRA. To the contrary, as we have already pointed out, FFAA implies a variety of the constitutivity claim – albeit a weaker version thereof: since, on FFAA, the very continuous existence of the practice of making and consuming assertions is explained by its having generated knowledge in hearers, and since the latter is ensured via regulating the speech act of assertion with KRA, it follows that KRA explains the very existence of the practice. In this way, the practice of making and consuming assertions is constituted at least in part by KRA.[12]

---

[12] It is worth noting that the claim that the practice of making and consuming assertions is constituted by KRA in this lightweight sense is compatible with the case that caused trouble for KAA construed as a claim about the practice of making and consuming assertions. Recall that the relevant case features a population of agents such that (i) all its members only ever say what they believe to be false, (ii) this is common knowledge and, consequently, (iii) whenever a member of the population says that p, members of the audience will infer and thereupon come to believe that not-p. The fact that assertions of agents in this population will violate KRA with near maximum systematicity means trouble for KAA. This is because, on the present reading of KAA, it is essential to the practice that it is governed by KRA. The lightweight alternative eschews this essentiality claim. In fact, it is plausible that, in the problem case, the practice of making and consuming assertions is not governed by KRA. In fact, since this would work against the reliability with which assertions that p generate knowledge that not-p in hearers, it wouldn't make sense to do so. It may make sense to govern assertion by a assert that p only if you believe not-p rule. It may even be that assertion isn't governed by any rule at all here. Since KRA doesn't contribute to the explanation of why assertion the practice of making and consuming assertions continues to exist, this is entirely compatible with our lightweight constitutivity claim. Crucially, note that this doesn't undermine our lightweight alternative to KAA. To see this, compare: my car is constituted in part by its carburetor. What's more, that it is thus constituted isn't a mere accident. There is excellent reason for it to be constituted in this way. At the same time, the carburetor isn't an essential constituent of my car. It's possible for my car to exist (and even to run) without it. The same holds, mutatis mutandis, for the practice of assertion and KRA. The practice is constituted in part by KRA and that it is thus constituted isn't an accident. At the same time, KRA isn't an essential constituent of the practice. As the above case shows, it's possible for the practice to exist (and even to generate knowledge) without KRA.

CHAPTER 8

KRA and Epistemic Contextualism

In Chapter 7, we inquired into whether KRA can also give us an insight into the very nature of assertion. More specifically, we looked in detail at the most promising attempt at achieving this, Williamson's knowledge account of assertion, according to which KRA is the unique constitutive rule governing assertion. We argued that the knowledge account of assertion is bound to fail and, what's more, that there is every reason to remain sceptical that an account that countenances further constitutive rules will do better.

In this final chapter, we will take a closer look at the relation between KRA and epistemic contextualism (EC).[1] EC is the view that the truth conditions of knowledge ascriptions vary with (attributor) context. In particular, we will look at one of the most famous arguments for EC, due to Keith DeRose, that KRA demands EC. While champions of EC will of course be very happy with this argument, there is reason to be more cautious for champions of KRA. This is because EC's main rival, epistemic invariantism (EI), is generally taken to be the default view in the semantics of knowledge attributions. By way of evidence, consider the following passage from a recent encyclopaedia entry on the issue:

> As its proponents generally admit, EC is something that one needs to be argued into [. . .] we seem, if anything, to be 'intuitive invariantists'. As one leading contextualist says, many 'resist [the contextualist] thesis – some fiercely. Moreover, those who do accept the thesis, generally do so only as a result of being convinced by philosophical reflection.' (Cohen 1999, 78, Rysiew 2016, §3)

If the argument from KRA to EC goes through, it means that champions of KRA will have an unexpected commitment to abandoning the default view on a completely different issue in epistemology. And that might just

---

[1] See also Simion (2021) for a book-length treatment of this.

sound like a cost for the view. Accordingly, it will not come as a great surprise that one central aim of this chapter is to show that DeRose's argument fails (Section 8.2). What's more, we will also show, and this is the other central aim, that DeRose's argument can be turned on its head: there is actually a tension between KRA and EC (Section 8.3). As a result, rather than putting the default view in the semantics of knowledge attributions in jeopardy, if anything KRA vindicates it. First things first, however, we will briefly sketch DeRose's argument (Section 8.1).

8.1   DeRose's Argument

To get DeRose's argument from KRA to EC into clear view, let's first consider the following two cases:

Aspirin Low
You remember having bought aspirin last month. As such, when you head together with your sister towards your place for dinner, and she lets you know she has a minor headache, you flat out assert: '*Don't worry, I have aspirin at home*'.

Aspirin High
You remember having bought aspirin last month. Your sister's two-year-old baby is having a fever, and needs an aspirin as soon as possible. Plausibly, were your sister to ask you: 'Do you have aspirin at home, or should we go to the pharmacy?' you would be less inclined to flat out assert that you have aspirin at home. You would rather say something along the lines of: '*Well, let's drop by the pharmacy, just in case*'.

In *Aspirin Low* you assert that you have aspirin at home. What's more, your assertion is intuitively permissible. In contrast, you are unwilling to do so in *Aspirin High*. And, crucially, making the same assertion in this context wouldn't have been permissible. In this way, there is reason to think that whether a given assertion is intuitively permissible varies with context (henceforth also *Intuitive Shiftiness*).

Next, DeRose argues from *Intuitive Shiftiness* to KRA. Here goes:

If the standards for when one is in a position to warrantedly [i.e. properly] assert that P are the same as those that constitute a truth condition for 'I know that P,' [as KRA would have it] then if the former vary with context, so do the latter. In short: [KRA] together with the context sensitivity of assertability [. . .] yields contextualism about knowledge (2002, 187).

What of the advocate of [KRA] who does not accept contextualism? Such a character is in serious trouble. Given invariantism about knowledge, [KRA] is an untenable attempt to rest a madly swaying distinction upon a stubbornly fixed foundation. [...] [KRA] demands a contextualist account of knowledge and is simply incredible without it (2002, 182).

Now, it has since become widely known that this argument is a bit too quick. Too see why, let's first take another and closer look at the Aspirin cases. Note that in *Aspirin Low* and *High* you are in exactly the same epistemic position towards the proposition that you have aspirin at home: you remember having bought it last month. At the same time, your practical situation is different. In *Aspirin Low* not much hinges on whether you have aspirin at home. Your sister will be somewhat uncomfortable but she'll not suffer any serious harm. In contrast, the stakes in *Aspirin High* are considerably higher than in *Aspirin Low*: your sister's baby's health depends on it. Since we may assume that everything else is equal between the two cases, there is reason to think that the difference in intuitive permissibility between *Aspirin Low* and *Aspirin High* is due to the fact that the stakes are higher in the latter case. In other words, there is reason to think that permissible assertion varies with stakes.

With this point in play, consider a version of EI that is also interest-relative (IREI) in that whether one knows supervenes at least in part on one's practical situation. In particular, consider a version of invariantism according to which when more hinges for one on whether p is true, one needs to be in a better epistemic position towards p in order to know that p (e.g. Fantl and McGrath 2009, Hawthorne 2004, Stanley 2005). On IREI, *Intuitive Shiftiness* is entirely compatible with KRA. Thus, KRA does not demand EC.

Even so, DeRose's argument promises to establish at least the entailment between KRA and the falsity of Classical Epistemic Invariantism (CEI). According to CEI, whether or not one knows does not vary with stakes. Rather, it depends only on one's doxastic and epistemic position towards the target proposition and its truth value. For instance, in the Aspirin cases, either remembering having bought aspirin last month puts you in a good enough epistemic position to know that you have aspirin at home or it doesn't. If it does, then you know in both *Aspirin Low* and *High* (assuming that you have the corresponding true belief, that is). If, on the other hand, it doesn't, then you know in neither. So, DeRose's point about the impossibility of resting 'a madly swaying distinction upon a stubbornly fixed foundation' would still appear to show that, given the shiftiness of permissible assertion, we cannot combine KRA with CEI. In other words, DeRose does appear to establish at least the following:

Conditional Incompatibility
If *Intuitive Shiftiness* is true, then KRA is incompatible with CEI.

Since we have already seen that there is excellent reason to think that *Intuitive Shiftiness* is true, we have equally good reason to think that KRA is indeed incompatible with CEI. And since it might be thought that having to deny CEI would be worrisome enough a commitment for champions of KRA, we think it is worth taking the time to show that even DeRose's argument for *Conditional Incompatibility* remains unsuccessful.[2]

8.2 Why DeRose's Argument Is Unsuccessful

Let's first return to *Intuitive Shiftiness*. Recall that DeRose argues from the intuitive variability in permissible assertion to the incompatibility of KRA and CEI. Crucially, however, recall that KRA is a distinctively *epistemic* norm of assertion, that is, a norm that specifies conditions for *epistemically permissible assertion*. But now recall what we saw in Chapter 3, to wit, that type-specific norms, including the epistemic norm of assertion, can be overridden by other norms. So suppose for a moment that our permissibility intuitions in cases like the Aspirin cases do not track distinctively epistemic permissibility but some other kind of permissibility. Since it is entirely possible that an assertion is impermissible in some other way whilst being permissible in the distinctively epistemic sense associated with the epistemic norm for assertion and vice versa, it simply does not follow from *Intuitive Shiftiness* that KRA and CEI are incompatible. By the same token, *Conditional Incompatibility* is false.

What DeRose needs in order to establish the incompatibility of KRA and CEI is that there is variability in the distinctively *epistemic* permissibility of assertion (henceforth also *Epistemic Shiftiness*):

> *Conditional Incompatibility**. If *Epistemic Shiftiness* is true, then KRA is incompatible with CEI.

Of course, *Intuitive Shiftiness* and *Conditional Incompatibility** will not serve to establish the incompatibility between KRA and CEI unless the following assumption holds:

> **Epistemic Tracking**
> The intuitive variation in permissibility of assertion tracks the distinctively epistemic permissibility of assertion.

---

[2] One of us has a book-length treatment of this issue (Simion 2021).

Unfortunately, *Epistemic Tracking* is not all that easy to defend: given that many norms govern assertions, our permissibility intuitions can be sourced in any of these norms, and indeed, most likely, will be sourced in all-things-considered permissibility. The latter, however, need not track epistemic permissibility. There is little reason to think, then, that merely appealing to our intuitions about when assertions are permissible will do the trick as there is little reason to think that our intuitions track distinctively epistemic permissibility here. Rather, DeRose will need to supplement his methodology with a principled way to distinguish the requirements of the distinctively epistemic norm[3] he is after, and he needs to show that there is variation concerning just these requirements in the relevant cases. This will give him *Epistemic Shiftiness*. And, since *Conditional Incompatibility** is fine, it will enable him to establish the incompatibility of KRA and CEI.

Now, what would clearly do the trick for DeRose is:

Content Individuation
If a norm *N* affects the amount of epistemic support needed for permissible assertion, than *N* is an epistemic norm.

After all, it seems plausible enough that one needs to have better epistemic support for asserting that one has aspirin at home in *Aspirin Low* than in *Aspirin High*. Given *Content Individuation*, there is reason to believe that what varies between the two cases are the requirements of the epistemic norm in particular and hence the conditions for specifically epistemic permissibility.

Unfortunately, we have already seen that *Content Individuation* is false. As a result, it does not serve to generate the needed support for *Epistemic Shiftiness*. Recall also that we argued that a promising alternative to *Content Individuation* is *Value Individuation*, which individuates types of norm by the values they are associated with. The problem is that, rather than helping DeRose mount a case for *Epistemic Shiftiness*, *Value Individuation* allows champions of KRA+CEI to offer a plausible alternative account of cases like *Aspirin Low* and *High*. To see how, note that they may argue that the value that determines how much epistemic support is needed for permissible assertion is very plausibly a practical (and/or moral)

---

[3] Jennifer Lackey expresses a similar worry regarding excuse manoeuvres brought in defence of KRA: 'For now, whenever evidence is adduced that concerns the epistemic authority requisite for proper assertion, it may bear on the norm of assertion or it may bear on these other [...] norms. [...] [I]t will be extremely difficult, if not impossible, to tell which is being defended' (Lackey 2011, 277).

one in these cases. In particular, in *Aspirin High*, it is very plausibly the value of averting a serious risk to your sister's baby's health that requires you to have exceptionally strong epistemic support in order to permissibly assert. Since this is a practical (or moral) value, by *Value Individuation*, it follows that it is really a practical (or moral) norm that requires you to have such strong support for your assertion here. But then, champions of KRA +CEI may continue, what's really going on is that the requirements of the practical (or moral) norm override the requirements of the epistemic norm with the result that the requirement for all-things-considered permissible assertion coincide with the requirements of the practical (or moral) norm here. In this way, *Value Individuation* allows champions of KRA+CEI to offer an attractive alternative account of the problematic cases. As a result, it is not as if DeRose has simply failed to provide sufficient support for *Epistemic Shiftiness*, it now looks as though a convincing case for this thesis is simply not going to be forthcoming.

What comes to light, then, is that DeRose's argument for the incompatibility of KRA and CEI fails. Since 'permissible' at issue in *Conditional Incompatibility* is not suitably restricted and taken to mean 'epistemically permissible', this thesis is false. If, on the other hand, 'permissible' is so interpreted, i.e. if we move from *Conditional Incompatibility* to *Conditional Incompatibility**, we will also have to replace *Intuitively Shiftiness* by *Epistemic Shiftiness* in order to get DeRose's argument off the ground. Crucially, however, the latter requires further support. And what we have seen now is that the prospects of gathering such support are dim to say the least. Either way, then, DeRose's argument for the incompatibility of KRA and CEI remains uncompelling. The unwanted commitment that champions of KRA might seem to incur can be avoided.[4]

---

[4] In fact, there is reason to think that things are actually even worse for DeRose and others who want to use DeRose's argument from KRA to mount a case against CEI. Here is why. *Value Individuation* ushered the way towards an attractive alternative account of what's going on in the kinds of case that DeRose took to support *Conditional Incompatibility* and so, in conjunction with KRA, the denial of CEI. This means, however, that we now have two accounts of these cases on the table, one essentially anti-CEI, the other entirely compatible with CEI. The trouble for DeRose and his followers is that the alternative explanation of the cases is arguably preferable. To see this, notice first that the alternative need only appeal to an independently plausible normative framework in order to explain the relevant cases. Second, DeRose and his followers, will also need to appeal to this framework to explain some cases. The trade-off case mentioned earlier is one case in point, Williamson's *Train* is another. In both cases, the speaker's assertion is clearly (all-things-considered) permissible and yet equally clearly violates KRA. The only explanation for this on the market is in terms of the normative framework (more specifically, in terms of overriding). This means that those who want to run DeRose's argument from KRA against CEI, will have to offer different explanations for cases like *Train* and our trade-off case (in terms of the normative framework) on the one hand, the cases like *Aspirin Low* and *High* (in terms of their non-CEI semantics of knowledge attributions) on the other.

8.3 DeRose's Argument Turned on Its Head

The fact that DeRose's argument from KRA fails is of course entirely compatible with the truth of EC. What we will do in the remainder of this section is to argue that DeRose's argument can be turned on its head. In other words, we will mount a case that KRA is actually in tension with EC.

To see how this works, it will be useful to remind ourselves what the difference EC and EI amounts to. In a nutshell, the idea is that according to EI, the truth conditions of a knowledge ascription do not vary with attributor context. Instead they depend only on facts about (i) the subject's epistemic as well as (ii) doxastic position towards the target proposition and (iii) her epistemic environment. (Now, if we opt for IREI, then the truth conditions of knowledge attributions depend, in addition, on (iv) the subject's practical environment. However, since we are not interested in settling the in-house dispute between classical and interest-relative versions of invariantism here, we will set this issue aside and work with a distinctively classical version of invariantism.)

In contrast, while EC grants that the truth conditions of knowledge ascriptions do depend on (i), (ii) and (iii), EC denies that it depends only on (i), (ii) and (iii). Instead, according to EC, they also depend on facts about the context of the ascriber of knowledge.

8.3.1 Bank Cases

While DeRose's argument from KRA has been thought to be one important argument for EC, there is another argument for EC that is arguably even more influential than the argument from KRA. In fact, if there is such a thing as the master argument for EC, this is it. The centrepieces of this argument for EC are pairs of cases like the following:

> *Bank Low.* It's Friday and X, Y and Z are on their way home from a strenuous business trip that lasted the entire working week. Z is sitting in the back of the car and is listening to music on her iPod. X and Y would like

---

It is easy to see, however, that this immediately puts them at a disadvantage vis-à-vis those who explain all of these cases in terms of the normative framework. After all, their account will be both more uniform – all cases afford the same explanation – and more parsimonious – less theoretical machinery is invoked to account for these cases. A closer look thus suggest that, far from playing in the hands of DeRose and his followers, if anything, cases like *Aspirin Low* and *High* contribute to undermining an important motivation for alternatives to CEI.

to deposit their paycheques at the bank on the way home. Whether they do so is of little importance: they still have enough money in the bank and no impending bills. As it turns out the bank is extremely busy and so X and Y consider postponing their project until the next day. Naturally, they wonder whether the bank will be open then. X says: 'Z passes by the bank every Saturday. Let's ask her.' And Y responds: 'Yes, let's. She knows whether the bank will be open tomorrow.'

Bank High. It's Friday and X, Y and Z are on their way home from a strenuous business trip that lasted the entire working week. Z is sitting in the back of the car and is listening to music on her iPod. X and Y would like to deposit their paycheques at the bank on the way home. Whether they do so is of utmost importance: they both have very little money left in their accounts and both of their accounts are due to be debited with a substantive sum on Monday. As it turns out the bank is extremely busy and so X and Y consider postponing their project until the next day. Naturally, they wonder whether the bank will be open then. X says: 'Z passes by the bank every Saturday. Let's ask her.' However, as Y points out: 'I don't know. Banks sometimes change their opening hours. I remember that a friend of mine once couldn't deposit a cheque because his bank had changed its Saturday hours.' to which X replies: 'I guess you're right. Let's not ask Z. She doesn't know whether the bank will be open tomorrow either.'[5]

The most important thing to note about these cases is that, at least when considered separately, the attribution of knowledge in *Bank Low* as well as the denial of knowledge in *Bank High* are natural and appropriate. Let's call this 'the linguistic data'.

In order to mount a case against CEI, its critics appeal to the so-called the methodology of the straightforward (MS), which DeRose characterises in the following passages:

> [The] 'methodology of the straightforward', as we may call it, takes very seriously the simple positive and negative claims speakers make utilizing the piece of language being studied, and puts a very high priority on making those natural and appropriate straightforward uses come out true, at least

---

[5] Notice that our versions of the cases feature attributions of knowledge *whether p*. This should be harmless, however, for two reasons: first, knowledge-whether is very plausibly constituted by knowledge-that: to know whether *p* is to know that *p* in case *p* is true and to know that not-*p* in case *p* is false (and not-*p* true). Second, the cases could, given a generous investment of space, be converted into cases of knowledge-that attributions. For a recipe how to do this see DeRose (2009).

> when that use is not based on some false belief the speaker has about some underlying matter of fact. (DeRose 2009, 153)

> Since the speaker is using the term seriously and properly, and this use isn't based on any false beliefs the speaker has about underlying matters of fact relevant to whether the subject knows, this is a use I think a theory about the meaning of 'know(s)' should try to make come out true, and it's a strike against a theory if it fails to do so. (DeRose 2009, 18)

In conjunction with MS, the linguistic data provided by the above 'bank cases' exert serious pressure on CEI. To see this, note first that Z's doxastic and epistemic position as well as his epistemic environment are exactly the same in both cases.[6] That is to say, in both cases she believes, say, that the bank will be open tomorrow based on the inductive evidence provided by having invariably found the bank to be open on Saturdays in the past. Moreover, there have actually not been any changes in opening hours in this bank or others and no other funny business is going on. As a result, CEI countenances exactly two options: either the attribution of knowledge comes out true in both cases or else the denial does. In this way, it comes to light that CEI simply doesn't have the resources to make both X's attribution of knowledge in *Bank Low* and his denial of knowledge in *Bank High* come out true. Given MS, invariantism doesn't seem to be able to give the right kind of explanation of cases like the above Bank Cases.

Unlike CEI, EC does have the resources to give the right kind of explanation of the Bank Cases. This is because EC allows for the truth conditions of knowledge ascriptions to depend on facts about attributor context. This gives EC the additional flexibility that is needed to secure both the attribution of knowledge in *Bank Low* and the denial of knowledge in *Bank High* come out true, at least in principle. To see this, note that there are differences in the attributor contexts. In *Bank Low*, not much hinges on whether the target proposition is true and no error possibilities are explicitly considered. In contrast, the truth of the target proposition is of vital importance in *Bank High* and the possibility that the bank might have changed its Saturday opening hours since last week is on the table. And it might just be that champions of EC can argue that these differences in attributor context induce a difference in the truth conditions

---

[6] Since *Bank Low* and *High* are third person cases, the subject's practical environment is also the same. As a result, the argument also serves to exert pressure on interest-relative versions of invariantism.

for the relevant knowledge ascriptions such that the attribution in *Bank Low* and the denial in *Bank High* both come out true. If so, then EC will make exactly the right predictions about the bank cases: the attribution of knowledge in *Bank Low* is true as is the denial in *Bank High*.

While this leaves open the question as to whether champions of EC can flesh out the view such that it does actually deliver these verdicts, for present purposes we will simply grant them that they can. In fact, we will grant them that they can fully respect MS. That is to say, we will grant them that, in all cases in which MS enjoins us to think that a certain knowledge ascription is true, EC will make this knowledge ascription true.

8.3.2 Further Linguistic Data

Let's assume that these linguistic data do provide evidence that EC is the true theory of the meaning of 'know'. What we want to argue next is that there is a tension between EC and KRA. To be more precise, if the argument is successful and EC is true as a result, then either KRA does not hold or at any rate, KRA is not a good norm of assertion.

To get there, we'd first like to look at the following pair of cases:

> *Zolex Low.* A and B are wondering whether it is already 9:30. They need to catch the 10 o'clock train to London and, if it is indeed 9:30 or later, they should get going in order to make it to the station on time. While they have a preference for taking the 10 o'clock train, not much hinges on whether they do so. They have open tickets, no important appointments and there is another train just half an hour later. B sees S, who is standing nearby, and notices that he is just looking at his watch. C says, 'Let's ask S, he is just looking at his watch.' and B agrees, 'Yes, let's. He knows whether it's past 9:30.'

> *Zolex High.* A and B are wondering whether it's already 9:30. They need to catch the 10 o'clock train to London and, if it is indeed 9:30 or later, they should get going in order to make it to the station on time. It is of utmost importance that they don't miss their train. Their tickets are valid only for the 10 o'clock train, they have no money to buy a new one and, on top of all that, they will miss an important business meeting if they miss their train. B sees S, who is standing nearby, and notices that he is just looking at his watch. B says, 'Let's ask S. She is just looking at her watch.' However, as A points out, 'I don't know. It's a Zolex watch and those sometimes run late. I remember that a friend of mine once missed a flight because his Zolex watch was running late.' They both agree that S doesn't know whether it's past 9:30.

As a first observation note that *Zolex Low* and *Zolex High* are exactly analogous to the Bank Cases. In fact, they constitute yet another instance of a range of cases (henceforth also *contextualist cases*) that, in conjunction with MS, serve to motivate EC. Unsurprisingly, they don't serve to show that EC is in tension with KRA. The reason we are bringing them up is that *Zolex High* does do so, at least in conjunction with the following cases:

> *Zongines Low.* A and B are wondering whether it is already 9:30. They need to catch the 10 o'clock train to London and, if it is indeed 9:30 or later, they should get going in order to make it to the station on time. While they have a preference for taking the 10 o'clock train, not much hinges on whether they do so. They have open tickets, no important appointments and there is another train just half an hour later. B sees S, who is standing nearby, and notices that he is just looking at his watch. C says, 'Let's ask S, he is just looking at his watch.' and B agrees, 'Yes, let's. He knows whether it's past 9:30.'
>
> *Zongines High.* A and B are wondering whether it's already 9:30. They need to catch the 10 o'clock train to London and, if it is indeed 9:30 or later, they should get going in order to make it to the station on time. It is of utmost importance that they don't miss their train. Their tickets are valid only for the 10 o'clock train, they have no money to buy a new one and, on top of all that, they will miss an important business meeting if they miss their train. B sees S, who is standing nearby, and notices that he is just looking at his watch. B says, 'Let's ask S. She is just looking at her watch, which is a Zongines and those are among top three most reliable types of watches there are. She knows whether it's already past 9:30.' A agrees.

I'd like to set *Zongines Low* aside for the time being. What I'd like to focus on instead is *Zolex High* and *Zongines High*. Note that *Zolex High* features a denial of knowledge and *Zongines High* an attribution of knowledge. (In what follows, we will also refer to these two cases as 'the watch cases'.) Notice that both are serious as well as natural and appropriate. Moreover, neither is based on a false belief about an underlying matter of fact, or so we may assume. The denial of knowledge in *Zolex High* is based on A's belief that Zolex watches sometimes run late and that he has a friend who once missed a flight because his Zolex was running late. And, of course, we may assume that both of these beliefs are true. In contrast, the attribution of knowledge in *Zongines High* is based on B's belief that Zongines watches are among the top three most reliable types of watch there are. Again, we may assume that this belief is true. By MS, a theory of the meaning of 'knows' should try to make both the denial of knowledge in *Zolex High* and the attribution of knowledge in *Zongines High* come out true. Since we are assuming that EC is true and fully respects MS, we get the result that the denial of knowledge in *Zolex High* and the attribution in *Zongines High* are both true.

At this point it is time to return to KRA. Recall that, according to KRA, it epistemically permissible for one to assert that p if and only if one knows that p. Given KRA, we get the result that it is epistemically permissible for S to assert that it's past 9:30, say, in *Zongines High* but not in *Zolex High*. And while it may be thought that this is perfectly fine, on reflection, there is reason to think that this is a bizarre consequence of the view. To see why, note that it is compatible with everything that has been stated in the watch cases (i) that Zolex watches are also among the top three most reliable types of watch there are, ahead of Zongines watches, and (ii) that the only difference between the two cases is that in *Zolex High* a Zolex watch is used while in *Zongines High* it's a Zongines. So let's assume that this is how things stand. In that case, however, it seems utterly bizarre to think that is epistemically permissible for S to assert that it is past 9:30, say, in *Zongines High* but not in *Zolex High*. After all, the only difference between the two cases is that the epistemic instrument that ultimately grounds the assertion is *more reliable* in *Zolex High* than in *Zongines High*. To operate a norm of assertion such that the mere increase in reliability of the epistemic instrument that ultimately grounds an assertion translates into a switch in epistemic permissibility of the assertion from permissible to impermissible simply makes no normative sense – especially not once we are clear that the rationale for the norm is that to ensure that the function of assertion is fulfilled reliably. If this isn't immediately obvious, consider the following non-epistemic analogue featuring two cases of you driving a vehicle and using a speedometer to regulate your speed of driving. Suppose the only difference between the two cases is that in one the make of your speedometer is more reliable than in the other. To operate a norm for vehicle fitness that permits driving your vehicle in the case in which you are using less reliable speedometer but not in the case in which you are using the more reliable one makes no normative sense – again, especially not once we are clear that the rationale for this norm is to ensure that the function of the vehicle, safe transportation, is fulfilled reliably. Any norm for vehicle fitness that has this consequence is not a good such norm. Likewise, any norm of assertion that has the consequence that it's epistemically permissible for S to assert that it's past 9:30 in *Zongines High* but not in *Zolex High* is not a good epistemic norm of assertion. Since, in conjunction with EC, KRA has exactly this consequence, in the hands of EC, KRA turns out not to be a good epistemic norm of assertion. And, in this way, there is a tension between EC and KRA.

It may also be worth noting that there are alternative norms of assertion that will allow champions of EC to avoid this problematic result. Consider, for instance, an epistemic norm of assertion according to which it is epistemically permissible for one to assert that p if and only if one is in a sufficiently strong epistemic position towards p. Now, all else equal, increases in the reliability of the instrument in acquiring one's belief that p translate into increases in the strength of one's epistemic position towards p. This means that S is in a stronger epistemic position towards the proposition that it is past 9:30 in *Zolex High* than in *Zongines High*. After all, Zolex watches are more reliable than Zongines watches. Moreover, everything else is equal between the two cases. This is because the only difference is in the watch used. The alternative norm of assertion under consideration will avoid the bizarre consequence that KRA has given EC. On this norm, it simply cannot be that S's assertion in *Zongines High* is epistemically permissible, while S's assertion in *Zolex High* isn't. If the assertion in *Zongines High* is epistemically permissible, S must be in a sufficiently strong epistemic position towards the proposition he asserts. But as we just saw, S is in a stronger epistemic position towards this proposition in *Zolex High*. This means that S makes the threshold for permissible assertion here also. The bizarre consequence of combining EC with KRA is avoided.

Alternatively, abandoning EC in favour of CEI will also enable champions of KRA to avoid the problem. To see this, recall that, according to CEI, whether one knows depends only on facts about (i) the subject's epistemic as well as (ii) doxastic position towards the target proposition and (iii) the subject's epistemic environment. Now, the only difference between *Zongines High* and *Zolex High* that may be relevant to whether S knows the target proposition is a difference in S's epistemic position towards it. More specifically, it is stronger in *Zolex High* than in *Zongines High*. Of course, this means that if S's epistemic position towards the target proposition is strong enough for S to know it in *Zongines High*, then it must also be strong enough for S to know it in *Zolex High*. And, as a result, it simply couldn't be that KRA renders it epistemically permissible for S to assert the target proposition in *Zongines High* but not in *Zolex High*.

What comes to light, then, is that there is tension between EC and KRA. In the hands of EC, KRA turns out not to be a good epistemic norm of assertion. Moreover, there is reason to think that this tension holds specifically between EC and KRA. After all, we just saw that the tension can be avoided for champions of both EC and KRA. The former can opt for a different norm of assertion, the latter can endorse EI instead. In this way, DeRose's argument that KRA demands EC is turned on its head. In fact, KRA demands not-EC, at least provided that KRA is a norm in good standing.

8.3.3 Objections and Replies

Isn't this too fast? Even if the argument works in the way envisaged, it targets only some versions of KRA that champions of EC might adopt, including the following:

> ATTRIBUTOR KRA (AKRA). It is permissible for S to assert that p if and only if S knows that p according to the standards operative in the context of the *attributor*. (DeRose 2009, 99)

However, champions of EC might opt for different versions of KRA. And, in fact, DeRose goes for the following instead of AKRA:

SPEAKER KRA (SKRA). It is permissible for S to assert that p if and only if S know that p according to the standards operative in the context of the *speaker*. (DeRose 2009, 99)

It might seem as though, even if the above argument succeeds in establishing a tension between EC and AKRA, it does not do so for EC and SKRA. After all, it would seem that, since all else is equal between *Zolex High* and *Zongines High*, S is in the same context in both cases. But given that they are, it is hard to see how it could be that S knows by the standards operative in her context in *Zongines High* but not in *Zolex High*. After all, she is in a stronger epistemic position towards the target proposition in *Zolex High*. And it's quite plausible that, as a result, for any two cases in which she is in the same context, if the only difference between the two cases is that she is in a stronger epistemic position towards the target proposition in former case than in the latter, if she knows in the latter, then she also knows in the former. And this will of course allow champions of EC to avoid the troublesome result. Since SKRA is not only a viable way of implementing KRA within an EC framework, but in fact the preferred one, it may now look as though the argument is of comparatively little consequence.

By way of response note that even if S is indeed in the same context in both watch cases as they are described, it is easy to imagine variations of these cases in which S is in different contexts. Suppose, for instance, that S is in the same boat with A and B in the sense that, she too, has a ticket for the 10 o'clock train, no money to buy a new one and needs to make the relevant business meeting. Perhaps, in much the same way as in the original *Bank Low* and *Bank High* cases, A and B are discussing the matter separately because S is currently on the phone or went to the bathroom. If the watch cases are described in this way, then S is part of the same context as A and B. In that case, however, EC will predict that, by the standards operative in the context of S, S knows that it's past 9:30 in *Zongines High* but not in *Zolex High*. As a result, even if EC is combined with SKRA, we get the bizarre result that it is permissible for S to assert the target proposition in *Zongines High* but not in *Zolex High*.

DeRose also tables a couple of further ways of implementing KRA within an EC framework. Could one of these ways (or perhaps a completely different one) help champions of EC to avoid this problem? In what follows, we will argue that the answer to this question is no. It may be worth noting, however, that in order to do so we will not look at a range of proposals and provide reason for thinking that they don't work. Rather, we argue that champions of EC ought to implement KRA in a particular way and that that way won't do the trick for them.

To get the argument off the ground, we'll need to make a brief digression. Cases that focus on what distant subjects ought to do or say in light of what they know seem to cause trouble for EC. The reason for this is that in such cases it should be the context of the subject that sets the standards for knowledge, not the context of the attributor. And that doesn't seem to fit will with EC according to which, on the face of it, it is always the attributor's context that sets the standards for knowledge.

In response, DeRose writes:

> First, there is nothing in contextualism to prevent a speaker's context from selecting epistemic standards appropriate to the practical situation of the subject being talked about, even when the subject being discussed is no party to the speaker's conversation – which is good, because speakers often do select such standards when their conversational purposes call for it! And second, not only does contextualism allow for the possibility that the speakers' context will select standards appropriate to the practical situation of the subject, but, in the relevant cases, it would actually lead us to expect that the speakers' context will select such standards, because the speakers'

own conversational purposes call for such subject-appropriate standards in the cases in question. (DeRose 2009, 240)

To begin with, we agree that this is exactly what a champion of EC should say in response to this worry. EC has more flexibility than those pressing the problematic cases may have thought. Although the context of the attributor do ultimately fixes which standards are operative in a given context, these standards don't always have to coincide with the standards that would be relevant to the practical situation of the attributor. Rather, the context of the attributor can select the standards of the subject as the one's operative in the context. What's more, we may expect this to happen when what's of interest at the attributor's context is the subject's standards.

Crucially, however, the motivations for this response seem to us to carry over to the issue of how to implement KRA within an EC framework. That is to say, EC can allow that the standards for permissible assertion operative in a given context are standards for knowledge operative in the speaker context, as SKRA would have. However, EC can also allow that the standards for permissible assertion operative in a given context are the standards for knowledge operative in the attributor context, as AKRA would have it. What's more, we may expect attributor context to select which standards are operative in accordance with the conversational purposes of at issue in the attributor context. If so, the way to implement KRA within an EC framework is as follows:

> OPEN KRA (OKRA).   It is permissible for S to assert that p if and only if S knows that p according to whatever standards (subject, attributor, etc.) have been selected by the context of the attributor.   (DeRose 2009, 99)

Some of the problem cases that DeRose's response was meant to address will serve to show that sometimes it is the subject's standards that will be selected as relevant to permissible assertion. This is unsurprising given that DeRose endorses SKRA. What's more interesting is that there are cases in which it is the attributor's standards that are selected as so relevant. In fact, the original watch cases are relevant examples. To make this point come out even more clearly, just imagine variations of the original watch cases in which A and B overhear S assert that it is 9.20, say. In the case in which S has a Zolex, A points out that Zolex watches are sometimes late, and so forth and A and B agree that S doesn't know. In the case in which S has a Zongines, B points out that Zongines are among the three most reliable types of watch and the like, and A and B agree that S does know. There can be no question here that the standards of knowledge relevant to permissible assertion here are the standards of the attributors. What A and B are doing when they say that S doesn't know is to criticise S's assertion on the grounds that S lacks knowledge. Moreover, in their context, this criticism is perfectly legitimate. But that couldn't be the case if the standards for permissible assertion were the standards for knowledge at issue in S's context. After all, S may very well know by the standards operative in her context. To make sense of the idea that in pointing out that S lacks knowledge, A and B are criticising S's assertion and, in their context, legitimately so, it needs to be the case that the standards for permissible assertion are the standards for knowledge at issue in A and B's context. Since there is reason to believe that the standards for permissible assertion will in some cases coincide with the standards for knowledge operative in the speaker's context and in others with the standards for knowledge operative in the attributor's context, there is reason to believe that the way to implement KRA within an EC framework is one according to which attributor context call the shots but may then select the standards of knowledge operative in either the subject's context or in the attributors'. In this way, there is reason to think that we will want the same kind of flexibility DeRose exploited in order to deal with other problem cases for EC. And that means that OKRA is the way forward for champions of EC. But, of course, if OKRA is indeed what supporters of EC should go for, then the above problem is bound to arise. In fact, all variations of the watches cases we have seen will arguably serve to generate it.

8.4 Conclusion

In this chapter, we have inquired into whether champions of KRA have to reject the default view in the semantics of knowledge attributions, CEI, in favour of EC. We have taken a close look at DeRose's famous argument to this effect. Fortunately, we have seen that the argument doesn't go through. As a result, the potentially troublesome consequence of KRA can be avoided. In addition, once we are clear that epistemic norms aren't just norms with epistemic content and once a more plausible proposal for individuating types of norm, i.e. by the associated value, is in place, an attractive alternative account of the kind of case that DeRose's argument relies on can be given.

Finally, we have shown that DeRose's argument can be turned on its head. There is good reason to think that EC is actually in tension with KRA, at least provided that the argument from cases like the bank cases and MS is what motivates EC. In particular, we argued that, in the hands of EC, KRA will not be a good norm of assertion. Since KRA is indeed a good norm of assertion, we have an argument from KRA against EC.

The Value of Knowledge

We care a lot about knowledge. As a society, we invest a lot of time and energy in the development of institutions whose aim is to accumulate or distribute knowledge. Universities, schools, libraries, and the internet are among the most prominent of these. On an individual level, we send our children to school and encourage them to go to university so that they can acquire knowledge about a wide range of topics. Some of us go to considerable financial lengths in order to make this possible. Finally, in philosophy, the study of knowledge has historically received a great deal of attention. A lot of effort has been made to get clear on what exactly is involved in knowing.

From a philosophical point of view, the fact that we seem to care so much about knowledge gives rise to a number of interesting questions: First, is our concern with knowledge warranted? In other words, does knowledge have value that is special at least in the sense that it would warrant this concern? Second, in what respect(s) exactly is knowledge valuable? These two questions are closely related. If knowledge does have the kind of value that would warrant our concern with it, then we may expect there to be a story about the specific respect(s) in which knowledge is valuable. The first question thus naturally gives rise to the second. On the other hand, an answer to the second question will allow us to make progress towards answering the first question. After all, if we have an account of the respect(s) in which knowledge is valuable, we will be better positioned to assess whether the value that attaches to knowledge warrants our concern with it.

The aim of this appendix is to provide novel answers to both of these questions. More specifically, we will try to develop a novel way in which knowledge is valuable, thereby answering the second question. In addition, we will argue that, as a result, the first question also receives a positive answer: the novel way in which knowledge is valuable serves to vindicate our concern with it.

A.1   The Value Problem: Two Challenges

What does it take to provide a satisfactory answer to the question whether knowledge has value that is special enough to warrant our concern with it? There are a number of proposed answers in the literature. They differ from one another in the strength of the demands imposed.

Let's begin with what is widely regarded as the most lenient proposal, which dates back as far as Plato's Meno. To begin with, notice that it is nearly universally accepted that knowledge requires true belief. Now suppose it turns out that knowledge is in no respect more valuable than true belief that isn't knowledge, i.e. mere true belief. In that case, it would seem wrong to care about knowledge rather than mere true belief. Our special concern with knowledge would seem misplaced.

This motivates a first constraint on satisfactory accounts of the value of knowledge:

> [C1] Any satisfactory account of the value of knowledge must explain why knowledge is in some respect more valuable than mere true belief.

Some have claimed that simply meeting C1 won't be enough to give a satisfactory account of the value of knowledge. Jonathan Kvanvig, for one, argues that more is needed: Suppose knowledge consists of a set of constituents. Suppose, next, it turns out that knowledge is in no respect more valuable than some proper subset of its constituents. In that case, it would be wrong to care specifically about knowledge rather than the proper subset of equally valuable constituents. Our special concern with knowledge would still seem misplaced. In view of these considerations, Kvanvig favours the following constraint:

> [C2] Any satisfactory account of the value of knowledge must explain why knowledge is in some respect more valuable than any proper subset of its constituents. (Kvanvig 2003, xii–xiii)

Furthermore, it has been widely assumed that the task of explaining the value of knowledge consists in showing that individual items of knowledge are more valuable than the corresponding individual beliefs that fall short of knowledge (Riggs 2009, 334).

Roughly, the idea here is that in order to meet C2 we need to show that it is better for one to know that p than to have a belief that p that falls short of knowledge, for all propositions p. While the challenge Riggs unpacks in the above quote is of course C2, it is not hard to see that C1 can be given the same treatment: for all propositions p, knowledge that p must be more valuable than mere true belief that p. Key to this way of fleshing out the challenges is that they require showing that every item of knowledge is more valuable than the corresponding belief that falls short of knowledge. (In what follows, we will refer to this requirement as 'Riggs's requirement'.)

Let's get one thing out of the way: Everything we will say in what follows is compatible with the idea that that knowledge is valuable in a way that satisfies Riggs's requirement. By way of explanation, consider first the following distinction between two types of value: final and instrumental. For something to be finally valuable is for it to be valuable for its own sake. For instance, it is widely acknowledged that happiness is finally valuable. In contrast, for something to have instrumental value is for it have value as a means to an end. For instance, it is widely acknowledged that money is instrumentally valuable, at least in the kinds of society we live in: it allows its possessors to buy things that enable them to achieve a certain level of comfort in life.

The reason everything we say is compatible with the idea that knowledge is valuable in a way that complies with Riggs's requirement is that it is compatible with all our claims that knowledge but not true belief that falls short of knowledge is finally valuable. If so, every item of knowledge is more valuable (and indeed enjoys a different kind of value) than the corresponding true belief that isn't knowledge. That said, for the purposes of this section, we'd like to bracket responses to the challenges in terms of the final value of knowledge and focus on responses in terms of instrumental value instead.[1]

Curiously, once we are clear that we are aiming for this kind of response, the prospects of success look somewhat dim. The reason for this is that, when focusing solely on instrumental value, some items of knowledge appear to be of no value whatsoever. (Let's call items of knowledge that have no instrumental value whatsoever items of 'useless knowledge'.) Knowing the exact number of grains of sand in the jar you brought back from last year's summer holiday is but one popular example (e.g. Sosa 2003). If some items of knowledge are useless, however, they are no more valuable than the corresponding beliefs that fall short of knowledge, which are useless as well. A satisfactory response to C1 and C2 appears no longer available.

---

[1] But see Simion and Kelp (2016) for discussion of accounts of the value of knowledge in terms of final value and Kelp (2021) for an account of final value of knowledge according to which knowledge enjoys final epistemic value because it is the aim of inquiry.

On the other hand, recall that C1 and C2 are to be motivated by our concern with knowledge. That is to say, we wanted an account of the value of knowledge that explains our concern with knowledge. If so, however, it is far less evident that a satisfactory account of the value of knowledge must satisfy Riggs's requirement. After all, our concern with knowledge does not appear to extend to all items of knowledge. In particular, we seem to have little concern for items of useless knowledge – and, we want to add, rightly so. If so, examples of useless knowledge are best understood as suggesting that a satisfactory account of the value of knowledge need not satisfy Riggs's requirement.

Once we abandon Riggs's requirement, we might attempt to replace it by a weaker requirement. Rather than venturing to show that each item of knowledge is more valuable than the corresponding mere true belief, we might think that it will do to show that enough items of knowledge are more valuable than the corresponding beliefs that aren't knowledge. We may try to rise to this challenge in at least two ways. First, we may try to explain the value of knowledge in terms of a property (or properties) of individual items of knowledge. While we do not mean to deny that this is a promising line to pursue, in what follows we'd like to explore a different approach, which starts from the thesis that knowledge is a commodity and aims to explain the special value of knowledge in terms of a property of the commodity.

A.2 Commodity Value

'Knowledge' is a mass term, like 'water,' and a kind of commodity – something one can have more or less of. Now suppose that it can be shown that the commodity of knowledge has special value and that an account of the value of the commodity can be given that satisfies C1 and C2. There is reason to believe that this will also be sufficient to adequately meet these challenges. After all, an account of the value of the commodity would make good sense of our concern with knowledge. What's more, if we did succeed in providing an account of the value of the commodity of knowledge we would still stand as a good chance as any of vindicating the special focus on knowledge in the history of epistemology.

For that reason, it seems that everything is to be gained and nothing to be lost by exploring the prospects for an account of the value of the commodity of knowledge.

Before moving on to the value of the commodity of knowledge, we'd like to take a look at the value of another central commodity in our lives, to wit, water. Water is of course valuable in many respects. For the purposes of this section, we'd like focus on one valuable quality of water, its power to quench our thirst. Suppose liquid hydrogen were just as well suited to quench our thirst as is water. The constituents of liquid hydrogen, H_2, are a proper subset of the constituents of water, H_2O (so that liquid hydrogen stands to water as, for instance, justified true belief stands to knowledge.) Now suppose you have before you two glasses, one containing water and the other liquid hydrogen. It is plausible that the glass with water is no more valuable than the glass with liquid hydrogen, at least not with respect to its power to quench your thirst. After all, ex hypothesi, liquid hydrogen is as well suited to do the job as water is. Does that mean that water, the commodity, couldn't have special value, value that warrants our concern with water? No. To see this, suppose (as happens to be the case) that liquid hydrogen is extremely rare and can exist only in very special environments. Suppose that, at the same time, water is easily available in a wide range of places and to a wide range of people. In that case water is plausibly valuable to us in a way that would warrant our concern with it. What makes water thus valuable is not just the fact that it has the power to quench our thirst. After all, we are supposing that water shares this property with liquid hydrogen. It is a combination of the fact that it has this property and the fact that it is so widely and easily available. To put a snappy label to it, water is of special value because it is our way of quenching our thirst.

Now, we want to suggest that the situation is in essence the same with knowledge on the one hand and true belief that falls short of knowledge on the other. One valuable property of knowledge is that it is a way of correctly representing the world around us. It is undeniable that the same holds for true belief that falls short of knowledge. Now compare two agents, A and B, such that A knows that p and B truly believes but doesn't know that p. It is very plausible that A's belief that p is no more valuable than B's, at least not with respect to its correctly representing the world – just as it is very plausible, in the imagined case above, that the glass of water is no more valuable with respect to thirst-quenching than the glass of liquid hydrogen. Arguably, however, just as in the case of water and liquid hydrogen, this result is compatible with knowledge being valuable in a way that would warrant our concern with it. In fact, the very same properties that account for the special value of water in the imagined case account for the corresponding special value of knowledge: in a wide range of areas, knowledge is widely and readily available.

To see this, consider first perceptual beliefs about middle-sized dry goods. On any non-sceptical account of knowledge, given formation by suitable processes (alternatively: on suitable grounds) in sufficiently hospitable epistemic environments, these beliefs will qualify as knowledge. For instance, my belief that there is a computer on the desk before me qualifies as knowledge: it is produced by a highly reliable ability to recognise tables in an epistemically hospitable environment. Now the crucial point is that, for beliefs in this range, formation by suitable processes in hospitable environments is the norm; formation of beliefs by unsuitable process, or in inhospitable environments is the exception. If this isn't immediately clear, consider again my belief that there is a computer on the desk before me and ask yourself what would have to be the case for my belief to remain true but fall short of knowledge. Those with some training in epistemology will find it easy to answer this question: I mistake a hologram for a computer, whilst unbeknownst to me there is a computer somewhere else on the desk, I acquire my belief by a highly unreliable process such as a coin-toss, and the like. While any of this might come to pass, it is undeniable that, as a matter of fact, it only rarely does. For that reason, cases of knowledge are the norm and cases of true belief that fall short of knowledge are the exception. Perceptual beliefs about middle-sized dry goods are not the only cases in point. Consider testimonial belief about propositions of crucial practical importance in our lives: propositions about bills that need to be paid, the nature of the sickness of your child and the medication that will cure it, what's available at the local restaurant, and the like. Or consider inferentially supported beliefs that exploit a variety of natural and social regularities: that my car is still parked outside the Department, that London is still the capital of the United Kingdom, and the like. Here too, when beliefs in these ranges are formed by suitable processes in sufficiently hospitable epistemic environments, they will qualify as knowledge. Here too, cases of knowledge are norm and cases of true belief that fall short of knowledge are the exception.

These considerations suggest that, in wide range of cases, knowledge is widely and readily available. All we have to do to acquire knowledge is open our eyes, listen to what other people tell us, attend to our feelings, and so forth. In comparison, in those areas true belief that falls short of knowledge is a rare commodity that exists only in very special environments.

In parallel with the case of water, then, what makes knowledge especially valuable is not just the fact that it involves a correct representation of the world. It is the fact that it has this property in combination with the fact that, in a wide range of areas, it is so widely and easily available. Just as water is of special value because it is our way of quenching our thirst, knowledge is of special value because, in a wide range of areas, it is our way of correctly representing the world.

One could point out that we tend to attach higher value to scarce commodities than to readily available ones. However, it is not market value that is at stake here; it is instrumental value related to our epistemic goals. Analogously, while the market value of truffles is higher than that of bread, it is undeniable that, due to its ready availability, bread is more instrumentally valuable for our survival.

Before moving on, we'd briefly like to say a few words about what exactly the proposed account of the special value of the commodity of knowledge amounts to. To this end, we'd like to return once more to the parallel account of the special value of the commodity of water. In particular, we'd like to point out that, on the present account, the surplus value of the commodity of water over the commodity of liquid hydrogen in the society under consideration is contingent and agent-relative. To see that it is contingent, note that there may be other possible worlds at which liquid hydrogen exists in abundance and water is rare. At those worlds, liquid hydrogen may well be more valuable to members of the counterpart of our society than water. It is agent-relative because there may be creatures inhabiting the world of our society for whom liquid hydrogen is more valuable than water, despite being so rare. One example are creatures who are severely allergic to any liquids containing oxygen.

And, of course, the same holds, mutatis mutandis, for the value of the commodity of knowledge: on the proposed account, the surplus value of knowledge over true belief that falls short of knowledge is contingent and agent-relative.

One worry one might have is that there is a crucial disanalogy between the case of water and the case of knowledge. In particular, one might think that, in the case of water, the following counterfactual is true: 'If there hadn't been any water, we wouldn't have been able to quench our thirst, at least not on a global scale.' After all, there wouldn't have been enough liquid hydrogen around to do the trick. In contrast, it might be thought that the parallel counterfactual for knowledge is not true: 'If there hadn't been any knowledge, we wouldn't have been able to correctly represent the world, at least not on a global scale.' After all, there would still have been enough true beliefs around to do the trick. In this respect, then, knowledge and water are disanalogous. What's more, the disanalogy is important. The truth of the counterfactual is just what makes it plausible that, in the thought experiment, water is of special value in the first place. Given that the parallel counterfactual about knowledge isn't true, the proposed account of the value of knowledge fails.

We want to make three points by way of response. First, the closest worlds at which there isn't any knowledge (or at least not enough to satisfy our needs for correct representation on a global scale) are very far off. Knowledge abounds, whilst true belief that isn't knowledge is rare not only at the actual world but a good way out into modal space, well past the boundary even of nearby worlds. That is to say that knowledge is very robustly our way of correctly representing the world. Given that this is so, it is less than clear that, even if the counterfactual is indeed false, this compromises the value of knowledge that, according to our proposal, attaches to knowledge at the actual world.

Second, we are somewhat suspicious of the idea that if there hadn't been any knowledge, there still would have been plenty of true beliefs around, enough to satisfy our need of correctly representing the world on a global scale. The reason for this is that it is not clear to us that the following counterfactual isn't true instead: if there hadn't been any knowledge, there wouldn't have been any beliefs around. Very roughly, the thought here is (i) that many of our beliefs are formed by processes that were selected for reliably producing true beliefs and (ii) that had these processes not been reliable enough to produce knowledge, we would not have been reliable enough in finding food, avoiding predators and other dangers etc. to make it as a species.

Third, suppose we stipulate that, at the world of our thought experiment, water abounds and liquid hydrogen is rare (S1) and that had water been rare, liquid hydrogen would have abounded (S2) with the result that the allegedly troublesome counterfactual is false for water as well. In that case, water is still of special value at the world of the thought experiment. After all, it is the only resource present at that world suited to quench our thirst on a global scale. At best, the counterfactual shows that something else might have been of special value instead of water (and would have been had water not been of special value). Note, however, that this is entirely unproblematic on the current account as the value of water is acknowledged to be contingent. Crucially, the case is exactly the same for knowledge and true belief that falls short of knowledge at the actual world. Although knowledge entails true belief and, in consequence, true belief abounds at the actual world, true belief that falls short of knowledge is not entailed by knowledge – in fact, it excludes knowledge. Even though knowledge and true belief are abundant at the actual world, true belief that isn't knowledge is rare. This gives us the analogue of S1. The counterfactual pressed by the objector is the analogue of S2, i.e. that if knowledge had been rare, true belief that isn't knowledge would have abounded. What we can now see is that even if our objector is right and the counterfactual is true, our proposed account of the value of knowledge will still get off the ground. Just as in the case of water the truth of S2 does not impugn the special value of water at the world of the thought experiment, the truth of the parallel counterfactual does nothing to impugn the special value of knowledge at the actual world. After all, just as in the case of water, knowledge is the only resource present at the actual world suited for correctly representing the world on a global scale.

Another worry one might have is that the proposed account of the special value of knowledge is too thin. Recall that the value of knowledge is both contingent and agent-relative. If that's really all there is to the value of knowledge, do we genuinely capture the special value we have long believed knowledge to have? Here is our response to this worry. First, it is entirely compatible with the proposed account that there are other ways in which knowledge is valuable. We already mentioned one such alternative, albeit only to put it aside for the purposes of this section, to wit, that knowledge is finally valuable. However, there may be even further ways in which knowledge may be valuable, including alternative ways of being instrumentally valuable. As a result, it is compatible with everything we said that the proposed account does not fully capture the value we believe knowledge to have. In that case, it doesn't matter that our account of the value of knowledge is too thin.

Second, suppose it turns out that our thin way is the only way in which knowledge is valuable over and above true belief that falls short of knowledge. Suppose furthermore that our account does not fully capture the special value we have believed knowledge to have. In that case, we believe that we have to revise our beliefs about how special knowledge is. However, it does not detract from the significance of the account. Even if knowledge turns out to be less special than we thought it to be, it will be of some importance to know that it is in some way better than true belief that falls short of knowledge.

That said, we do believe that the observation we started from is pretty solid: as a society we care about knowledge in the sense that we invest a lot of time and energy in institutions aiming at the accumulation or distribution of knowledge and so on. Even if our account is too thin to capture the special value some (or even all) of us may have believed knowledge to have, it will be of considerable significance whether or not knowledge is valuable in a way that vindicates this concern. Crucially, there is reason to think that our account delivers on this front. To see this, let's return one more time to the case of water. Suppose the society under consideration cares about water in much the same way in which we care about knowledge: it invests a lot of time and energy in institutions investigating its nature, as well as institutions involved with the management of water, its sourcing, distribution, quality control and so on. Suppose it turns out that the only thing that makes water more valuable than liquid hydrogen is that water is a more widely and readily available commodity than liquid hydrogen. Even so, this result will vindicate the society's concern with water. By way of evidence, note that it makes sense for them to continue caring about water in the way they have done: to invest time and energy in institutions investigating its nature and to be concerned with its management. Moreover, it would not make sense to significantly alter the way they have cared for water. In particular, it would not make sense for them to stop caring more for water than for liquid hydrogen, to allocate 50 per cent of their resources to research into the nature and management of liquid hydrogen and so on. In this way, there is reason to believe that the result concerning the value of water vindicates the society's concern with water. And the same holds, mutatis mutandis, for our concern with knowledge.

A.3 The Superiority of Knowledge: A Third Challenge

We outlined two challenges that any satisfactory account of the value of knowledge will have to meet. While these challenges enjoy rather widespread support, some think that there is a further condition of adequacy on accounts of the value of knowledge. In particular, Duncan Pritchard argues that a satisfactory account of the value of knowledge must, in addition, show that knowledge enjoys a different kind of value than true belief that falls short of knowledge. According to Pritchard, then,

> [C3*] Any satisfactory account of the value of knowledge must explain why knowledge is in some respect more valuable than any proper subset of its constituents not just as a matter of degree but as a matter of kind. (Pritchard et al. 2010, 7–8).

On the account developed here, knowledge is valuable because it is our way of correctly representing the world. Note that this will serve to address challenges C1 and C2, as it explains why knowledge is more valuable than mere true belief and more valuable than beliefs that fall short of knowledge. At the same time, it is not hard to see that our account does precious little to address C3*, according to which knowledge must have a different kind of value than beliefs that fall short of knowledge. For that reason, we'd now like to take a closer look at Pritchard's challenge.

First, we'd like to express a worry about the challenge. Suppose it can be shown that knowledge is finally valuable. In that case, it would seem that we have everything we could hope for. By the same token, any plausible challenge for an account of the value of knowledge should at this stage be met. Unfortunately, there is no guarantee that C3* will be met. To see this, suppose that true belief turns out to be finally valuable as well. Given, additionally, that all other kinds of value are equally shared between true belief and knowledge, there will no kind of value that attaches to knowledge that does not attach to true belief that isn't knowledge. C3* will not be met. As a result, there is reason to believe that C3* is too demanding. At the same time, we think that Pritchard may have been on to something when he introduced C3*. To see this, let's take a look at how he motivates it:

> [I]f one regards knowledge as being more valuable than that which falls short of knowledge merely as a matter of degree rather than kind, then this has the effect of putting knowledge on a kind of continuum of value with regard to the epistemic, albeit further up the continuum than anything that falls short of knowledge. The problem with this 'continuum' account of the value of knowledge, however, is that it fails to explain why the long history of epistemological discussion has focused specifically on the stage in this continuum of value that knowledge marks rather than some other stage (such as a stage just before the one marked out by knowledge, or just after). Accordingly, it seems that accounting for our intuitions about the value of knowledge requires us to offer an explanation of why knowledge has not just a greater degree but also a different kind of value than whatever falls short of knowledge. (Pritchard et al. 2010, 7–8)

What becomes clear here is that Pritchard takes it, first, that no account of the value of knowledge on which it is on a continuum with the value of true belief that isn't knowledge can be successful. He also seems to think, second, that the only way in which we can avoid placing knowledge on such a continuum is by showing that knowledge enjoys a different kind of value.

Importantly, the second claim is false. Even if a difference in kind of value is sufficient to get knowledge off the value continuum with true belief that falls short of knowledge, it isn't necessary. There are other ways in which one type of good, A, can be discontinuous in value with another type of good, B. For instance, it may be (i) that any amount of A is better than any amount of B (henceforth also 'Strong Superiority') or (ii) that some amount of A is better than any amount of B (henceforth also 'Weak Superiority'). Mill famously put forth such a discontinuous account of value relations:

> It is quite compatible with the principle of utility to recognise the fact that some kinds of pleasure are more desirable and valuable than others. Of two pleasures, if [...] one of the two is, by those who are competently acquainted with both, placed so far above the other that they [...] would not resign it for any quantity of the other pleasure which their nature is capable of, we are justified in ascribing to the preferred enjoyment a superiority in quality, so far outweighing quantity as to render it, in comparison, of small account. (Mill 1963, 210)

Both Strong and Weak Superiority will take knowledge off a value continuum with true belief that isn't knowledge. At the same time, neither requires a difference in kind between these two. It comes to light that, even though C3* is arguably too demanding, Pritchard's motivations for C3* may still justify a condition of adequacy for accounts of the value of knowledge over and above C1 and C2, to wit:

> [C3] Any satisfactory account of the value of knowledge must show that knowledge is not on a value continuum with true belief that falls short of knowledge.

Crucially, even if showing that knowledge enjoys a different kind of value than true belief that falls short of knowledge is sufficient to meet C3, it is not necessary. Rather, to rise to C3 it will be enough to show that knowledge is, in some respect, at least weakly superior to true belief that falls short of knowledge. That is to say, we need to show, at a minimum, that some amount of knowledge is in some respect better than any amount of true belief.

While we aren't certain that even C3 constitutes a reasonable demand on adequate accounts of the value of knowledge, in what follows, we want to try and provide some support for the claim that knowledge is weakly superior to true belief that isn't knowledge. Roughly, the idea is that a certain amount of knowledge is required to achieve one of the highest goods in life: human flourishing or what Aristotle called 'eudaimonia'.

Eudaimonia is a type of happiness. Crucially, however, it is not happiness of any old sort. As Rosalind Hursthouse points out, eudaimonia is 'the sort of happiness worth seeking or having' (2007, §2). We will assume that a eudaimonic life is at least weakly superior to a life without eudaimonia. To put it in Mills's terms, no one fully acquainted with both lives would sacrifice a eudaimonic life for a life without it, no matter how good the non-eudaimonic life may be in other respects. Derek Parfit nicely illustrates the spirit of this idea in the following passage:

> I could live for another 100 years, all of an extremely high quality. Call this the Century of Ecstasy. I could instead live forever, with a life that would always be barely worth living [...] the only good things would be muzak and potatoes. Call this the Drab Eternity. I claim that, though each day of the Drab Eternity would be worth living, the Century of Ecstasy would give me a better life. Though each day of the Drab Eternity would have some value for me, no amount of this value could be as good for me as the Century of Ecstasy. (Parfit 1984, 17–18)

Now suppose it can be shown that a eudaimonic life requires a certain amount of knowledge and that no amount of true belief that falls short of knowledge will do the trick. In that case, knowledge will also be weakly superior to true belief that isn't knowledge. After all, there will be an amount of knowledge that cannot be sacrificed for any amount of true belief that falls short of knowledge without losing something of superior value, to wit, the eudaimonic life.

To see how it works, let's first take a closer look at the eudaimonic life. Human beings are multi-faceted creatures leading complex intellectual, emotional and physical lives. Humans can attain flourishing in each of these domains. We believe that to attain a life of eudaimonia, one must attain flourishing in all of them. A human being leading a flourishing physical and intellectual life may fall short of a eudaimonic life if s/he does not attain a flourishing emotional life and so on. We want to suggest that one important condition on flourishing in a given domain consists in sufficiently realizing one's potential in that domain.

There are of course many ways in which one can fail to sufficiently realize one's potential in a given domain. Perhaps the most obvious one is to systematically and dramatically fail to attain what one should and could very easily have attained. For the intellectual domain, in order to attain intellectual flourishing one must sufficiently realize one's potential in that domain. Again, one way of failing to sufficiently realize one's potential in this domain is to systematically and dramatically fail to attain what one should and could very easily have attained. Now recall that knowledge is widely and easily available to us human beings in a wide range of areas. As a result, in these areas we humans often have the ability to know, knowledge is within our reach as intellectual agents. What's more, it is also plausible that among the things that it is easy for us to know, there is a wide range of things that we should know. If so, any human being who systematically and dramatically fails to attain knowledge that he could easily have attained will systematically and dramatically fail to attain knowledge of things in that range. As a result, any such human will fall short of sufficiently realizing his potential in the intellectual domain and so will fail to attain a life of intellectual flourishing. Given that a life of eudaimonia requires flourishing in all of the above mentioned domains, including the intellectual, any human agent who systematically and dramatically fails to attain knowledge s/he could easily have attained will be precluded from a life of eudaimonia. For us humans, then, the eudaimonic life is a life rich (enough) in knowledge.

JRA and Knowledge-First Justification

A question that we left hanging at the end of our discussion of the dialectic between KRA and JRA is whether it might be possible to arrive at a viable version of JRA by combining JRA with a knowledge-first account of justification.[1] This question will take centre stage in what follows.

There are two broad types of knowledge-first views of justification in the literature: *prescriptive* knowledge-first views – which we have ourselves defended at length in previous work – impose knowledge-first conditions on the mechanisms of belief *formation* (e.g. Kelp 2018, Miracchi 2015, Simion 2019b). We don't think that JRA in conjunction with these (types of) views will deliver the goods that KRA delivers: very roughly, that is because the precise focus of these views on belief formation rather than belief itself. For this reason, what we will do in what follows is, instead, focus on the competition, i.e. *evaluative* knowledge-first views of justification. These views are evaluative rather than prescriptive in that they impose knowledge-first conditions on belief itself rather than its formation. Arguably, the most influential variety of this view is what we will henceforth dub 'the Would-Be-Knowledge View of Justification.' Roughly, according to the champions of this account, what justification maps on to is what is happening internally in cases of knowledge. According to people like Alexander Bird (2007), Jonathan Jenkins Ichikawa (2014) and Steven Reynolds (2013), justification is, in a sense to be specified further, would-be-knowledge; that is, it maps on to some internal features of the believer, which, in conjunction with friendlier external conditions, constitute knowledge.

The question that we will address in what follows is: would a Would-Be-Knowledge View of Justification in conjunction with JRA offer a satisfactory account of the normativity of assertion? In order to answer this question, we will focus on the particular varieties of this view defended

---

[1] Thanks to an anonymous referee for pressing us on this.

by Alexander Bird (2007) and Jonathan Jenkins Ichikawa (2014).[2] We will set Reynolds's view aside, in view of the fact that (1) Reynolds himself has defended KRA rather than JRA in print and (2) Reynolds employs KRA to explain why we should conceive of justification as would-be-knowledge in the first place.[3]

When it comes to fleshing out what the relevant state involved in would-be-knowledge may be, the accounts are quite different: for Bird, what matters is that the believer at stake have the same mental states at this world as a knower does at a different possible world. Roughly, then, the view takes it that justification 'is a certain kind of approximation to knowledge, [...] where the failure to know (if any) is explained by factors external to the subject's mental states' (Bird 2007, 86). Crucially for our purposes, Bird also endorses externalism about mental states: thus, what it will take for a believer to have a particular mental state or another – and thus to count as a would-be-knower or not – will partially depend on environmental factors, external to the believer's skull.

In contrast, Jenkins Ichikawa's account is more thoroughly internalist-friendly: according to Jenkins Ichikawa, 'a subject's belief is justified just in case her intrinsic state is consistent with her having knowledge' (2014, 189).

Importantly, would-be-knowledge JRA accounts (henceforth WKJRA) will arguably deal well with several of the problems that we identified for their traditional JRA cousin as follows:

(1)   WKJRA will explain the intuition of un-assertability in lottery cases. After all, lottery believers fail to instantiate both the metal states (externalistically conceived) and the intrinsic state of a knower.

(2)   WKJRA will also nicely explain the unassertability of Moorean statements of the form 'p but I don't know that p.' After all, if it is impossible to know that 'p but I don't know that p,' one cannot be instantiating the mental states/intrinsic state of a knower of this conjunction.

(3)   WKJRA can easily explain why, when prompted via 'How do you know?' or 'Do you know this?' questions, an answer along the lines of, e.g. 'I don't, I was just saying' is impermissible. After all, having the mental sates/internal states of a knower that p is plausibly incompatible with e.g. believing that one does not know that p, on pain of cognitive dissonance.

---

[2] Jenkins Ichikawa (2017) defends an Incremental Knowledge Norm of Assertion.
[3] See Simion (2019b) for discussion.

The most pressing problem for this view, however, comes from how it deals with criticisability and blame. To see this, it will be informative to make a small detour to see how the authors themselves motivate WK accounts of justification.

One question that naturally arises for these accounts is: why should we care about would-be-knowledge? Why should we think it has the normative significance ascribed to it by these views? This is a central concern for the internalist-friendly knowledge firster to address. The champions of the view are themselves fairly concerned with answering this worry. We will look at their proposals in turn.

In a nutshell, here are the proposals they put forth: Jenkins Ichikawa takes matters internal to the believer to map on to blamelessness. According to him, then, justified belief is a kind of blameless belief, which explains its normative significance (Jenkins Ichikawa 2014, 193). In the same way in which blameless belief is a good thing, belief that would be knowledge in the relevant sense is a good thing also.

The problem with this way to motivate a WK account of justification is that it will be incompatible with a widespread and already discussed assumption in normativity theory, i.e. that norm compliance and blameless norm violation come apart. According to WKJRA conceived along Jenkins Ichikawa's lines, this distinction disappears: speakers who are internally similar to knowers are asserting permissibly *in virtue of* asserting blamelessly.

Mutatis mutandis, in virtue of this, an Jenkins Ichikawa WKJRA will also fail to account for what we have dubbed above Legitimate Criticisms and Illegitimate Rebuttals.

Bird disagrees with equating justification with blamelessnes; according to him, there is a clear normative difference between blamelessness and justification; justified belief is not merely blameless, but praiseworthy (2007, 108). Accordingly, then, on Bird's view, we get three important normative distinctions: successful belief (knowledge), praiseworthy belief (justified belief) and blameless belief. In aiming at knowledge, one can fail to reach one's aim while doing nothing wrong (blamelessly); that is, for instance, the case of someone who is brainwashed into believing a falsehood. In contrast, one can fail to believe knowledgeably while, at the same time, doing something right, i.e. praiseworthy. This latter normative dimension, according to Bird, maps on to justified belief, and regards one's proper 'ordering' of one's mental life (2007, 108).

It is easy to see that, at least at first glance, WKJRA conceived on Bird's view will be normatively superior in virtue of being able to accommodate the distinction between speakers who blamelessly violate JRA and speakers who are in breach of JRA.

Unfortunately, on closer inspection, Bird's account of praiseworthiness will not easily pass normative muster either. To see this, note, first, that praiseworthiness is, plausibly, and according to Bird himself, a property 'to be laid at the door of the believer': it makes sense to have some positive evaluation for agents who do internally perfectly fine in one respect or another, but fail to reach their goal due to external factors. Bird himself motivates his view along the following lines:

> [Some] some failures can be laid at the door of the believer, because the source of failure is one or more of the believer's mental states, and some failures can be ascribed to mischance, in that the failure is due to some mentally extraneous factor. The role of the concept of justification is to mark the difference between these different sources of failure. (Bird 2007, 96)

According to Bird, then, the crucial role played by the concept of justification – i.e. epistemic praiseworthiness – is to mark the difference between failure that is due to our environment and failure that is due to us.

Now, here is the problem: we have seen that Bird accepts externalism about mental content. As such, what mental states one is in will not merely supervene on internal features of the subject, but on the environmental conditions as well – by definition. If so, Bird's account of justification preserves externalism in that 'would be knowledge' is not entirely dependent on matters internal to the believer: since whether one is in a mental state or not also depends on the environment (as per externalism), it will follow that whether one has would-be knowledge – and thus justification, and praiseworthiness – or not will depend on the environment. But then, it is not clear how Bird's account of justification – and, in turn, epistemic praiseworthiness – fits the motivations put forth in its support. After all, given that my mental states are not entirely an internal affair, they are still dependent on environmental cooperation. Failure to be in the right mental state is not, as Bird puts it, something that can be 'laid at the door of the believer' exclusively, any more than knowledge is. They both depend on cooperation of the environment. In this, the view remains silent on the normative significance of would-be-knowledge after all.

More importantly for our purposes here, note that Bird's account, when combined with JRA, will also fail to explain Legitimate Criticisms and Illegitimate Rebuttals: on his view, it will be illegitimate to criticise assertions sourced in false belief, and perfectly legitimate to rebut such criticisms. Furthermore, on closer inspection, Bird's view will make the intuition behind Legitimate Criticisms even more mysterious than Jenkins Ichikawa's; after all, it would appear that Legitimate Criticisms, if correct, licences criticism of permissible assertions sourced in praiseworthy beliefs.

Constitutivity in General

In what follows, we will briefly argue that the argument from Chapter 7 against Williamson's Knowledge Account of Assertion generalises. To begin with, let CAA be the thesis that CRA is the unique constitutive rule of assertion. Recall:

CRA
One must: assert p only if p has property C.

Now consider the following condition:

Factivity
p has C only if p is true.

Engagement Condition' and *Systematic Falsity* (alternatively: *Systematic Counter-Knowledge*) serve to show that CAA is incompatible with any version of *C Rule* such that *C* that satisfies *Factivity*. Here is how: Suppose that CAA is true and that *C* satisfies *Factivity*. By *Systematic Falsity* (alternatively: *Systematic Counter-Knowledge*), *A* (*B*) makes assertions that, with near maximum systematicity, are false. Since *C* satisfies *Factivity*, *A* (*B*) violates *C Rule* with near maximum systematicity. It follows that *A* makes assertions that, with near maximum systematicity, violate *C Rule*. We thus have our relevant instance of (iii*) for assertion and *C Rule* such that the key property *C* at issue in *C Rule* is factive.

But now recall that establishing an instance of (iii*) will be enough to show the falsity of the thesis that r is the only constitutive rule governing *A* for any putative constitutive rule r and any *A*. Since according to CAA, *C Rule* is the only constitutive rule of assertion, this means that CAA will be false on any version of the view on which *C Rule* satisfies *Factivity*.

Given that CAA is incompatible with factive *C*, one might wonder whether CAA could not be combined with a property *C* that is non-factive such as justification or belief. Unfortunately, however, the negative result generalises beyond factive *C*. Consider the following two conditions:

Knowledge-Condition
If one knows that p, then p has C.

Consistency
If p has C, then not-p does not have C.

Engagement Condition' and *Systematic Counter-Knowledge* serve to show that CAA is incompatible with any C that satisfies *Knowledge-Condition* and *Consistency*. Here is how: Suppose that CAA is true and that C satisfies *Knowledge-Condition* and *Consistency*. By *Systematic Counter-Knowledge*, B makes assertions that, with near maximum systematicity, run counter to what B knows. That is to say, with near maximum systematicity, when B asserts p he knows not-p. Since C satisfies *Knowledge-Condition*, not-p has C.[1] Since C satisfies *Consistency*, p does not have C. In consequence, B violates C *Rule* with near maximum systematicity. It follows that B makes assertions that with near maximum systematicity, violate C *Rule*. We thus have a second instance of (iii*) for assertion and any version of C *Rule* such that C satisfies *Knowledge-Condition* and *Consistency*.

Again, as we have already seen, this will be enough to establish the falsity of any such version of CAA. Since justification satisfies both *Knowledge-Condition* and *Consistency*, it follows another main candidate for fleshing out CAA cannot be made to work either.

Finally, it is easy to see that the CAA cannot be combined with the claim that C is belief by the speaker. In fact, *Engagement Condition'* and *Systematic Counter-Knowledge* again serve to make this point. To see how, suppose CAA is true and that C is belief by the speaker. By *Systematic Counter-Knowledge*, B makes assertions that, with near maximum systematicity, run counter to what B knows. That is to say, with near maximum systematicity, when B asserts p he knows not-p. But now recall that, ex hypothesi, nearly all of B's beliefs qualify as knowledge. As a result, when B knows that not-p, he nearly never believes that p. It follows that with near maximum systematicity, B asserts that p only when he does not believe that p. In consequence, B violates C *Rule* with near maximum systematicity. Hence, B makes assertions that, with near maximum systematicity violate C *Rule*. We have our final instance of (iii*) for assertion and a version of C *Rule* according to which C is belief by the speaker.

It comes to light that CAA is false on the main proposals for the crucial property C at issue in the C *Rule* in the literature. This means that unless we have been heading down the wrong track in the debate on the identity of C entirely, there is reason to believe that CAA is false. There is no unique constitutive rule of assertion.

---

[1] Note that we might not even need *Knowledge-Condition* here. Rather, it will be enough if the case can be set up in such a way that, in the case of B, not-p has C whenever he asserts p.

Bibliography

Adler, J. (2002). *Belief's Own Ethics*. Cambridge, MA: MIT Press.

Aristotle (1985) [350 BCE]. *The Nicomachean Ethics*. Indianapolis, IN: Hackett.

Bach, K. (2008). Applying Pragmatics to Epistemology. *Philosophical Issues* 18: 68–88.

Ball, B. (2014a). Deriving the Norm of Assertion. *Journal of Philosophical Research* 39: 75–85.

(2014b). Response to Hindriks and Kooi. *Journal of Philosophical Research* 39: 93–99.

Benton, M. A. (2011). Two More for the Knowledge Account of Assertion. *Analysis* 71: 684–87.

(2016a). Expert Opinion and Second-hand Knowledge. *Philosophy and Phenomenological Research* 92(2): 492–508.

(2016b). Gricean Quality. *Noûs* 50: 689–703.

Bigelow, J. and Pargetter, R. (1987). Functions. *Journal of Philosophy* 86: 181–96.

Bird, A. (2007). Justified Judging. *Philosophy and Phenomenological Research* 74: 81–110.

Blaauw, M. (2012). Reinforcing the Knowledge Account of Assertion. *Analysis* 72: 105–8.

Bolton, G. (1991). A Comparative Model of Bargaining: Theory and Evidence. The *American Economic Review* 81: 1096–136.

Bondy, P. (2007). *Epistemic Rationality and Epistemic Normativity*. London: Routledge.

Brown, J. (2010). Knowledge and Assertion. *Philosophy and Phenomenological Research* 81: 549–66.

Buller, D. (1998). Etiological Theories of Function: A Geographical Survey. *Biology and Philosophy* 13: 505–27.

Capes, J. (2012). Blameworthiness without Wrongdoing. *Pacific Philosophical Quarterly* 93(3): 417–37.

Cappelen, H. (2011). Against Assertion. In Brown, J. and Cappelen, H. (eds.), *Assertion: New Philosophical Essays*. Oxford: Oxford University Press.

Chisholm, R. (1964). The Ethics of Requirement. *American Philosophical Quarterly* 1: 147–53.

Cohen, S. (1999). Contextualism, Skepticism, and the Structure of Reasons. *Philosophical Perspectives* 13: 57–89.

Copp, D. (1997). Defending the Principle of Alternate Possibilities: Blameworthiness and Moral Responsibility. *Noûs* 31: 441–56.

(2003). 'Ought' Implies 'Can', Blameworthiness, and the Principle of Alternate Possibilities. In Widerker, D. and McKenna, M. (eds.), *Moral Responsibility and Alternative Possibilities: Essays on the Importance of Alternative Possibilities.* Aldershot: Ashgate.

(2008). 'Ought' Implies 'Can' and the Derivation of the Principle of Alternate Possibilities. *Analysis* 68: 67–75.

Davis, E. (2016). Typecasts, Tokens, and Spokespersons: A Case for Credibility Excess as Testimonial Injustice. *Hypatia* 31: 485–501.

DeRose, K. (1991). Epistemic Possibilities. *Philosophical Review* 100(4): 581–605.

(2002). Assertion, Knowledge, and Context. *Philosophical Review* 111: 167–203.

(2009). *The Case for Contextualism: Knowledge, Skepticism, and Context.* Vol. 1. Oxford: Oxford University Press.

Dotson, K. (2011). Tracking Epistemic Violence, Tracking Practices of Silencing. *Hypathia* 26(2): 236–57

Douven, I. (2002). A New Solution to the Paradoxes of Rational Acceptability. *The British Journal for the Philosophy of Science* 53: 391–410.

(2006). Assertion, Knowledge, and Rational Credibility. *Philosophical Review* 115: 449–85.

(2009). Assertion, Moore and Bayes. *Philosophical Studies* 144: 361–75.

Douven, I. and Kelp, C. (2012). In Defense of the Rational Credibility Account: A Reply to Casalegno. *dialectica* 66: 289–97.

Fantl, J. and McGrath, M. (2009). *Knowledge in an Uncertain World.* New York: Oxford University Press.

Fischer, J. (2006). *My Way: Essays on Moral Responsibility.* New York: Oxford University Press.

Frankfurt, H. (1969). Alternate Possibilities and Moral Responsibility. *Journal of Philosophy* 66: 829–39.

Fricker, E. (2012). I – Stating and Insinuating. *Aristotelian Society Supplementary Volume* 86(1): 61–94.

Fricker, M. (2007). *Epistemic Injustice: Power and the Ethics of Knowing.* Oxford: Oxford University Press.

García-Carpintero, M. (2004). Assertion and the Semantics of Force-Markers. In Claudia Bianchi (ed.), *The Semantics/Pragmatics Distinction.* Stanford, CA: CSLI Publications.

Gazdar, G. (1979). *Pramatics: Implicature, Presupposition, and Logical Form.* New York: Academic Press.

Geach, P. (1956). Good and Evil. *Analysis* 17: 32–42.

Gerken, M. (2011). Warrant and Action. *Synthese* 178: 529–47.

Gibbard, A. (1990). *Wise Choices, Apt Feelings: A Theory of Normative Judgment.* Cambridge, MA: Harvard University Press.

Gibbons, J. (2013). *The Norm of Belief.* Oxford: Oxford University Press.

Godfrey-Smith, P. (1993). Functions: Consensus without Unity. *Pacific Philosophical Quarterly* 74: 196–208.

(1994). A Modern History Theory of Functions. *Noûs* 28: 344–62.

Goldberg, S. (2015). *Assertion: On the Philosophical Significance of Assertoric Speech.* Oxford: Oxford University Press.

(2020). *Conversational Pressure: Normativity in Speech Exchanges.* Oxford: Oxford University Press.

Graham, P. (2010). Testimonial Entitlement and the Function of Comprehension. In Haddock, A., Millar, A. and Pritchard, D. (eds.), *Social Epistemology.* New York: Oxford University Press.

(2012). Epistemic Entitlement. *Noûs* 46: 449–82.

(2014a). The Function of Perception. In Fairweather, A. (ed.), *Virtue Epistemology Naturalized. Bridges between Virtue Epistemology and Philosophy of Science.* Dordrecht: Springer.

(2014b). Functions, Warrant, History. In Fairweather, A. and Flanagan, O. (eds.), *Naturalizing Epistemic Virtue.* Cambridge: Cambridge University Press.

Green, M. (2015). Speech Acts. In Zalta, Edward N. (ed.), *The Stanford Encyclopedia of Philosophy* (Summer 2015 Edition), http://plato.stanford .edu/archives/sum2015/entries/speech-acts/

(2020). Speech Acts. In Zalta, Edward N. (ed.), *The Stanford Encyclopedia of Philosophy* (Winter 2020 Edition), https://plato.stanford.edu/archives/ win2020/entries/speech-acts/

Grice, P. (1989). *Studies in the Way of Words.* Cambridge, MA: Harvard University Press.

Griffith, P. (1993). Functional Analysis and Proper Functions. *British Journal for the Philosophy of Science* 44: 409–22.

Haji, I. (1998). *Moral Appraisability.* Oxford: Oxford University Press.

Hawthorne, J. (2004). *Knowledge and Lotteries.* Oxford: Oxford University Press.

Hinchman, E. S. (2005). Telling as Inviting to Trust. *Philosophy and Phenomenological Research* 70: 562–87.

(2013). Assertion, Sincerity, and Knowledge. *Nous* 47: 613–46.

Hindriks, F. (2007). The Status of the Knowledge Account of Assertion. *Linguistics and Philosophy* 30: 393–406.

Hindriks, F. and Kooi, B. (2014). Reaffirming the Status of the Knowledge Account of Assertion. *Journal of Philosophical Research* 39: 87–92.

Hohfeld, W. (1919). *Fundamental Legal Conceptions.* New Haven: Yale University Press.

Hornsby, J. (1995). Disempowered Speech. *Philosophical Topics* 23(2): 127–47.

Hornsby, J. and Langton, R. (1998). Free Speech and Illocution. *Legal Theory* 4: 21–37.

Hursthouse, R. (2007). Virtue Ethics. In Zalta, Edward N. (ed.), *The Stanford Encyclopedia of Philosophy* (July 2007 Edition).

Jenkins Ichikawa, J. (2014). Justification Is Potential Knowledge. *Canadian Journal of Philosophy* 44(2): 184–206.

(2017). *Contextualising Knowledge: Epistemology and Semantics.* New York, NY: Oxford University Press.

Kelp, C. (2011). Not Without Justification. *dialectica* 65: 581–95.

(2014). Two for the Knowledge Goal of Inquiry. *American Philosophical Quarterly* 51: 227–32.

(2016). Justified Belief: Knowledge First-Style. *Philosophy and Phenomenological Research* 93: 79–100.

(2017). Lotteries and Justification. *Synthese* 194: 1233–44.

(2018). *Good Thinking: A Knowledge First Virtue Epistemology.* London: Routledge.

(2021). *Inquiry, Knowledge, and Understanding.* Oxford: Oxford University Press.

Kelp, C. and Simion, M. (2017a). Commodious Knowledge. *Synthese* 194: 1487–502.

(2017b). Criticism and Blame in Action and Assertion. *Journal of Philosophy* 114(2): 76–93.

Kitcher, P. (1994). Function and Design. *Midwest Studies in Philosophy* 18: 379–97.

Kneer, M. (2018). The Norm of Assertion: Empirical Data. *Cognition.* https://doi .org/10.1016/j.cognition.2018.03.020.

Kvanvig, J. L. (2003). *The Value of Knowledge and the Pursuit of Understanding.* Cambridge: Cambridge University Press.

(2009). Assertion, Knowledge and Lotteries. In Pritchard, D. and Greenough, P. (eds.), *Williamson on Knowledge.* Oxford: Oxford University Press.

(2011). Norms of Assertion. In Brown, J. & Cappelen, H. (eds.), *Assertion: New Philosophical Essays.* Oxford: Oxford University Press.

(2017). Reply to Simion. *Logos and Episteme* 8(1): 113–16.

Lackey, J. (2007). Norms of Assertion. *Noûs* 41: 594–626.

(2008). *Learning from Words: Testimony as a Source for Knowledge.* Oxford: Oxford University Press.

(2011). Assertion and Isolated Second-hand Knowledge. In Brown, J. and Cappelen, H. (eds.), *Assertion: New Philosophical Essays.* Oxford: Oxford University Press.

(2016). Assertion and Expertise. *Philosophy and Phenomenological Research* 92: 509–17.

(2018). Credibility and the Distribution of Epistemic Goods. In McCain, K. (ed.), *Believing in Accordance with the Evidence.* Dordrecht: Springer.

(2020). False Confessions and Testimonial Injustice. *Journal of Criminal Law and Criminology* 110: 43–68.

Langton, R. (1993). Speech Acts and Unspeakable Acts. *Philosophy and Public Affairs* 22(4): 293–330.

Lenzen, W. (1980). *Glauben, Wissen und Wahrscheinlichkeit.* Vienna: Springer.

Littlejohn, C. (2014). Know Your Rights: On Warranted Assertion and Truth. *Erkenntnis* 79(6):1355–65.

(Forthcoming). A Plea for Epistemic Excuses. In Dorsch, D. and Dutant, J. (eds.), *The New Evil Demon Problem*. Oxford: Oxford University Press.

Luzzi, F. (2016). Testimonial Injustice without Credibility Deficit (or Excess). *Thought: A Journal of Philosophy* 5(3): 203–11.

Madison, B. (2010). Is Justification Knowledge? *Journal of Philosophical Research* 35: 173–91.

Maitra, I. (2011). Assertion, Norms and Games. In Brown, J. and Cappelen, H. (eds.), *Assertion: New Philosophical Essays*. Oxford: Oxford University Press.

McGlynn, A. (2014). *Knowledge First?* New York: Palgrave Macmillan.

McHugh, C. (2012). The Truth Norm of Belief. *Pacific Philosophical Quarterly* 93: 8–30.

McKinnon, R. (2015). *The Norms of Assertion. Truth, Lies and Warrant*. New York: Palgrave Macmillan.

McKinnon, R. and Turri, J. (2013). Irksome Assertions. *Philosophical Studies* 166: 123–26.

Mill, J. S. (1963). *Essays on Ethics, Religion, and Society*. The Collected Works of John Stuart Mill, vol. 10. Toronto: University of Toronto Press.

Miller, D. (2017). Justice. In Zalta, E. (ed.), *The Stanford Encyclopedia of Philosophy*. https://plato.stanford.edu/archives/fall2017/entries/justice/

Millikan, R. G. (1984). *Language, Thought, and Other Biological Categories*. Cambridge, MA: MIT Press.

(2004). *Varieties of Meaning: The 2002 Jean Nicod Lectures*. Cambridge, MA: MIT Press.

Miracchi, L. (2015). Competence to Know. *Philosophical Studies*, 172 (1): 29–56.

Montminy, M. (2013). Why Assertion and Practical Reasoning Must Be Governed by the Same Epistemic Norm. *Pacific Philosophical Quarterly* 94 (1): 57–68.

Moore, G. E. (1942). A Reply to My Critics. In Schilpp, P. (ed.), *The Philosophy of G.E. Moore, The Library of Living Philosophers*. La Salle, IL: Open Court.

(1962). *Commonplace Book: 1919–1953*. London: George Allen & Unwin.

Moran, D. (2006). Getting Told and Being Believed. In Lackey, J. and Sosa, E. (eds.), *The Epistemology of Testimony*. Oxford: Oxford University Press.

Neander, K. (1991a). Functions as Selected Effects: The Conceptual Analyst's Defence. *Philosophy of Science* 58: 168–84.

(1991b). The Teleological Notion of 'Function'. *Australasian Journal of Philosophy* 69: 454–68.

Nolfi, K. (2014). Why Is Epistemic Evaluation Prescriptive? *Inquiry* 57: 97–121.

Ochs, J. and Roth, A. E. (1989). An Experimental Study of Sequential Bargaining. *American Economic Review* 79: 355–84.

Pagin, P. (2016). Problems with Norms of Assertion. *Philosophy and Phenomenological Research* 93: 178–207.

Parfit, D. (1984). *Reasons and Persons*. Oxford: Clarendon Press.

Pelling, C. (2013a). Assertion and Safety. *Synthese* 190: 3777–96.

(2013b). Assertion and the Provision of Knowledge. *The Philosophical Quarterly* 63: 293–312.

Pritchard, D. (2014). Epistemic Luck, Safety and Assertion. In Littlejohn, C. and Turri, J. (eds.), *Epistemic Norms: New Essays on Action, Belief and Assertion*. Oxford: Oxford University Press.

Pritchard, D., Millar, A. and Haddock, A. (2010). *The Nature and Value of Knowledge: Three Investigations*. Oxford: Oxford University Press.

Reuter, K. and Broessel, P. (2018). No Knowledge Required. *Episteme*. https://doi.org/10.1017/epi.2018.10.

Reynolds, S. (2013). Justification as the Appearance of Knowledge. *Philosophical Studies* 163: 367–83.

Ridge, M (2014). *Impassioned Belief*. Oxford: Oxford University Press.

Riggs, W. (2009). Getting the Meno Requirement Right. In Pritchard, D., Haddock, A. and Millar, A. (eds.), *Epistemic Value*. Oxford: Oxford University Press.

Rudy-Hiller, F. (2018). The Epistemic Condition for Moral Responsibility. In Zalta, Edward N. (ed.), *The Stanford Encyclopedia of Philosophy* (Fall 2018 Edition), https://plato.stanford.edu/archives/fall2018/entries/moral-responsibility-epistemic/

Rysiew, P. (2016). Epistemic Contextualism. In Zalta, Edward N. (ed.), *The Stanford Encyclopedia of Philosophy*, https://plato.stanford.edu/archives/win2016/entries/contextualism-epistemology/

Schroeder, M. (2021). Value Theory. In Zalta, Edward N. (ed.), *The Stanford Encyclopedia of Philosophy* (Spring 2021 Edition), https://plato.stanford.edu/archives/spr2021/entries/value-theory/

Simion, M. (2016a). Assertion: Knowledge Is Enough. *Synthese* 193(10): 3041–56.

(2016b). Assertion: Just One Way to Take It Back. *Logos and Episteme* 7(3): 385–91.

(2016c). Knowledge, Rational Credibility and Assertion: The Scoreboard. In Grajner, M. and Schmechtig, P. (eds.), *Epistemic Reasons, Epistemic Norms and Epistemic Goals*. Berlin and Boston, MA: DeGruyter.

(2019a). Assertion: The Context Shiftiness Dilemma. *Mind & Language* 34: 503–17.

(2019b). Knowledge-first Functionalism. *Philosophical Issues* 29(1): 254–67.

(2019c). Saying and Believing: The Norm Commonality Assumption. *Philosophical Studies* 176(8): 1951–66.

(2020a). A Priori Perceptual Entitlement, Knowledge-first. *Philosophical Issues* 30(1): 311–23.

(2020b). Testimonial Contractarianism: A Knowledge First Social Epistemology. *Noûs*. https://doi.org/10.1111/nous.12337

(2021). *Shifty Speech and Independent Thought: Epistemic Normativity in Context*. Oxford: Oxford University Press.

Simion, M. and Kelp, C. (2016). The Tertiary Value Problem and the Superiority of Knowledge. *American Philosophical Quarterly* 53(4): 397–411.

Simion, M., Kelp, C. and Ghijsen, H. (2016). Norms of Belief. *Philosophical Issues* 16: 374–92.

Slote, M. (1979). Assertion and Belief. In Dancy, J. (ed.), *Papers on Language and Logic*. Keele: Keele University Press.

Smith, H. (1991). Varieties of Moral Worth and Moral Credit. *Ethics* 101: 279–303.

Smith, M. (2005). Norms and Regulations: Three Issues – Discussion. *Philosophical Studies* 124: 221–32.

Sosa, E. (2003). The Place of Truth in Epistemology. In Zagzebski, L. and DePaul, M. (eds.), *Intellectual Virtue: Perspectives from Ethics and Epistemology*. New York: Oxford University Press.

  (2011). *Knowing Full Well*. Princeton: Princeton University Press.

  (2015). *Judgment and Agency*. Oxford: Oxford University Press.

Sperber, D. (2001). An Evolutionary Perspective on Testimony and Argumentation. *Philosophical Topics* 29 (1/2): 401–13.

Speak, D. (2005). PAPistry: Another Defense. *Midwest Studies in Philosophy* 29: 262–68.

Stanley, J. (2005). *Knowledge and Practical Interest*. New York: Oxford University Press.

Sutton, J. (2005). Stick To What You Know. *Noûs* 39: 359–96.

Tappolet, C. (2014). The Normativity of Evaluative Concepts. In Reboul, A. (ed.), *Mind, Values and Metaphysics: Philosophical Essays in Honour of Kevin Mulligan*, Vol. 2. New York: Springer.

Thijsse, E. (2000). 'The Doxastic-Epistemic Force of Declarative Utterances.' In Black, W. and Bunt, H. (eds.), *Abduction, Beliefs and Context in Dialogue: Studies in Computational Pragmatics*. Amsterdam: John Benjamins.

Thomson, J. (2008). *Normativity*. Chicago, IL: Open Court.

Turri, J. (2010). Prompting Challenges. *Analysis* 70: 456–62.

  (2011). The Express Knowledge Account of Assertion. *Australasian Journal of Philosophy* 89(1): 37–45.

  (2013). The Test of Truth: An Experimental Investigation of the Norm of Assertion. *Cognition* 129: 279–91.

  (2014). Knowledge and Suberogatory Assertion. *Philosophical Studies* 167: 557–67.

  (2015). Knowledge and the Norm of Assertion: A Simple Test. *Synthese* 192: 385–92.

  (2016). *Knowledge and the Norm of Assertion: An Essay in Philosophical Science*. Cambridge: Open Book Publishers.

Turri, J., Friedman, O. and Keefner, A. (2017). Knowledge Central: A Central Role for Knowledge Attributions in Social Evaluations. *Quarterly Journal of Experimental Psychology* 70: 504–15.

Unger, P. (1975). *Ignorance: A Case for Scepticism*. Oxford: Clarendon.

Walsh, D. and Ariew, A. (1996). A Taxonomy of Functions. *Canadian Journal of Philosophy* 26: 493–514.

Weiner, M. (2005). Must We Know What We Say? *Philosophical Review* 114: 227–51.

Whiting, D. (2013). Stick to the Facts: On the Norms of Assertion. *Erkenntnis*
        78: 847–67.
    (2015). Truth Is (Still) the Norm for Assertion: A Reply to Littlejohn.
        Erkenntnis 80(6): 1245–53.
Widerker, D. (1991). Frankfurt on 'Ought Implies Can' and Alternative
        Possibilities. *Analysis* 51: 222–24.
Williamson, T. (1996). Knowing and Asserting. *Philosophical Review* 105(4):
        489–523.
    (2000). *Knowledge and Its Limits*. Oxford: Oxford University Press.
    (2009). Replies to Critics. In Greenough, P. and Pritchard, D. (eds.),
        Williamson on Knowledge. Oxford: Oxford University Press.
Zimmerman, M. (1997). Moral Responsibility and Ignorance. *Ethics* 107(3):
        410–26.

Index

action, 1, 4, 32–33, 35–36, 40, 42, 52, 55–56, 59, 63, 106, 119, 128
Adler, Jonathan, 46, 151
Ariew, André, 74
Aristotle, 31, 34, 188
assertion
  epistemic function of, 5
  good, 4–5, 7, 73, 90–91, 94–95, 97–98
  nature of, 6, 84
  normativity of, 5, 73, 91, 115
  selfless, 4–5, 84, 92, 94–97
assurance view of testimony, 118, 125, 136
attributive goodness, 5, 77

Bach, Kent, 3, 7, 98, 105–6, 116, 118
Ball, Brian, 100, 116
belief-assertion parallel, 46, 108–9
Benton, Matt, 2, 18–19, 60–63, 116
Bigelow, John, 74
Bird, Alexander, 28, 191–94
blamelessness, 4, 7, 24, 30–38, 42, 48–49, 95, 122, 144, 149, 193
blameworthiness, 7, 30, 33–35, 37, 42, 48
Bolton, Gary, 128
Bondy, Patrick, 33
Brown, Jessica, 7, 51–54, 56–59, 67, 69
Buller, David, 74

Cappelen, Herman, 145–47
Cases
  Affair, 52–54, 56–58
  Aspirin High, 160–61, 163
  Aspirin Low, 160–61, 163–64
  Bald, 53–54, 56
  bank cases, 166–67, 176
  Bank High, 166–67, 173
  Bank Low, 165–67, 173
  Case 1, 150
  Case 2, 151
  Case 3, 154
  Creationist Teacher, 48, 92–94, 96

Doctor, 59
Drive 1, 55–56
Drive 2, 55–56
Drive 3, 55
Fake Barns, 31–32, 38–39, 41–42
Fake Snow, 30–32, 38–39, 42
Food, 63
Recommendation, 65
Stepping-Stone Physics, 94
Train, 58, 164
watch cases, 168–69, 171, 173–74
Zolex High, 169–73
Zolex Low, 168–69
Zongines High, 169–73
Zongines Low, 169
Chisholm, Roderick, 33
claim right, 123–24, 135
Coates, Paul, 35
consequentialism, 79
contextualism, 6, 8, 159–61, 165, 167–75
conversational patterns, 20, 28, 38–40, 42, 49
conversational pressure, 8, 118, 125, 129
Copp, David, 33
criticism, 1, 4, 7, 23–32, 35, 37–38, 41, 44–45, 48, 95, 105–6, 110–11, 113–14, 133–34, 141, 175, 193–94
  legitimate, 23–26, 33–34, 36, 95, 105

Davis, Emmalon, 122
deontology, 57, 79
derivations of KRA, 100–2, 104, 106–7, 109–10, 116
DeRose, Keith, 2, 6, 8, 17, 159–66, 172–75
Dotson, Kristie, 120
Douven, Igor, 2, 8, 13–16, 28, 30, 44–47, 50, 92, 95, 98, 107–10, 116, 118, 151
duty to believe, 6, 8, 118, 124–35
  presumption-based accounts, 125–30, 132
  purport-based accounts, 125, 130–32

For EU product safety concerns, contact us at Calle de José Abascal, 56–1°, 28003 Madrid, Spain or eugpsr@cambridge.org.

www.ingramcontent.com/pod-product-compliance
Ingram Content Group UK Ltd.
Pitfield, Milton Keynes, MK11 3LW, UK
UKHW020352140625
459647UK00020B/2419